INFORMATION SYSTEMS DEVELOPMENT: PRINCIPLES OF COMPUTER-AIDED SOFTWARE ENGINEERING

ALBERT F. CASE, JR.

Nastec Corporation

PRENTICE-HALL
Englewood Cliffs, New Jersey 07632

Library of Congress Cataloging-in-Publication Data

Case, Albert F.
  Information systems development.

  Bibliography: p.
  Includes index.
  1. System design.   2. Computer software—
Development.   I. Title.
QA76.9.S88C39   1986   005.1   85-25567
ISBN 0-13-464520-0

Editorial/production supervision and
  interior design: *Carol L. Atkins*
Cover design: *Lundgren Graphics, Ltd.*
Manufacturing buyer: *Gordon Osbourne*

Printed in the United States of America

10 9 8 7 6 5 4 3 2

ISBN 0-13-464520-0   025

Prentice-Hall International (UK) Limited, *London*
Prentice-Hall of Australia Pty. Limited, *Sydney*
Prentice-Hall Canada Inc., *Toronto*
Prentice-Hall Hispanoamericana, S.A., *Mexico*
Prentice-Hall of India Private Limited, *New Delhi*
Prentice-Hall of Japan, Inc., *Tokyo*
Prentice-Hall of Southeast Asia Pte. Ltd., *Singapore*
Editora Prentice-Hall do Brasil, Ltda., *Rio de Janeiro*
Whitehall Books Limited, *Wellington, New Zealand*

To Deb, Kim, Chris, Mom, and Dad

Contents

Preface

OBJECTIVES OF THIS BOOK

One can rarely pick up a trade journal or systems management text without finding an article on the subject of managing the systems development process, ensuring the satisfaction of systems users, or keeping project budgets under control. Now the subject of the "software challenge," the challenge of producing computer software systems of high quality and low cost in a timely fashion, is becoming a topic of interest to the popular and business press.

There are, today, tools, techniques, methodologies, and strategies available to software development management to meet the software challenge. The intention of *Information Systems Development: Principles of Computer-Aided Software Engineering* is to outline an integrated strategy and methodology for improving information systems development productivity. This strategy calls for:

1. A structured, well-defined planning process that drives systems development
2. An engineering approach to developing software and managing projects
3. Specifications for a computer-aided software engineering (CASE) system, an automated tool kit to support managers and software developers

Although the strategy and procedures outlined in this book are oriented to the process of developing business-oriented information systems, the techniques and processes outlined support engineered products/embedded systems and

xii   Preface

large-scale special-purpose systems (such as those of the Department of Defense and the aerospace industry) as well.

AUDIENCE

Information Systems Development presents a comprehensive management and technical overview of the process of developing information systems. Its management and planning procedures and implementation recommendations would be of great value to a director or vice president of management information systems (MIS). Since the specific technical processes for designing software are covered, this book would also be an excellent guide for managers, analysts, or consultants charged with selecting and implementing development techniques.

Project and systems development managers will find the discussions of the systems development life cycle and project management techniques most helpful in managing their projects. Some of the techniques can be implemented immediately with visible, short-term results.

Since this book examines and defines the software development process from planning to implementation, it could be used as either a primary or supplementary textbook for advanced courses in MIS or project management.

WHY THIS BOOK WAS WRITTEN: THE SOFTWARE CHALLENGE

The "software challenge" refers to the conflict between the desire on the part of data processing users to have new, high-quality* information systems, and the ability of the systems development organization or department to deliver them in a timely, cost-effective manner.

The software challenge is really two problems. The first problem is immediate. It is relatively common knowledge that development projects rarely come in on target. Systems installed typically have extensive "bug-fixing" maintenance periods after installation, frequently disrupting the normal operations of the enterprise. Software development is expensive and unreliable.

The second problem is more insidious and less visible. There are limited software development resources. A recent U.S. Department of Defense (DoD) study entitled "Software Technology for Adaptable Reliable Systems" indicated that demand for computer software is increasing at a 12% compound rate annually, while the supply of expert computer software professionals is growing

---

*Throughout this book, the term "high-quality" will represent both absence of defect *and* adherence to the user's needs.

at only a 4% compound rate. Present productivity tools can be expected to increase productivity only 4%. This study concludes, therefore, that by 1990, there could be a shortage of qualified software development personnel of as many as 1 millon persons. This means that while demand for software is growing, the resources that can provide it are not. This translates directly into higher labor costs, hence higher software costs. Even if the developers are available, they may not be affordable.

FUELING THE GROWTH IN SOFTWARE DEMAND

What is fueling this tremendous growth in demand for computer software?

First, tremendous advances in hardware engineering and technology, combined with the plummeting cost of computers (mainframe, mini, micro, and home), are fueling demand for application software to make these computers operate.

Second, during the 1970s, quality of product and productivity of the American work force threatened the very survival of the U.S. economic system. Executive management recognized that the computerization of America was the key to regaining American industrial and economic supremacy. The latest software applications to support this computerization are significantly more complex than the applications developed in the 1960s and 1970s.

Third, the world of consumer products has discovered the microchip. Everything from automobiles, dishwashers, and microwave ovens to industrial photocopiers and robotics systems are now computer controlled. This new world of embedded systems, or engineered computer products, represents a whole new vista of software applications.

Fourth, a growing awareness of the "Information Age," spurred by such works as Alvin Toffler's *Third Wave* and John Naisbitt's *Megatrends,* has made mainstream America more computer literate. Hence they are more demanding of organizations that provide computer software.

WHAT DOES THIS MEAN TO SOFTWARE DEVELOPMENT MANAGEMENT AND PROFESSIONALS?

It means primarily that we are being challenged to produce an increasing number of more complex information systems. And we are being challenged to do so within the constraints of limited resources, compounded by the fact that each new system built requires an increase in maintenance or support resources, thus detracting from the resources available to build new systems.

HOW CAN WE MEET THIS CHALLENGE?

The engineering and manufacturing industries were faced with a similar problem—to produce more, higher-quality products within limiting resource constraints. Their solution was to provide a systematic, engineering discipline to the development effort, controlled by advanced management techniques and supported by new technologies such as computer-aided design and manufacturing (CAD/CAM) and computer-aided engineering (CAE). Engineers and manufacturers became *smarter* about how they did their work. Systems development managers and professionals must now follow suit. Software developers must be able to keep pace, in productivity and quality, with hardware developers.

There has been much work done in this area already. The purveyors of methodologies and design techniques, the vendors of programming and generation tools, and the suppliers of project control systems all offer partial solutions. To be effective, however, these solutions must be *INTEGRATED.* Some effort toward integration has already been made in the government arena. For example, the DoD STARS (Software Technology for Adaptable Reliable Systems) program is endeavoring to specify a complete environment for developing software in a controlled, managed environment. What is needed is an identification of these advances and a translation from the research environment to the real-world business of information systems development.

Information Systems Development is a comprehensive, practical manual for evaluating software engineering technology and applying it to the development of information systems. It examines the planning, management, control, and development processes involved in systems development, and provides a blueprint for a software engineering management information system to integrate these processes.

USERS' GUIDE FOR INFORMATION SYSTEMS DEVELOPMENT

This book, itself a system, is a set of specifications for a system to build information systems. A system to build systems is relatively complex and contains recursion and iteration of various processes. This is not bad if you are describing the system to a computer in a programming language that contains *DO-WHILE, PERFORM,* and/or *CALL* constructs. English, on the other hand, is not so structured. Because people cannot read in a parallel processing mode, each of the four parts contains enough information to stand alone. This helps to eliminate the need to constantly cross-reference to other parts of the text.

Although every author hopes and dreams that readers will hang on his or her every word, reality indicates that this is not true. Since each part is capable of being read independently, the reader can random-access the part of the book that addresses a specific informational need. This is a by-product of the high cohesion/low coupling of the individual parts of the book.

Since every good system needs a users' guide, such a guide for this text is included below. For each part, the general content and major audience are included.

PART I: Introduction.

The introduction provides the student, professional, and manager with a historical perspective of the challenges (both immediate and long term) facing the software development industry, and defines software engineering. This section is important to an understanding of the other sections.

PART II: Systems Planning Process.

A prime contention of the management aspects of the software engineering approach to systems development is that management is a function of planning. This is "must" reading for managers, but could be skipped by project managers and software development professionals if Chapter 6 were read.

PART III: Software Engineering Transformation Process.

This section deals primarily with the technical aspects of managing systems projects. Life cycles and development techniques are described. This is an important section for the professional and the project manager. Senior management would benefit from reading Chapter 11.

PART IV: Computer-Aided Software Engineering.

This part looks at the management information system (SE/MIS) required to support the software engineering transformation process. The emerging CASE technology as a mechanism to automate the SE/MIS, where it is headed, and what it means to software development are discussed. The premise is that CASE is the mechanism which will enable the software engineering approach to be implemented in a consistent, cost-effective manner. The impact of artificial intelligence on CASE is discussed. This section is highly recommended for all readers and is required reading for senior and middle management.

A NOTE ON CHARTS AND DIAGRAMS

There are numerous diagrams in this book depicting the relationship between the various entities and processes involved in developing information systems.

The representation used in many of these diagrams is process-flow notation. In Part IV, an analysis of the various system development techniques is portrayed in which process-flow development techniques are discussed. It is important to note that process-flow notation is an excellent method of modeling or representing a known environment and is widely recognized and understood by information systems professionals. However, as will be evident from reading Part IV, it is not necessarily the best or the only method for discovery and definition when applied to information systems analysis and design. Process-flow notation was adopted for convenience and should not be construed as an endorsement of process-flow design techniques.

ACKNOWLEDGMENTS

This book is the culmination of more than three years of research, tinkering, and thinking about improving the way information systems are developed. Like any other major project, it cannot be done by a single person. Although my name appears on the cover, numerous people have contributed to the success of this endeavor.

First, I would like to thank the following executives of Nastec Corporation: Ken Hill, Jim McGuire, Dick Ramsdell, Al Connor, Tom Long, and John Manley (who is now the director of the Software Engineering Institute at Carnegie-Mellon University). They not only tolerated my considerable pre-occupation with this book, but contributed to the effort with ideas, encouragement, and resources. (The entire original manuscript, both graphics and text, was prepared at Nastec on a CASE 2000 Workstation.) Furthermore, they gave me the opportunity to validate many of the concepts in this book. This would not have been possible under other circumstances.

While most of my professional colleagues contributed in some fashion to this book, some in particular, should be mentioned. Jim Blake applied many of the principles in this book to his projects, and tempered some of my more avant-garde ideas with practical experience. Vaughn Frick is a walking encyclopaedia of information on development techniques and provided considerable insight. Byron Burke assisted me in the area of automating life-cycle methodologies.

Much of the work for this book was done while I was at Ryder System— Automotive Carrier Division. Greg Vogel (then Group Controller for the M&G Convoy subsidiaries) welcomed the use of the concepts in this book for the systems development work in his area of responsibility. David Caswell, also from Ryder, strongly encouraged the project.

There are two other associates who deserve credit for prodding me to completion on this project. Dr. Eric Streiff, Dean of Continuing Education, State University of New York at Buffalo, was enough of a risk-taker to let me develop and teach a new course on data processing project management in the

Millard Fillmore College Division. The class notes for that course ultimately evolved into this book. I would also like to thank Karl Karlstrom, my editor at Prentice-Hall. Karl tolerated three missed deadlines, yet continued to support the project and prodded me to completion.

Last, but certainly not least, I would like to thank my wife, Deborah, my daughter Kimberly Marie and my son, A. F. Christopher Case III who suffered through late nights, missed dinners and absent weekends (while I tried to make up for three missed deadlines). Not once did they waver in their support and encouragement for me to complete this project or complain about my share of the chores which went undone.

In addition to those mentioned there were many others who contributed to this effort: former students, business associates, and friends who gave me ideas, tried out the concepts, and provided valuable critiques of this approach to building systems. I thank them all. The successful and beneficial aspects of this book are the result of all of these contributions; however, any shortcomings, errors, or omissions are my own responsibility—those I will share with no one else.

TRADEMARK ACKNOWLEDGMENTS

PRIDE and *PRIDE/asdm* are registered trademarks of M. Bryce and Associates, Inc. *NASTEC CASE 2000* and *DesignAid* are registered trademarks of Nastec Corporation. *LifeCycle Manager* and *GraphiText* are also Nastec Corporation trademarks. *SPECTRUM* and *SPECTRUM/Structured* are trademarks of Spectrum International, Inc. *SDM/70* and *SDM/Structured* are trademarks of AGS Management Systems, Inc. *Data Structured Systems Design* and *DSSD* are registered trademarks of Ken Orr and Associates, Inc. *IBM, IBM Personal Computer/XT, IBM Personal Computer/AT* and *IBM 3270 PC* are registered trademarks of International Business Machines Corporation.

1

The Software Challenge

1.1 INDUSTRY GROWTH MEANS MORE SOFTWARE

- *Point:* In 1983, IBM sold more personal computers (IBM/PC) than it had sold all other types of computers since it was founded. More than 90% of these IBM/PCs were sold to business and government.

- *Point:* In less than five years Apple Computer Company moved from being a garage operation to the Fortune 500.

- *Point:* In the 1970s, the Radio Shack Division of Tandy Company moved into the personal computer business. The TRS-80 computer line now accounts for the majority of Tandy's revenue.

- *Point:* In 1983, *Time* magazine's "Man of the Year" was the computer.

- *Point:* In 1983, President Ronald Reagan announced the Strategic Defense Initiative (SDI), known to the press as the "Star Wars Defense Program," a program of high-technology defense systems predicated on a fewer number of "smart" (i.e., software controlled) weapons rather than larger numbers of troops and conventional (dumb) weapons.

In the last decade, there has been an explosive growth in the rate of proliferation of computers. Daily, new companies are springing up offering faster, cheaper, more powerful devices. As the number of new computers grows, so too grows the need for computer software, which is required to make the computers perform. The demand for software is being driven by the proliferation and cost-effectiveness of computer hardware. This is putting pressure on the software developers to deliver.*

In part, this trend toward computerization has been fueled by the sluggish economy the nation experienced in the late 1970s. American industry was being beaten by foreign competition in the race to produce higher-quality, less expensive products. American industry's response was a national initiative to increase quality and productivity, and the key to this initiative was the use of automation. Not only were computers becoming cheaper, they were becoming more desirable.

1.2 THE NEED FOR MORE COMPLEX SYSTEMS GROWS

At present, most standard business applications have been automated. Payroll, general ledger, and payables and receivables systems abound and are far cheaper to buy than to build. With this foundation of software maturing, computer users are finding newer, more advanced, and more complex applications for computers and software. As the number of software systems and their complexity grows, there is an increasing need to interface these systems so that they communicate with each other. Integration among systems is a problem that needs to be addressed—and becomes more difficult as each new system is built.

An example of the level of complexity being faced today is the hybrid business application combining microcomputer software with mainframe software. Just a few short years ago, micros were rare. Then they became "personal computers," which help managers and professionals do their job with stand-alone files and application programs—in a world apart from the mainframe-based information systems. Now, with the advent of micro-mainframe data link systems such as those provided by Micro-Tempus, Cullinet, Applied Data Research, Cincom, and a host of others, applications are being built in which portions of the processing occur in personal computers on a professional's desk using data from and providing updated data to mainframe-resident databases. Add to this scenario, personal computer local-area networks that share data among themselves and the mainframe, and application control and data integrity become significant design and implementation problems.

*The high-technology recession of 1985, in fact, has been attributed to the fact that computer software has not kept pace with the availability of computer hardware. Data communications software is one of the biggest culprits. There was a distinct lack of high-performance software which would allow microcomputers running application programs to interact with mainframe databases. Many systems development organizations acquired personal computers only to find that they were under utilized because of lack of software. Apple Computer's declining fortunes can be attributed to the lack of application software for business computer users. These factors indicate that it is software, and not hardware, that is the pacing factor in the computerization of America.

2

The Management Dilemma

As the demand for software grows, systems development organizations are pressured to deliver. As users of computer systems become more sophisticated and systems become more integral to the success of the user organizations, the need for reliable, high-quality software escalates. This has created a dilemma of unprecedented proportions for software development organizations.

2.1 THE EFFECT OF LIMITED RESOURCES

One of the largest consumers of software development resources is the federal government, particularly the Department of Defense (DoD). The government must compete for resources from the same pool as private industry. Concern over the scarcity of resources led the DoD to conduct a study from which Figure 2.1 was derived.

While the demand for software systems is growing at an annual compound rate of 12%, the resources available to develop software are growing at only 4% annually. Productivity improvements obtained through current technology boost the resource growth rate by only 4%, leaving a compounded 4% shortfall in resource annually. The DoD estimates that by 1990 there could be a deficit of as many as 1 million software developers.

Anyone who has recently tried to hire experienced software development personnel (analysts, programmers, project managers) is aware that qualified, experienced people do not grow on trees. Furthermore, the diversity of hardware and software is forcing specialization among software personnel.

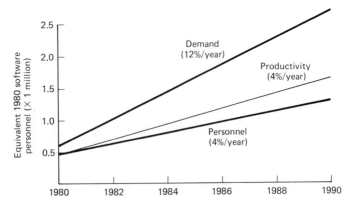

Figure 2.1 Software supply and demand trends. Source: U.S. Department of Defense.

Developers with specific skill areas such as telecommunications, database, or microcomputer applications can be difficult to find.

2.2 THE COST OF SOFTWARE/ SYSTEMS DEVELOPMENT

Even if highly skilled and specialized software development resources were available, in many organizations they may not be affordable in the numbers necessary to execute all the software projects in the queue. Computer hardware has steadily decreased in price and increased in performance. Technology has advanced significantly due to massive research and development efforts and breakthroughs in production techniques. Computer software, on the other hand, has steadily increased in cost. This inversion is depicted in Figure 2.2. Why the difference?

First, software development is labor intensive. Requirements definition, design, coding, and testing are largely composed of manual tasks to be performed by software developers. Hardware development and manufacture, on the other hand, although still performed by skilled engineers, is heavily automated. Computer-aided design and manufacturing (CAD/CAM) systems, circuit libraries, automated hardware emulators, and simulators abound and measurably increase the productivity of hardware engineers. Although there are some automated software development tools available, they tend to focus on the coding functions, which represent as little as 20% of the entire software development work effort. This leaves 80% of the effort largely unaided by automated tools.

Second, software development is viewed and managed largely as a creative effort. Hardware development, on the other hand, is an *engineering process*. Although creativity is highly prized, the development process is highly structured. Firm work-breakdown structures exist for engineering efforts. Standards are applied to each step of the work breakdown, and quality is measured and checked at every step. Sound project management principles and practices are applied to the management of the work-breakdown structure. In hardware engineering, creativity is applied to the execution of the work effort, not in deciding what the work effort is or in managing it. In software development, conversely, very few engineering principles are applied. Although numerous work-breakdown structures, standards, and development methodologies and techniques exist and are available commercially, fewer than 30% of software development organizations use them.

Third, hardware development builds on previously developed technology. Catalogs of reusable components and bills of material for electronic subassemblies are readily available. There are test systems to test the validity of assemblies constucted from these components. Newly engineered components are added to the library as they are designed. None of these techniques are applied with regularity to software development. Each new program, each new enhancement, represents largely a new and creative effort on the part of the software developer.

The result—substantially more labor is expended per dollar of value on software than on hardware. The return on investment of the development effort is significantly lower. Hence software costs rise while hardware costs drop.

2.3 GROWING PROJECT BACKLOGS: THE IMPACT OF SUPPORT

There has always been a backlog of software development projects. It has been commonly accepted that a two- to five-year backlog of projects is normal

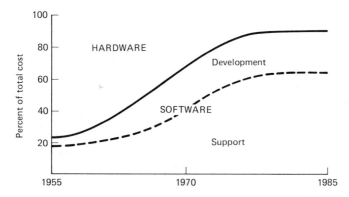

Figure 2.2   Hardware/software cost trends. Barry Boehm, *Software Engineering Economics,* p. 18, © 1981. Reprinted by permission of Prentice-Hall.

in a software development environment. This problem is worsened by the shortfall of resources and the growing demand for software.

There is another, less visible culprit adding to the backlogs. The addition of one new software program to an organization's operating environment takes a certain amount of resource to create, but that is not the end of the resource requirement. After implementation, software takes on a life of its own and requires periodic care and feeding, commonly known as maintenance or support. If the support requirement for a new program is 10% of the development effort annually, each set of 10 new programs will require one full-time person for maintenance—forever.

Many organizations today are pressured by extreme maintenance/ support requirements which consume in excess of 50% of their available resource. A major problem affecting the software development industry is the misconception that maintenance is fixing bugs and hence requires less management attention and control. A study performed by Lientz and Swanson for their book *Software Maintenance Management* indicates that of that body of work called maintenance, over 75% is actually enhancement and adapting software to meet new needs—which is really development work and requires the same level of management effort to control and manage—only 21% is actually fixing bugs.

2.4 LATE PROJECTS

Most software development professionals would grudgingly admit that many instances of late projects are due to poor estimating. Many disciplines outside software development require professionals to estimate, but few have as poor a reputation for accuracy.

In other disciplines, the estimator relies on statistical analysis, historical data, and a scientific method of measuring the size of the job. In manufacturing environments, job costing systems and standard-cost accounting methods provide controls over the estimating process. These processes are not widely implemented in the software development arena.

Also, in other disciplines, the nature of the work is somewhat repetitive, which over the course of time, has been carefully measured and analyzed within a standard work-breakdown structure. We have already established that this process is not widely used in software development. Software development professionals typically develop their estimates from personal observation of the size of the task and develop an estimate based on personal experience in developing similar applications. Since the human mind is not notorious for exact, instantaneous recall, this contributes to the inaccuracy of estimates. Admittedly, there have been some efforts targeted at improving the confidence-factor of systems development efforts; However, many of these estimating models (like the COCOMO model)* base their resource estimates on lines-of-code. That's great, except that we rarely know how many lines of code will result when we first peruse the work-request.

Many project delays are blamed on changes in specifications by the users, underestimation of the programming effort, reprogramming caused by bugs discovered in the testing process, and machine downtime. Although these problems may cause delays in the project, frequently, as we shall see in subsequent chapters, these factors are under the control of the project manager.

2.5 USER DISSATISFACTION

User dissatisfaction occurs when the functionality of the system delivered to the customer (user) does not correspond to the user's expectations. Although there are, admittedly, some irrational and unreasonable users in the business community, they are probably a small minority.

In a simple analysis, this problem is caused by miscommunication between the software developer and the user. This miscommunication can arise for three reasons:

1. In the haste to achieve results, requirements definition and design are ignored and user requests are viewed as "simply a matter of programming."
2. The user's requirements are not verified and reviewed in sufficient, mutually agreeable detail prior to implementation.
3. Users and software developers do not have a set of rules to follow in communicating with each other.

Again, this is a problem with a solution.

---

*Barry Boehm, in his book *Software Engineering Economics* (1981) gives a detailed, procedural description of the COCOMO estimating model. Like many models, COCOMO does a fairly good job of telling you how long the project will take—after you've written the code and then counted the lines.

3

The Software
Engineering Solution

3.1 WHAT IS SOFTWARE ENGINEERING?

Engineering is the process of designing, planning, and constructing an artifact (a bridge, car, computer, etc.) employing standard procedures, techniques, and tools within a controlled, managed environment. The engineering process has been consistantly applied over the past 15 to 20 years and was pioneered in the aerospace industry. The NASA Apollo project is probably one of the best examples of the success of the engineering process in implementing complex, large-scale projects. The engineering process is largely responsible for the dramatic advances in computer hardware technology and the resurgence of the American automotive industry.

Software engineering is the application of the engineering process to the development of computer software. By engineering software, we can improve the productivity of the software developers (software engineers), increase the quality of the software product, and achieve greater management control over the process.

The software engineering approach to developing information systems is not necessarily a new methodology for managing or developing software systems, but rather a "meta-methodology" which integrates and optimizes available technologies for building systems and managing development, allowing for flexibility in assimilating new techniques and technologies as they occur.

The key difference between the software engineering approach and more traditional approaches is that software engineering stresses *integration* among the various planning, management, and development or engineering processes which are interleaved, closely coupled procedures that result in the creation of information systems.

Most traditional approaches, including many of the commercially available "systems development methodologies" and individual productivity tools, take a narrow, piecemeal view of the overall systems management and development process, focusing on such discrete areas as project management, project control, requirements definition, or system design or programming. These canned solutions to systems development problems attack a segment of the overall problem and are rarely integrated with one another.

Software engineering, as presented in this book, however, provides a procedure with which an enterprise can identify, select, and implement a corporate systems development methodology which begins with strategic systems planning and ends with the maintenance of existing information systems applications. Some of the procedures presented are unique to the software engineering approach—focusing on meeting the informational needs of various levels of management and developers. Other software engineering

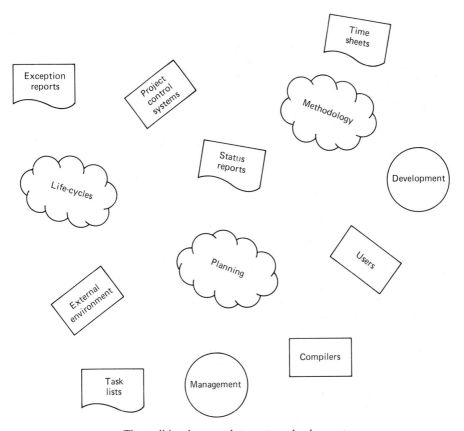

The traditional approach to systems development

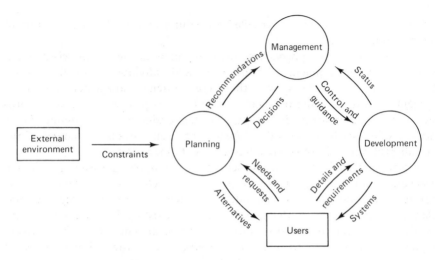

The software engineering approach to systems development

procedures focus on the requirements for and evaluation of existing pieces of the solution and provide guidelines for integrating them.

As a "meta-methodology," the software engineering approach to information systems development addresses:

- Global systems architecture development for the enterprise
- Strategic systems planning for funding systems projects
- Tactical systems planning for allocating and managing project resources
- Operational systems planning for controlling projects
- Engineering procedures (process flow and/or data structured) for specifying, programming, documenting, installing, and maintaining information systems

all as a single method of process, rather than as disjointed, sometimes unrelated entities.

3.2 THE BENEFITS OF THE SOFTWARE ENGINEERING APPROACH

The application of software engineering results in:

- The ability to meet the demand for software within limiting resource constraints
- The reduction in software maintenance or support associated with new software systems

- Increased user satisfaction with the software product
- Timely, on-budget completion of software engineering projects
- Increased ability to plan and schedule future development projects and optimize the allocation of software engineering resources

In aggregate, these benefits can be summed up as improved productivity and management control.

3.3 SOFTWARE ENGINEERING'S PRIME OBJECTIVE: IMPROVING PRODUCTIVITY

Frequently, when people speak of improving productivity, they refer to the "dictionary" definition, which focuses on *efficiency,* or increasing the rate at which software project deliverables can be completed (i.e., decreasing the completion time). This definition usually considers code the only deliverable and ignores the impact of software quality.

A measure of *quality* is the absence of defects found in the software and the supporting user documentation. Defects can refer to hard bugs, such as inaccurate calculations or postings of data. Defects can also refer to soft bugs, such as screens being implemented in a manner unsuitable to the user. These soft bugs are generally a result of communications problems between the designer and the user during the requirements and design phases of the software project. Poor-quality software must either be repaired or lived with. Repairing defective software is expensive, counteracts the speed with which the software was built, and lowers post-project efficiency. Perhaps a better definition of a high-quality system would simply be a system which meets the needs of the user. This would imply that:

- the system is easy for the user to operate
- it provides the information needed in a timely manner
- the system is adaptable to a dynamic user environment
- it does not break
- occasionally required maintenance can be performed at a low cost

For our purposes, we shall define *productivity* as a function of both efficiency and quality. If I can produce software faster, with the same defect rate, I have become more productive. If I can product higher-quality software (i.e., a lower defect rate) in the same amount of time, I am still more productive, for I will not have to spend time, post-installation, correcting defects.

Considering both quality and efficiency in the productivity equation adds another dimension to the problem. Typically, spending more time in analysis, design, and testing (actions that increase quality) also decreases the efficiency with which the software project is completed. It may be possible to produce zero-defect software, but it may cost 10 times as much to build. Figure 3.1 depicts the relationship between quality (measured in defects) and efficiency (measured in time).

Productivity is a curve along which management must select the point that it wishes to achieve. Simply trading-off quality for efficiency merely moves the organization along the curve at the same level of productivity. The curve in this figure represents the bounded universe in which today's software developers live. Figure 3.2, however, represents an actual shift in productivity. In this figure, if management moves the software development organization from any point on curve A to any point on curve B, productivity has been improved. Management must still make the same "guns and butter" economic trade-off decision between efficiency and quality, but the organization, regardless of the point achieved on curve B, is still economically better off.

The objective of the software engineering solution to the software challenge, then, is to provide a mechanism for the enterprise to shift its software development productivity curve—and to provide management with the controls necessary to choose the point of higher productivity best suited to the organization.

3.4 SOFTWARE ENGINEERING: A SYNTHESIS OF METHODOLOGIES, TECHNIQUES, AND TOOLS

Virtually all of the essential elements of the engineering process (procedures, techniques, and tools) required for software engineering are available today. The challenge is to integrate the elements into a workable system. The following is an overview of software engineering procedures, techniques, and tools. A more detailed analysis of specific products and technologies is covered in Chapter 16.

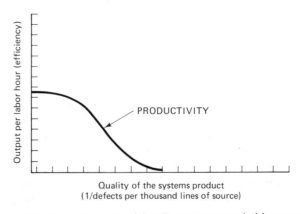

Figure 3.1 Improving productivity: The management decision curve

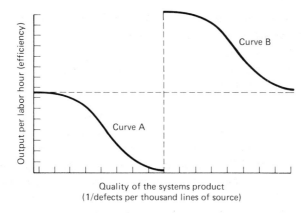

Figure 3.2   Improving productivity: Shifting the management decision curve

The Life-Cycle Approach:
Software Engineering Methodologies

The development or engineering of computer software is a project-oriented process. Before proceeding, let's establish a definition for the term "project" which can serve as a standard through the rest of this book:

> A *project* is an event with a defined beginning and end which produces a specific deliverable. The event can be subdivided into units of work that occur in a particular sequence which may create, modify and transform discrete deliverables into the final project deliverables—programs and documentation.

The work to develop software has defined steps, a starting point and a definitive end. Software engineering projects follow a life cycle from beginning to end. The blueprint for this life cycle is the software engineering methodology, which contains:

- A *work-breakdown structure,* which decomposes a project into successively smaller units of work. A project is divided into phases, or major categories of work, such as requirements definition, design, programming and unit testing, and implementation. Phases represent major milestones in the project during which the approach to implementing the software can be evaluated and major decisions can be made. Phases can be further divided into subgroupings of work, and additional decomposition occurs until a series of unique steps performed by a single person can be identified.

- *Step relationships,* which identify the relationships between steps of the project, the sequence in which the steps must be performed, and any dependencies between steps which exist.

- *Identification of standard deliverables,* which are tangible results of each step, such as data-flow diagrams, program specifications, user procedures, source code, and so on.
- *Procedures* for the management of the project and the execution of the steps to produce deliverables.

The software development methodology defines *what* must be done on the project and serves as a master project blueprint which can be tailored to a specific software engineering project. The earliest software engineering methodology was PRIDE, released in 1972 by M. Bryce and Associates of Cincinnati, Ohio. Since that time, a number of significant advances have been made in the area of software development methodology development. Methodologies such as Spectrum International's SPECTRUM life cycles and SDM/70-SDM/STRUCTURED from AGS Management Systems, Inc., are commercially available.

Methodologies are also employed in software engineering planning. While there are many books describing systems planning and data modeling methodologies by such authors as Larry Long and James Martin, there are also commercially available planning methodologies such as IBM's BSP (Business Systems Planning) process. A number of consulting firms also provide methodologies and services in this area, such as Ernst & Whinney and Arthur Anderson & Company.

Software Development Techniques

While the software development procedure methodology focuses on *what* work must be performed and *when,* the software development technique focuses on *how* to build the software. If the methodology indicates that a data-flow diagram must be prepared, the technique identifies the procedure for developing the diagram, the standard symbols that must be used, and the relationships between system elements that must be depicted. There are software development techniques that govern requirements definition, business system design, software design, and programming. The most commonly used graphic techniques in the commercial sector at present are the Yourdon, Orr, and Gane and Sarson. The area of techniques also includes such linguistic specification techniques as PSL/PSA.

Even though software development methodologies and software development techniques are separate elements of the software engineering process, they are related. Adopting a development technique may necessitate minor modifications to the work-breakdown structure of the methodology since there may not be a one-to-one mapping of required deliverables. Structured analysis and design techniques, for example, have been integrated quite successfully into the SPECTRUM methodology. Some methodologies, however, such as PRIDE, contain their own, embedded design techniques.

Tools

Tools are implements employed by people to reduce manual effort in accomplishing work. In ancient computing history, Hollerith cards and key-punches were the primary tools that people used to communicate with machines. The human–machine interface has been significantly improved, and such tools (both hardware and software) as interactive program development systems (such as IBM's TSO), database management systems, code optimizers, and application software generators (such as CGI, Inc.'s PACBASE) have evolved to reduce the human effort involved in developing software.

The requirements and design process, however, has remained largely a paper-and-pencil process. Flowcharts tend to be drawn today as they were in the 1940s when Eckert and Mauchley were developing ENIAC. A new genera-tion of computer-aided software engineering (CASE) tools, however, is emerging to automate the earlier phases in the software development life cycle. We are finding that word processors and microcomputers (IBM's line of personal computers) are finding their way onto analysts' desks.

The deployment of software engineering tools enables software engineers to execute steps using design techniques faster and to produce higher-quality results. There are also tools for project managers to control the software engi-neering process. Project control systems such as AGS Software's PAC-II and Nichols N5500 have been around for quite a while.

In addition to these tools which address special engineering tasks, there are tool kits, such as NASTEC CASE 2000 and PRIDE/ASDM, which pro-vide tools for groups of software development and management tools.

3.5 IMPLEMENTING SOFTWARE ENGINEERING

Implementing software engineering in a data processing/software develop-ment environment represents a significant technological and cultural change to both managers and developers. As with any change, there is some level of stress. The trade-off is between the acceptable level of stress versus the reward of the change. The software engineering approach to developing systems can be quite beneficial, as described above, and in fact, may be the only way to meet the software challenge. To minimize the level of stress and improve the chances of successful implementation, a planned, phased approach, as shown in Figure 3.3, is required.

As with all processes, implementing software engineering begins with planning. The necessary elements of the software engineering implementation plan are:

- Senior management commitment to deploy financial and human re-sources to implement the process

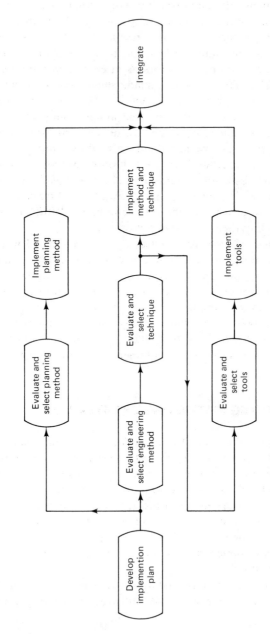

Figure 3.3 A phased approach to software engineering implementation

- Senior management commitment to participate in the strategic systems planning process
- Selection of a software engineering implementation team
- Selection of a strategic systems planning team

Since the implementation of a comprehensive software engineering process can be clearly segmented into the need for planning, engineering methodology and techniques, and tools, the process can be pursued in limited-scope phases. This limits the magnitude of the cultural change and allows for the complete assimilation of new technology in smaller groups.

3.6 STRATEGIC SYSTEM PLANNING

The strategic systems planning process for software engineering is primarily a senior management function which may or may not require staff assistance (depending on the size and complexity of the organization). The two phases of the software engineering implementation process associated with strategic planning are evaluation and selection of a planning methodology, and implementation of the strategic planning process.

Evaluating and Selecting Planning Methodology

The two main schools of thought associated with strategic systems planning are process-oriented planning and data modeling–oriented planning. These techniques are discussed in more detail in Chapter 6.

Implementing the Strategic Planning Process

The implementation of the strategic systems planning process involves the initial development of a systems architecture or global outline for all of the software applications that are required to manage the organization. Second, it involves macro-level estimating of the work associated with the implementation of the architecture, from which a strategic systems plan can be developed. Third, it involves the establishment of a senior management committee which can review the plan and resource requirements and fund the development effort. At regular intervals, the senior management committee convenes to evaluate the progress against the plan and approve changes to, or diversions from, the plan.

3.7 SOFTWARE DEVELOPMENT

The software development process, and the software engineering implementation plan associated with it, tend to focus on project management rather than senior management. Since the issues associated with the software development process tend to be more detailed and technical, the majority of the implementation process can be assigned to project management personnel. Therefore, the software development–related planning and implementation process can usually be implemented concurrently with strategic systems planning.

The four phases of the software engineering implementation plan associated with technical software development are the evaluation and selection of a methodology or life cycle, the selection of techniques to support the life cycle, and implementation of both, followed by the selection and implementation of tools that automate the process.

The tools selection process is generally constrained by the selection of methodologies and techniques for two reasons. First, software engineering tools typically (although, not always, as we shall see in Chapter 16) support a specific life or design technique. Second, it may, in some cases, be less traumatic to learn the processes involved before learning how to communicate with a machine or software program. This follows the same reasoning as sending pilots to ground school before they learn how to actually fly a plane.

3.8 INTEGRATION

Although integration is listed as the final phase, it is truly an ongoing process. As the methodologies, techniques, and tools are evaluated, a prime consideration should be the ease with which they fit together. Integration is also an ongoing process as new technologies become available. The software engineering process is not static and should be flexible enough in implementation to allow new techniques and processes to be easily integrated.

3.9 SUMMARY

Adopting a software engineering process allows development organizations to meet the software challenge, to be responsive to user requirements, to be more productive, and to have better control over projects and asset deployment. As with any environmental or cultural change, there is some stress; however, by using a phased, planned, and controlled approach to implementation, the significant benefits of software engineering can readily be achieved.

4

Management Theory and Software Engineering

Adopting the software engineering process requires a logical structuring of systems development management to incorporate engineering disciplines. To develop this structure, let us first examine the role of management. Early in the twentieth century, a Frenchman, Henri Fayol of the classical school of management, described the functions of management as *planning, organizing, staffing, directing,* and *controlling.* These functions are performed at three levels: *strategic* (top), *tactical* (middle), and *operational* (lower). If we view software engineering as a school of management thought, then each of these functions and levels relates to specific systems planning and management areas of responsibility.

4.1 CLASSICAL MANAGEMENT FUNCTIONS

From the classical school of management, *planning* is the process of determining what work must be performed. *Organization* is the development of a structure or framework to allow implementation of the plan. Once the effort has been planned and organized, *staffing* occurs to acquire the resources (labor and materials) necessary to perform the work. After the acquisition of the resources, the work must be *directed;* that is, the resources must be instructed and guided through the plan to see that the work is executed. Throughout the process of executing the work, the process must be *controlled.* Management must examine the process to ensure that the work is being performed in accordance with the plan. There must be feedback from the transformation process which management can analyze and interpret to develop controls or instructions with which to alter the performance of the work and the behavior of the workers. All of these functions are performed to varying degrees at each management level.

Strategic management is concerned with the long-term goals of the organization, planning three to five years ahead, determining global resource allocations to achieve the goals. Strategic management determines the organizational management structure, funds the resources required to meet the objectives of the organization, directs activities primarily through establishing priorities, and controls through adjusting budget allocations for resource and establishing new goals.

Tactical management is responsible for developing action plans for the organization to achieve the goals set by strategic management, and establishes objectives. Tactical management typically advises strategic management of the level of resource required to achieve the goals, and then staffs to the level funded by strategic management. Tactical management's planning horizon is typically one to two years. This level of management typically controls by reallocating existing, funded resources.

Operational management is responsible for executing the action plans and achieving the objectives established by tactical management. Operational management implements projects, oversees day-to-day work, and controls the transformation process directly by modifying work schedules and short-term plans, and typically must work within the resource allocation made by tactical management. Operational management's planning horizon may be daily, monthly, or quarterly, and rarely exceeds the duration of a particular project.

Although we can segment types of management by their scope of responsibility and planning horizon, that is not to say that any particular manager does not or cannot have some responsibilities for other management levels. Nor does it imply that the three levels of management operate independently of each other. There must be constant vertical communication among the management levels. It does no good for strategic management to set new goals and horizons if the organization is incapable of achieving them. Nor will the subordinate levels of management be successful without a clear sense of purpose and direction supplied by upper management. Each level of management must communicate, through formal and informal channels, to achieve integration. In addition, each level must, in some fashion, participate in the other levels, either through participative decision making or by acting as part of the information processing system, passing on to other levels of management information that it has processed from data gleaned from its own operations.

While these levels of management and their functions apply to corporate organizations, they apply to lower-level macro-systems as well, particularly the systems planning and management process, which is, in fact, a microcosm of the organization it supports. Within the context of software engineering, each level of management assumes specific roles in the planning and management of the systems development process.

4.2 STRATEGIC SYSTEMS MANAGEMENT

Information systems development is primarily a staff or service function which exists to support the operations of the business enterprise. One could picture it as an enterprise wholly contained within a larger enterprise which has only one customer. This customer purchases information systems either though a charge-back system, wherein the systems development organization sets prices for its services, or through budgetary control, where the host enterprise establishes the level of funding in advance. In either environment, it is necessary for the strategic level of management to assess the needs of the customer and changes in service requirements to establish goals, objectives, and priorities which will serve as the parameters by which systems development will allocate and manage its resources.

Successful strategic systems management must maintain an awareness of the state of the systems development organization: its strengths, weaknesses, productivity, and utilization of resources. Also, it must expand the scope of its analysis beyond the systems development organization. It must understand the business environment of its customer, changes in business plans and operations, and most important, must constantly monitor and understand the information requirements of the customer, and the sources and uses of data which are important to the enterprise, now and in the future.

Strategic systems management must act on this information and determine the necessary information systems which must be enhanced, created, or replaced. Furthermore, strategic systems management must determine the level of funding that will be required to provide the resources to undertake this task.

Because of the close relationship with the host enterprise, the strategic systems management function must be undertaken by both corporate and systems development management. This function is generally undertaken by an information systems steering committee composed of senior systems and executive management of the enterprise. The participants in the strategic management process are typically the senior systems manager, the senior development manager, and the executive managers of the various user groups.

4.3 TACTICAL SYSTEMS MANAGEMENT

Once strategic systems management has determined the directions and goals of systems development, provided the funding necessary to execute the work, and established the priorities of the development efforts to be completed, tactical systems management must control the resource. Tactical systems management must define specific project parameters, allocate resources among the projects, establish quality controls, and keep the resources in balance among the projects to ensure that they are allocated to optimize the utilization of resources during the peaks and valleys of resource requirements in a multiple-project environment.

In addition, tactical systems management must constantly monitor the systems development process to refine its estimating techniques and keep strategic management abreast of required resource levels to achieve present and projected projects. This implies a two-way flow of information between tactical and strategic management. Typically, senior systems development management is responsible for tactical decisions. The participants in the tactical management process are typically the senior systems manager and the senior development manager.

Since tactical management is responsible for quality assurance and the control of the project process, it is tactical management that must implement development standards, quality and productivity metrics, and manage the estimating, project control, and standards database.

4.4 OPERATIONAL SYSTEMS MANAGEMENT

Once tactical systems management has established the projects and resource allocations, projects are assigned to operational management—the project managers. *Project managers* are typically assigned to one or more projects and are given charge of the resources required to execute those projects. Typically, the level of resource assigned to a project will rise and fall with the requirements of the project. In many environments, project managers are true matrix managers and are the closest level of management to the actual systems development transformation process.

Project managers, being responsible for particular projects, must have the information necessary to estimate the duration of specific units of work and a detailed knowledge of the capabilities of the resources that must be applied to accomplish their objectives. In turn, they must provide tactical management with information regarding the level of effort and resource required to perform certain types of tasks, the availability and level of commitment remaining for their resources, and the performance of their project compared with the plan.

4.5 MANAGEMENT AND ORGANIZATION

Having determined the levels of management responsibility, it is important to determine who is responsible for each level. Figure 4.1 represents a fairly

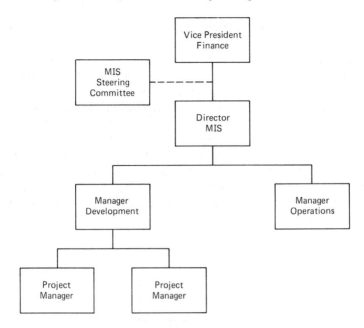

Figure 4.1 A simple data processing organization

common organizational structure for the small data processing organization. Here we can see the clear distinction between the various management levels. In this organization, the vice president of finance [who is the chief management information systems (MIS) officer for the corporation] is responsible for the approval of funding. The director of MIS develops strategic plans, which are approved by the vice president and the steering committee, and allocates resources between computer operations and development. The development manager initiates projects, sets quality and performance guidelines, and assumes the role of tactical manager. In many cases, the development manager has the authority to *initiate* projects that are not in conflict with the strategic plan, and *recommends* changes to the strategic plan when required. The project managers administer individual projects and assume the operational management role.

In larger organizations, particularly in enterprises that sell software products, financial organizations (such as banks and insurance companies), and other organizations that depend heavily on data processing systems as a central component of their business, the distinctions among strategic, tactical, and operational management are delineated less clearly because more levels of management participate. Furthermore, there is a crossing of level boundaries by the various managers. Figure 4.2 depicts an organizational structure of a large banking organization.

In this type of organization, the group vice president of information services clearly has responsibility for strategic management; however, so do the senior vice presidents, for their areas of responsibility. For example, the senior vice president for development is responsible for all the software engineering activities within the organization—which are divided into three primary areas: consumer, corporate, and international systems. Given that the group vice president for MIS determines the budget allocation for the software engineering area, the senior vice president for development must determine the allocations among the three areas. In addition, while there is a corporate steering committee, there may also be steering committees dedicated to development; and since consumer, corporate, and international banking may represent subsidiary companies, they may have their own priority setting and strategic planning groups.

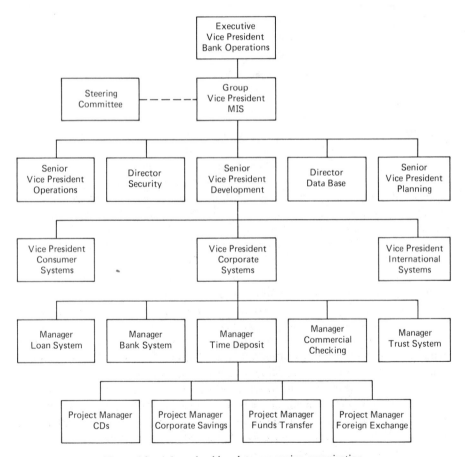

Figure 4.2 A large banking data processing organization

In this type of organization, the senior vice president of planning is responsible for the development and documentation of strategic plan alternatives is involved in strategic planning for operations, security, development, and database, and acts as a consultant to other subsidiary organizations which must perform strategic planning. Strategic planning at the highest level in an organization with subsidiary level strategies is concerned primarily with coordination among the subsidiaries to avoid gross inconsistencies and to facilitate communication where common goals, objectives, and systems occur.

Tactical management, in this context, becomes the shared responsibility of the vice-presidential level and the managers (such as the managers of loans, bank systems, time deposits, commercial checking, and trust). It is at this level that the actual projects are compared against the strategic plan and approved, or recommended to senior management as changes to the plan. The various department managers are also responsible for their budget and for allocating their budgeted resources among the approved projects.

Operational management is the responsibility of the project managers who directly supervise the transformation process. In organizations where project managers manage multiple projects, headed individually by team leaders, some tactical allocation responsibilities may fall to the project manager. Indeed, in many organizations, the project manager is an administrative manager with line responsibilities.

4.6 SUMMARY

There are three levels of software engineering management: strategic, tactical, and operational. Strategic management determines the organization's level of investment in software resource and approves the strategic plan for developing software. Tactical management allocates software development resources, approves projects (consistent with the strategic plan), and administers the software development budget. Operational management plans, controls, and reports on status for software engineering projects.

The participants in the various levels of management vary among organizations based on size and corporate structure. There is a high degree of overlap between adjacent levels, which allows cross participation in the management process. Typically, from a planning standpoint, the lower level of management assists in the preparation of the higher-level plan, and regularly makes recommendations for alterations to the plan.

5

The Systems Management Macro-System

5.1 SYSTEMS AND MACRO-SYSTEMS

Ludwig von Bertallanfy, the father of the systems concept and author of *General Systems Theory*, defined the term *system* as a group of components organized in a particular fashion, which worked together to achieve a certain outcome or objective.

Throughout the management information services industry, systems development professionals and management speak of systems in terms of application software—for example, management information systems, process control systems, modeling systems, and engineering systems. These systems are composed of hardware, software, and manual processes and procedures. The general architecture of these systems is depicted in Figure 5.1.

Although this use of the term "system" is correct, it is somewhat limiting. For purposes of discussing the application of software engineering to planning and managing systems development, it will be necessary to define a new level of systems, which we shall refer to as *macro-systems.*

The macro-system is a group of organized and related systems and subsystems, which, working together, achieve a desired result. Macro-systems occur at numerous levels. Higher-order macro-systems are composed of lower-order macro-systems, systems, and subsystems. An excellent example of a macro-system is the business enterprise. The enterprise is composed of marketing, sales, accounting, production, labor relations, purchasing, and a myriad of other components (or systems) working in conjunction to produce a product or service at a profit. Each of these component systems has its own

Figure 5.1 Basic system model

subsystems, programs, procedures, and objectives, yet they must work together efficiently, in an integrated process, in order to achieve the objectives of product and profitability. In the context of the business enterprise macro-system, the application software systems, and even the software engineering planning and development systems, are only small components. Management information systems, developed by the systems development organization, are data gathering and transformation systems which provide corporate management with the information needed to make decisions that control the enterprise's transformation process. Figure 5.2 depicts an organizational or enterprise macro-system.

Integration of the components of the macro-system is the key to the success of the enterprise. Each component must provide input to the subsequent components. The marketing system must identify appropriate products and set competitive prices, sales must generate orders, purchasing must

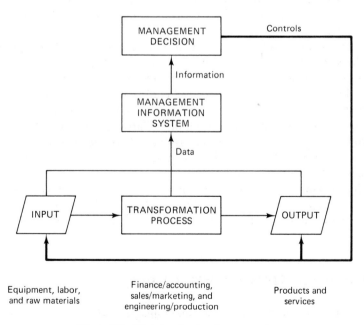

Figure 5.2 The organizational macro-system

acquire the appropriate level of raw materials, and production must build enough product to satisfy demand and provide sufficient capacity to meet changes in demand level. Accounting and finance must measure the profitability of the end product. To achieve this, each system must communicate with the other systems. The enterprise's management information system(s) must capture these data to be communicated, and summarize, organize, and format them for use by management, who will use the information to make decisions to control the business enterprise macro-system.

It is management's responsibility to enforce, optimize, and control the integration of the components of the macro-system. Integration is the key to the success of the enterprise. If any component of the enterprise compromises integration, a problem develops that must be attended to by executive management.

5.2 SYSTEMS DEVELOPMENT AS A MACRO-SYSTEM

In the same sense that a business enterprise is a macro-system, so is the data processing/systems development function. The systems development process or macro-system includes planning, project control, systems analysis, design, programming and implementation, machine utilization, personnel, and a host of related functions. Each of these components must have objectives, and in concert, work together to produce a product (software/data processing application systems) for the customer (user), which is quality controlled and cost-effective.

Each of the systems development components must be integrated with the others so that information flows freely among them. Systems development management must monitor the components of the macro-system to ensure integration and make management and control decisions based on an analysis of information about the state of the systems development process. A breakdown in any of the systems will result in late projects, cost overruns, personnel shortages and/or inferior software products delivered to users. A successful systems development organization must have an integrated systems planning and management macro-system.

By viewing the systems development process as a macro-system, it is possible to apply generally accepted systems analysis and design techniques to the process to improve the system, and automate as many of the processes as possible.

5.3 MACRO-SYSTEM ARCHITECTURE

The systems planning and management macro-system can be divided into several component systems, as depicted in Figure 5.3.

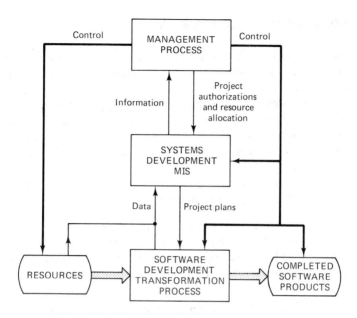

Figure 5-3   The software development macro-system

Starting at the bottom is the *software development transformation process,* which is the system for converting labor (programmers, analysts, designers), equipment (development software, computers, paper, pencils), and raw materials (data and specifications) into completed software system products.

The *management process* plans systems development at the strategic, tactical, and operational levels. It is through this process that resources get allocated, quality is assured, and projects are controlled. The management process evaluates present resource allocations against projected needs and determines which assets are deployed to execute which projects. The management process also establishes work-breakdown structures, performance, and development standards and methods that will be employed in the transformation process.

The systems development *management information system* (MIS) performs two functions. First, it collects data from the transformation process and the resource pool and assembles it into a useful format from which management decisions can be made. In addition, the MIS provides standards and project plan information to the resources executing the project.

From this general architecture we can develop an integrated, controllable software engineering planning and management process which will enable both corporate and systems development management to assess the success of the systems development organization, and to take steps to ensure success, despite the periodic stresses that affect development, and the ever-present evolution of the organization which systems development must support.

5.4 INFORMATION REQUIREMENTS

The systems development organization is a subset macro-system of the parent macro-system. No one would conceive of managing a business enterprise or governmental agency without application systems to monitor the process, collect data, and summarize and report to management. When software developers build these types of application systems, the first step in the process is to develop the information requirements that must be met by the application. In developing a software engineering macro-system, the same requirements analysis must be performed.

The key role in the software engineering process is the management decision process, which is a three-step process:

1. *Objectives:* There must be some expected results from the software engineering process. These objectives include the set of work that must be performed in the transformation process, the time frame in which the work must be executed, and the level of quality expected in the software product.

2. *Evaluation:* The state of the transformation process must be determined, and the variance from the desired objectives (if any) must be evaluated. The manager must determine whether the variance is within acceptable limits (Not a Problem) or whether corrective action must be taken (Problem).

3. *Control:* Once the manager knows the relation between the present state of the system in relationship to the objectives, the manager must determine what the acceptable alternatives are, what control measures can be taken, what the impact of the controls will be on the state of the system, and decide what controls to impose. Once controls have been imposed, a new set of objectives is established and the cycle continues.

The management decision process is an information processing system implemented on the most complex (and perhaps most efficient) computer—the human mind. As with any other information processing system, the management decision system requires input—information.* The information requirements for the systems planning and management process represent the information needed by management to execute the management decision process. The basic information requirements are:

- Which application systems need to be developed to support the objectives of the organization

---

*Computerized systems accept data as input and generate transformed data to other systems or information to people. The management decision process is a human-processing system which accepts information as input and generates additional information or action as output.

- How these systems interface or interrelate
- The criteria by which the application systems will be evaluated as successes or failures
- The current distribution of systems development resources and the duration for which these resources are committed to present projects
- The level of performance and quality being achieved by the application of current resources

To acquire and process this information, systems development management, by means of its own management information system, must constantly monitor:

- The current systems environment, including the organization's current management objectives, business plans and systems, and the data that are needed in these systems to meet the needs of the users
- The users' expectations and requirements with respect to system responsiveness and the ability of the systems development function to meet their requirements
- Projected systems development support resource levels based on anticipated project load as determined from the organization's objectives and business plans
- The present level of utilization of systems development resources and the current project queue to which these resources must be assigned; also, changes in the project queue generated by changes in estimated work remaining on outstanding projects
- The standards of quality expected of the systems development process, the degree to which these standards are being met, and the level (quantity) of work being completed with respect to planned performance levels

These basic requirements for the parameters by which a formalized, integrated systems planning and management process is designed. Through a software engineering approach, the metrics, work-breakdown structure, methods, and tools can be employed to capture this information, and develop and implement software development plans that meet the organization's objectives.

6

A Systems
Planning Overview

Management is the art and/or science of ensuring that events occur and that results get achieved in a predetermined manner. Management controls are those influences over events which management can exert to ensure that desired results are achieved. It is apparent, then, that the primary prerequisite to successful management is a good plan—a baseline against which results can be measured. Successful implementation of application systems requires a sound management process, founded on well-executed planning.

The software engineering process requires planning at three levels, which correspond to the management levels discussed in Section 4.1: strategic, tactical, and operational planning. These three levels of planning provide software engineering/application development management with a baseline of performance, productivity, requirements, and cost against which software development effort can be measured. These measurements become information or input to the management decision-making process, providing the parameters by which management controls will be executed. In this chapter we examine the requirements for each of the three levels of planning and define a planning process that is integrated into the overall software engineering macro-system.

6.1 STRATEGIC SYSTEMS PLANNING

A large number of business system development organizations approach strategic systems planning from the bottom up. That is, they evaluate work orders for systems development effort, prioritize them, and then execute them. The work orders typically emanate from the lower management levels and bubble up to senior management through the software development organization. All too frequently, applications developed using this technique require subsequent adaptation to account for uses of the information which were not previously considered, or because changes in the business environment necessitate changes in functionality—or enhancements to the system—frequently in a very short time span after development.* This method of planning also makes it difficult, if not impossible, to gain a perspective on the impact of ad hoc requests for systems on the corporate database. Furthermore, since this method of planning is based on external input, it makes it difficult to view software/systems development as a capital investment competing with other, non-data processing projects for funding. Finally, evaluating projects in this mode, on a piecemeal basis, does not afford the advantage of viewing the entire corporate information system (composed of a semi-infinite number of modules built as a result of individual work requests) in context. When viewed in context, reusable modules, components, applications, and subsystems can be identified, consolidated, and/or jointly developed. This optimizes systems development resource, lowers the ultimate development costs of the systems, and delivers applications to end users faster.

Taking a software engineering approach, in the strategic planning stage, the entire enterprise is viewed as a macro-system and the strategic plan is developed from the top down. The objective of strategic systems planning is to develop a global systems architecture for the firm which examines the enterprise's transformation process, extracts data, and outputs information to management from which decisions can be made to control the firm's transformation process. The outputs from the strategic systems planning process are the systems architecture and the strategic systems plan. The strategic systems planning process establishes the budget or funding levels for systems development.

The *systems architecture* models the enterprise and defines the application systems that must be developed to provide management with the information they need to make decisions that will enable the firm to meet both its short-term and long-term business objectives. The systems architecture identifies those components of the overall systems/database environment which are already in place, need to be modified, or need to be developed from scratch or purchased. The systems architecture is, in essence, a very high level system design.

The *strategic systems plan* is a mapping of the architecture over time. Typically, the strategic systems plan begins life as a series of options—depicting different segments of the architecture being completed in different amounts of

---

*Frequently is a relative term. In this sense, the occurrence is frequent if it happens often enough to impair the ability of the development organization to meet deadlines on important projects.

time with varied resource commitments, and ends up as a long-range blueprint for software development against which individual projects are measured and against which the endless number of ad hoc user requests can be evaluated.

The "final" versions of the architecture and plan, however, are updated at regular intervals to account for changes in business objectives, technology, and issues discovered as a result of evaluating ad hoc requests. Typically, the strategic systems planning process will be under the management of the most senior manager whose entire responsibility is data processing.

6.2 TACTICAL SYSTEMS PLANNING

Tactical systems planning is primarily a resource allocation issue, focusing on an annual time frame. Based on the assumption that a strategic plan and architecture have been developed for the organization, individual projects need to be initiated in concert with the plan. In addition, it must be recognized that it is unlikely that the strategic plan and architecture will resolve all of the shorter-term issues that will arise in the working environment.

The tactical planning process maps existing (and budgeted but not acquired) resources against the strategic plan and establishes preliminary project schedules, budgets, and resource allocations. It is against the tactical plan that projects are evaluated. In addition, the tactical planning process allocates resources, authorized by the strategic systems plan, among both strategic projects (i.e., those called for by the strategic plan) and high-priority work orders that were not incorporated in the plan. In essence, tactical systems planning is project management at the multiproject level.

While the tactical planning process focuses on an annual time frame, the plan is detailed at the monthly level and evaluated at least quarterly. Tactical systems planning is usually managed and/or conducted by the most senior manager whose responsibility is circumscribed by software/application systems development.

6.3 OPERATIONAL SYSTEMS PLANNING

Most organizations perform some level of *operational systems planning,* which is otherwise known as *project planning.* Once resources have been assigned to a project, via the tactical planning process, operational planning details the work that must be performed on an individual team-member basis. The planning horizon for operational systems planning is typically the duration of the project.

6.4 SUMMARY

In essence, the software engineering planning process is a tiered process of planning and requirements definition which functionally decomposes the software environment from the top down—and feeds recommendations and changes to the architecture from the bottom up. Since the planning process mirrors the responsibilities of software/systems development management, it provides criteria at all levels against which performance can be measured, allowing management control to be exerted over the entire software development process rather than simply at the project level. This planning process also allows the delineation of accountability for executing systems development, to ensure that sound management principles are imposed at all development levels.

7

Strategic Systems Management

7.1 INTRODUCTION

The business enterprise is a macro-system that transforms inputs (raw materials, capital equipment, labor) into outputs (products and/or services), usually in return for a profit from the effort. The management of the firm is chartered to observe the transformation process, which typically can be considered to include distribution of output, and to optimize the application of resources to ensure profitability. Around this corporate objective is an entire management/administrative infrastructure designed to provide management with relevant data about the transformation process so that management can make decisions and exert influence or control for optimization. This infrastructure incorporates data processing systems in the acquisition of data and generation of information, and frequently also provides control mechanisms (such as in process-control manufacturing systems).

Historically, these MIS/process-control applications evolved over long periods of time, without necessarily considering integrating either the functionality of the applications or the databases (in the loose sense). Today, these organizations are evolving even more systems through new development, enhancement of existing systems (to increase functionality), and adaptation (to provide substantially new application potential for systems that were originally designed for another purpose). Typically, this work is done in a piecemeal fashion as requests for new applications development and modification are received from the user community. Ad hoc requests are received from user management and prioritized by some mechanism (which frequently incorporates some decision-making body such as an MIS steering committee).

The problem with this approach is that it is a passive management process. That is, decisions as to which systems to build and which enhancements to incorporate result directly from inputs which were generated from a very narrow point of view. Each MIS work request is typically generated by a manager with a narrow scope of responsibility (in the overall corporate sense) and with that manager's perspective on the processing and data/information requirements. This tends to produce a randomization in the application development process and does not foster systems integration.

Why Systems Integration?

By itself, randomization is not bad; however, it can potentially lead to an increase in the work load (and ultimately the cost) of software applications. First, randomization of development generates multiple databases that store duplicate data—duplicating storage costs, file/database design effort, and programming effort to create substantially different mechanisms for accessing what is essentially identical data.

Second, randomization takes a narrow view of the overall systems architecture. Jones (1984) espouses the value of reusable code and reusable design. Viewing discrete work requests without a global analysis of the corporate information systems needs frequently causes new designs to be developed and new programs to be written, all of which increases the cost of information systems. It would be much more efficient to reuse design and programs; however, even this task can be difficult if the other potential or planned uses of the software are not known at the time of technical implementation.

Third is simply the cost of adaptation. There has long been a realization that a bug identified in programming costs roughly 10 times as much to correct as a bug caught in design, and a bug caught after implementation can cost as much as 100 times to fix. This is analogous to the cost of enhancing or adapting software. Other intended features and/or uses of processes and data are much less costly to incorporate in the original design and implementation than to incorporate once a first version of the system has been incorporated. However, developers must be aware of the need for data and/or features at the time of original design. This means that all known requirements, other than those of the specific requestor, must be considered at initial implementation. This requires some advanced planning.

Strategic Planning Objectives

The primary objective of strategic systems planning is to allow the development organization to be aware of planned uses of data and processes at design time so that the initial design can at least have "hooks" for required data and functionality, even if it does not provide it in the initial implementation. Also, the strategic systems planning process enables a macro-level look at organizational information requirements for database and development effort optimization which would not otherwise be available. During the strategic planning process, the entire information systems architecture can be analyzed for data and process redundancy, resulting in development of reusable design.

Strategic Planning Methodology

While there are a number of specific process- or procedure-oriented techniques that can be applied to the strategic systems planning process, there is a general methodology or planning life cycle into which those techniques can be mapped. In Figure 7.1, the general information flow for the strategic planning process is depicted.

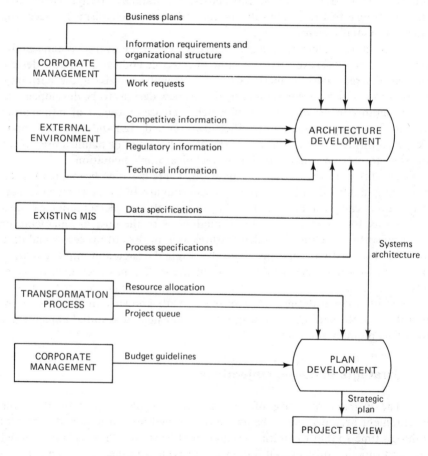

Figure 7.1   Strategic systems planning data flow

Define the architecture.   Architecture development begins by assessing the corporation from within, polling the senior and middle management team about their requirements and the business plans of the organization in general. In addition, the known, outstanding work requests are accumulated. From the external environment, competitive information (i.e., information on how competitors to your industry are applying information technology, and/or how information technology can provide your firm with a competitive edge), regulatory information, and data on new advances in hardware/software/application technology are gathered. From the enterprise's own documentation, data and process specifications for existing application systems can be assembled. From these data, the systems architecture can be developed using any number of specific development techniques discussed in the next section.

The resulting systems architecture describes the optimum information systems design for the enterprise. The major components of the architecture are:

- Model of the firm
- Matrix of information requirements and using organizations
- First-level information requirements description
- Definition of the major databases
- Definition of the major application systems required
- Identification of the system interfaces and intersections
- Identification of reusable/nonmodified existing system components
- Identification of new system components that must be developed
- Preliminary definition of the new system components
- Assessment of the hardware/software technology changes required

Once the architecture has been defined, it is possible to lay out a plan or schedule that depicts how the architecture will be implemented over time, given various resource alternatives.

Develop the strategic implementation plan.   The first requirement in developing the strategic implementation plan is estimating how much resource is required to implement the architecture. Second, the architecture must be reviewed and any dependencies must be identified to determine any sequence-oriented constraints that may apply to development.

Once these two steps have been accomplished, the architecture implementation can be segmented into projects, planned resource levels (based upon current budgetary plans) can be assigned, and the projects can be superimposed over a calendar.

This preliminary strategic implementation plan can then be massaged, based on varying priority and resource scenarios, and presented to management. Upon acceptance by senior management this plan can then serve as a road map to future development and a baseline against which project performance and new requests can be measured.

Strategic Management Decision Making

Developing the plan is only half of the planning process. The plan by itself is valueless unless there is a mechanism to implement it and to control the implementation. Furthermore, it is a rare organization that can set a global plan such as the one described and implement it without modification, especially since the plan probably spans more than one year. In reality, the plan is merely a basis for, and input to, the management decision-making process.

There are several things than can happen once the plan has been developed:

1. It can be followed rigorously (not likely).
2. It can be ignored (frequently).
3. It can be used as a guideline for selecting projects for implementation.

We have already stated why plans are not followed rigorously. Plans are often ignored because they are too cumbersome to implement or because they become outdated. Frequently, plans pass from option 1 to option 2; that is, firms believe that, for the plan to be of value, it must be followed to the letter. When this becomes impossible for business reasons, they diverge from the plan, which then becomes out of date and unusable, and ultimately falls into oblivion. In option 2 there are two problems: First, a lot of money and time is wasted developing a plan, and second, all of the problems of randomization and lack of planning resurface.

Gaining value from planning.   To gain value from planning, the strategic systems plan must be used as a guideline for selecting projects for development and for assigning and allocating resources. To keep the plan workable, it must grow and be evolved over time as business conditions change. This implies, then, that the plan is incorporated into some overall management process.

All too often, maintaining a strategic plan is seen as a labor-intensive, overhead activity which is performed on a quarterly basis. When resources become tight, maintenance of the plan is dropped. The reason for this is that the maintenance of the plan is done in batch-processing mode rather than interactively. True, the first time a plan is executed, it is a major commitment of resources; however, a shift from batch-oriented plan maintenance to a more interactive mode can be both more efficient and timely. Interactive planning implies that the plan is modified as the need arises. Figure 7-2 describes an

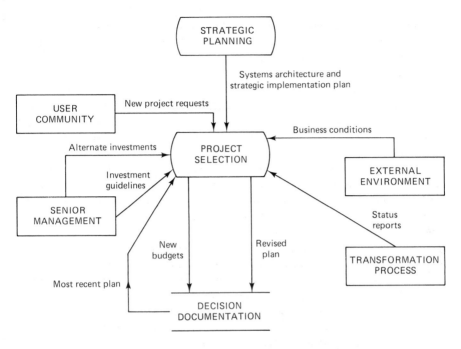

Figure 7.2   Strategic systems planning: management decision-making process

overall management decision-making process based on the existence of a strategic plan, but also incorporates interactive plan maintenance.

The process described in Figure 7.2 is essentially that of any MIS steering committee which has been implemented in data processing today. The difference is in having *specific deliverables* which are presented at the meeting and which document the decisions resulting from the session. Most steering committees are very similar in *what* they do; the difference lies in *how* the meetings are executed and the formats of the specific deliverables. The subtle difference between the process described in this figure and most others is that the strategic implementation plan is a living turnaround document, in a specific format, which both provides input to the session and documents its results. Earlier in this section specific procedures for administering this process were detailed which permit and enforce interactive planning.

7.2 THE SYSTEMS ARCHITECTURE

The Role of the Systems Architecture

In Chapter 5, the enterprise was defined as a macro-system that produced outputs (products and services) from inputs labor, raw materials, and capital equipment). This macro-system was managed by decisions and controls imposed by management over the transformation process. These decisions were supported by information provided to management by the enterprise's management information system (MIS). To a large degree, the effectiveness of the organization, measured in terms of profitibility, cost containment, or other convention particular to the type of enterprise, is dependent on the decisions made by management, therefore dependent on the quality of the MIS. It is the mission of the systems development organization to maximize the value of the information provided to management.

But what is the measure of effectiveness of the systems development organization? As a service organization, the systems development organization must respond to the needs and wishes of executive management. The systems development organization may then be measured on the effectiveness with which it develops an MIS response to the information requirements of management. The systems architecture is the documentation of the information requirements of the organization in the form of a model of the optimum MIS.

Defining the strategic systems architecture for a business enterprise is very similar to defining user requirements for an application system. The major difference is in the scope of the project. In application system development, the operating environment is typically well defined (such as payroll processing, inventory control, or general ledger). Even in those cases where it is not particularly well documented, the domain of the application is so small that it can often be implied. The scope of the systems architecture, on the other hand, is much wider, covering the entire enterprise macro-system. Typically, the exact nature of the corporate macro-system is much more nebulous. Indeed, many large corporations invest large sums of money in consulting fees to define the existing organization and make recommendations for new organizational structures.

The first two phases of the systems architecture development process deal with the definition of the environment or macro-system of the firm. The balance of the architecture development process deals with defining the data and information requirements to support the existing (or planned) organizational system. Many of the specific, commercially available systems design and development techniques (such as data-flow modeling, domain analysis, process analysis, and IPO) can be applied to the architecture development process for the global information macro-system, as well as to the domain of a particular application system. However, the perspective of the planner needs to be reoriented from that of the systems analyst/software engineer.

Carl Gustav Jung, a noted post-Freudian psychologist, coined the term "glosses" to refer to the different perspectives that individuals had of the world around them. Even though two people witnessed the same events, smelled the same odors, and felt the same tactile sensations, they described their perceptions differently. According to Jung, this was because they experienced different growth or development environments, which colored their perceptions of reality. Although the same techniques and same physical deliverables can be applied to systems architecture development and application system development, the analysts/planners need to have different "glosses," different ways to perceive the organization. Since we cannot grow planners or systems analysts in environmentally controlled nurseries (yet), we need to influence the planner's "gloss" externally, thereby influencing his or her perception of the enterprise and its information systems. This can be done by applying the development techniques in the context of a different development life cycle or work-breakdown structure. It is this work-breakdown structure that we discuss below. In subsequent sections we deal with the specific development techniques that can be applied to the development of the deliverables.

Figure 7.3 represents the positioning of the systems architecture within the enterprise-level macro-system. The systems architecture represents both the high-level specifications for the MIS and the plan or baseline against which the implemented MIS is measured. The systems architecture also represents a level of design that can be validated prior to implementation. It is a major investment to implement an information system. It is even more costly to maintain an information system in which defects, or "bugs," have been discovered. If one is having a house built, it is easier and cheaper to change the plumbing or electrical layout on the blueprint than after the drywall has been installed. If defects can be identified and resolved in the architecture, it is much less costly

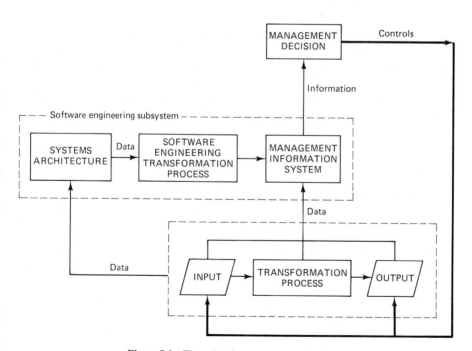

Figure 7.3 The role of the systems architecture

than waiting until implementation. Deciding on a database or file structure common to accounting, payroll, and production before the systems are built is much cheaper than converting later. Changes after implementation, first, obviate work that has already been completed. Code written to support different file structures is an investment that has no value in the common database or file environment. Second, there is a new investment of resource to create the common modules. These issues can be resolved "on paper" in the systems architecture, well in advance of implementation at the project level.

The Systems Architecture Work Plan

The initial development of a systems architecture is itself a project. As with any project, it can be defined in terms of specific units of work (tasks or work steps) that must be performed and deliverables that must be produced. Figure 7.4 depicts a typical, hierarchical work-breakdown structure for the phases and activities of a systems architecture development project.

Regardless of the specific techniques applied to the development of the systems architecture at the task and work-step levels. the phases and activities remain relatively stable. For this reason, in this section we confine our discussion of specific deliverables in the systems architecture development process to those levels of the work-breakdown structure. Later in the section, mapping specific techniques (such as IBM's BSP) into the work plan is discussed.

Phase 1: Develop a transformation process model.   Before modeling the MIS for an enterprise, one must know what the enterprise looks like—what its transformation processes are, and how those transformation processes relate to specific products and/or services of the enterprise. This process is not as trivial as it might seem. For example, let's examine an enterprise, well known among most business information systems professionals, IBM.

Everyone knows that IBM produces computers (mainframes from the data processing division, minis and micros from the entry systems division, terminals from who knows what division, etc.) as well as the following:

- Software (application software and operating systems)
- Office equipment and supplies (typewriters, paper, ribbons, word processors, etc.)
- Manuals (product documentation, user manuals, educational manuals)
- Educational services (product-oriented courses, Systems Science Institute, Systems Research Institute, self-study courses)
- Consulting services (software engineers, contract programming, custom system development)
- Time-sharing and network services (since the Justice Department decided to leave them alone)

- Textbooks for college courses and other scholarly works (from Science Research Associates, Inc., a wholly owned subsidiary of IBM)

Systems Architecture Development: An Eight-Phase Work-Breakdown Structure

Phase 1: Develop transformation process model

1.1. Identify existing products and services
1.2. Identify planned/new products and services
1.3. Identify production/provider facilities
1.4. Map production/provider domains

Phase 2: Develop enterprise organizational management model

2.1. Develop corporate organization chart
2.2. Identify management responsibilities
2.3. Map organizational responsibilities to production/provider domains

Phase 3: Define information requirements

3.1. Identify management control triggers
3.2. Develop information decomposition model
3.3. Identify data sources
3.4. Develop data/organization matrix

Phase 4: Define process requirements

4.1. Identify processes
4.2. Identify data flows
4.3. Develop process/organization matrix
4.4. Identify application process domains

Phase 5: Map the existing MIS

5.1. Model existing MIS database
5.2. Model existing MIS processes
5.3. Identify variances

Figure 7.4 Systems architecture development: an eight-phase work breakdown structure

The fact is that IBM has literally thousands of products and services provided to customers, which are, for the most part, highly integrated. Yet these products and services have vastly different transformation processes.

Although IBM is admittedly a giant, complex organization, smaller firms frequently have the same situation on a smaller scale. Al's Auto Dealership sells new cars, service, spare parts, and rental cars. It is still important to know what products and services are provided today—how they are produced or provided and what those transformation processes look like. This information is the key to providing an information system that will not only support

**Products and services analysis
AL's Auto Dealership**

P/S	Description
P	New cars—retail
P	Used cars—retail
P	Repair parts—retail
P	Extended service contract
S	Lease cars
S	Rental cars
S	Repair service

Figure 7.5   Products and services analysis for Al's Auto dealership

each of the transformation processes, but also provide cross-domain information.

The objective of developing a transformation process model is to identify all the businesses of the organization and their relationships to each other so that common and unique data can be identified. Unique data can be protected and common data can be shared and controlled to maintain the integrity of the information provided by the MIS.*

Activity 1.1: Identify Existing Products and Services.   In Activity 1.1, the major products and services of the enterprise are identified and listed. It is important to consider that many "products" are actually product families and that each product must be listed separately. For example, a vendor of microwave ovens who gives away cookbooks with the ovens probably should consider the cookbooks and the ovens as separate products. This is clearly the case with vendors who sell service contracts with their products. Service contracts are a separate product, as is the actual service performed.

Sources of the data to develop the list of products and services are the brochures and documentation provided by the enterprise, as well as interviews with corporate management. An example of a products and services list for Al's Auto Dealership is given in Figure 7.5.

Activity 1.2: Identify New Products and Services.   Important to the long-term feasibility of information systems is the ability to create adaptable systems—that is, systems which allow for changes in the business environment of the enterprise. Either systems can be built to accommodate pending environmental changes, or can be constructed such that they are independent of specific data requirements. In either case, it is required that the known and pending business changes are reflected in the systems architecture.

The primary source of information regarding changes in products or services is the strategic business plan of the organization. In addition, it may

---

*In many organizations, products and services can be classified into lines of business or product families.

be advisable to examine such external factors as competition, regulatory changes, and demographics, which could affect the products and services of the firm. As can be seen from Figure 7.6, some new lines of business will represent new management problems (such as wholesaling parts to garages) and therefore require additional consideration when building new information systems.

Activity 1.3: Identify Production/Provider Facilities.   Once the products and services of the enterprise have been identified, the sources of those products and services must be determined. Again, looking at our IBM example, a computer is ordered through either the National Accounts Division (NAD) or the National Marketing Division (NMD). The product was manufactured by the Data Processing Division (DPD), the Office Products Division (OPD), the Entry Systems Division (ESD), or some other division which has design, software engineering, and manufacturing facilities around the United States and the world. The documentation for the system probably came from their documentation center in Mechanicsburg, Pennsylvania, and may have been written (or at least managed) under the auspices of Science Research Associates in Palo Alto, California. In our less complex Al's Auto Dealership example, the production/provider facility analysis might look as shown in Figure 7.7.

The production/provider facilities analysis must include the entities within the enterprise which plan, develop, package, and sell and distribute products. Administrative entities (such as accounting, finance, and human resources) as well as operational entities (such as manufacturing, distribution, and marketing) must be included in the analysis.

Which production/provider transformation processes must exist can be determined from the list of products and services. Each product or service must have some mechanism for it to be acquired or manufactured and marketed. How the transformations actually occur, on the other hand, and which organizational units perform the functions requires an analysis of the

Products and Services Analysis
New Products and Services Planned
Al's Auto Dealership

	P/S Description
P	Wholesale parts to garages and parts stores
P	Sell repair manuals for new and out-of-production cars
P	Sell optional equipment to non–new car customers
	—Cruise control
	—Power mirrors
	—Custom stereo equipment

Figure 7.6 Products and services analysis: new products and services planned for Al's Auto dealership

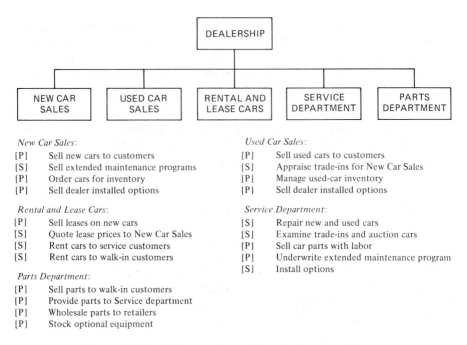

New Car Sales:

[P]	Sell new cars to customers
[S]	Sell extended maintenance programs
[P]	Order cars for inventory
[P]	Sell dealer installed options

Rental and Lease Cars:

[P]	Sell leases on new cars
[S]	Quote lease prices to New Car Sales
[S]	Rent cars to service customers
[S]	Rent cars to walk-in customers

Parts Department:

[P]	Sell parts to walk-in customers
[P]	Provide parts to Service department
[P]	Wholesale parts to retailers
[P]	Stock optional equipment

Used Car Sales:

[P]	Sell used cars to customers
[S]	Appraise trade-ins for New Car Sales
[P]	Manage used-car inventory
[P]	Sell dealer installed options

Service Department:

[S]	Repair new and used cars
[S]	Examine trade-ins and auction cars
[P]	Sell car parts with labor
[P]	Underwrite extended maintenance program
[S]	Install options

Figure 7.7   Production/provider facilities for Al's Auto dealership

enterprise itself. Typically, organization charts, regional office and plant listings, and interviews with senior management are all required to complete this deliverable.

Activity 1.4: Map Production/Provider Domains.   Once the products, services, and transformation processes have been identified, it becomes apparent that some products have multiple transformation processes involved in their planning, production, and distribution. The managers and controllers of each of these transformation processes must share data and information to manage effectively the profitable delivery of products and services. To establish the relationships between the various transformation processes and the products a *domain analysis* is performed.

Domain analysis assumes that each product or service has a primary transformation process which controls the production and delivery of the product. All other transformation processes are subsidiary to the primary. In Figure 7.8, an extremely simple domain analysis for Al's Auto Dealership is constructed to illustrate these relationships. In this example, the domain of the product/service is determined by reading across the Product/Service line. From this analysis it is evident that some products, such as new cars, are essentially in a transformation process by themselves; however, other products, such as dealer-installed options, repair service, and optional retail equipment, have very wide domains and affect virtually every transformation

Domain Analysis—Transformation Processes
Al's Auto Dealership

Product/Service	Transformation Process					
	New-Car Sales	Used-Car Sales	Service	Rent and Lease	Parts	Finance and Administration
New cars	P					U
User cars	I	P				U
Extended maintenance	D	D	M	D		U
Dealer-installed options	P	D	I	I	M	U
Auto leases	I			P		U
Auto rentals				P		U
Wholesale parts			D		M	U
Repair service	D	D	P	I	A	U
Repair parts			I		M	U
Optional equipment retail	D	D	I	I	P	U

Legend:
P = primary responsibility for product or service
I = integrator of one product/service into another product/service
M = manufacturer or provider of product/service
D = distributor/marketer of product/service
U = user of information
A = affected by product or service

Figure 7.8   Domain analysis: transformation processes

process. This analysis indicates, therefore, that some form of information relating to optional equipment, retail sales, and repair service needs to be shared by all entities. One can also ascertain, by identifying the primary responsibility for the product or service, which entity owns and is responsible for the integrity of the data and information.

Phase 2: Develop an organizational management model for the enterprise.   In developing the transformation model, in Phase 1 it was possible to see which operational entities (plants, departments, divisions) needed to interact and share data by virtue of their integrated product/service relationships. Frequently, however, the organization does not directly reflect the transformation process domains. While an MIS must use transformation process domains as a development constraint, it must reflect the information and control needs of the management structure. For this reason, an organizational model must also be developed. The objective of developing the organizational management model is to determine which individuals (by position) are responsible for making decisions governing the various transformation processes, indicating which managers need what data/information.

Activity 2.1: Develop Corporate Organization Chart.   The first level of documentation, which begins to relate positions within the management structure to the transformation processes, is the corporate organization chart. Typically, this already exists and simply needs to be updated.

Activity 2.2: Identify Management Responsibilities. In addition to the organization chart, it is also helpful to have a responsibility narrative, a written description of the responsibilities and authority of each position on the organization chart. As discussed in Chapter 4, there are various levels of management: strategic, tactical, and operational. Each level of management has differing authority and responsibilities with regard to the transformation processes, which correspond to differing information requirements. In addition, the level of management may frequently dictate access or security levels regarding the data within the system. The responsibility narrative for each entity should include strategic, tactical, and operational responsibilities. Figure 7.9 is an example of the type of information required on the responsibility narrative. Typically, the narratives will be drafted from available information—

Responsibility Narrative	
Position:	
Incumbent:	
Prepared by:	Date:
A. Strategic management responsibilities	Transformation process affected
1. 2. 3. 4.	
B. Tactical management responsibilities	Transformation process affected
1. 2. 3. 4.	
C. Operational management responsibilities	Transformation process affected
1. 2. 3. 4.	
Additional observations:	

Figure 7.9   Responsibility narrative

policy manuals, organizational documentation, and so on; however, the final iteration of the descriptions should come from interviews with the incumbent senior managers.

Activity 2.3: Map Organizational Responsibilities to Transformation Process Domains. Once the organization charts and responsibility narratives have been completed, they can be mapped to the transformation process domains completed in Phase 1. The objective here is to ensure that there is consistency between the actual transformation processes and the management controlling them. It is not uncommon for significant discrepancies to surface, or for there to be significant but resolvable conflicts between the incumbent managers. These conflicts are resolved and the final deliverables completed. The end result is depicted in Figure 7.10.

Armed with this detailed information about how the organization really operates, the systems architect is prepared to begin defining the managerial information requirements.

Phase 3: Define information requirements. The first two phases of the systems architecture development process serve primarily to define the macro-level environment in which the application systems (collectively the MIS) must reside. In addition, by collecting these data, we are able to influence the planner's perspective on the organization—in essence, we are able to construct a proper "gloss" for viewing an MIS architecture, at a much higher level than a single application system.

Once the environment has been defined, it is possible to develop specific information requirements: what data need to be collected from which transformation processes and provided to which organizational management entities so that management can exert control and influence over the entire macro-system.

Activity 3.1: Identify Management Control Triggers. Management, from one point of view, is a stimulus–response process. The manager looks at the transformation process (or some model of it represented in the form of information in a report produced by an information system) and responds to the information by exerting influence over the transformation process. The secret of a successful information system is the ability to produce a stimulus to the manager to take some action when necessary. Most, if not all managers, have some key data that cause them to respond. Typically, these data can evoke a range of responses in the manager, based on the values of the data. The key function to be performed by the planner in this activity is to identify the key data or *management control triggers*. This can be quite a challenge, as many software developers know, because users (especially experienced, effective managers) accept input and make decisions almost instinctively, without stopping to define their information requirements.

Organizational Responsibilities Analysis

Product/Service Domain	Responsibility								
	Vice President Sales	Vice President Manufacturing	Vice President Finance	General Manager, Plant 1	General Manager, Plant 2	General Manager, Plant 3	Director Customer Service	Vice President Marketing	Production Manager	Production Manager

LEGEND: M = Manage (tactical responsibility)
R = Advise or recommend
C = Must concur

A = Authority to Approve (strategic responsibility)
E = Executes (operational responsibility)
I = Incorporates into another

Figure 7.10 Organizational responsibilities analysis

In identifying management control triggers, the planner must begin with the basic data that managers recognize they need. These data are things such as return on investment, age of receivables, net income before taxes, inventory turns, or similar facts derived from analyzing the transformation process. These can usually be ferreted out by the planner with little difficulty. The challenge comes in identifying the control triggers that the managers do not yet realize that they need. This is accomplished by reviewing the transformation process domains and the organizational responsibilities with senior managers and discussing and analyzing the information requirements. Through individual reviews and group sessions, typically these control triggers can be defined—primarily because the organization is now modeled and can be viewed empirically.

Activity 3.2: Develop Information Decomposition Model. Once the universe of control triggers has been defined, the planner can begin to decompose the control triggers into their data/information components. Each trigger datum is analyzed to determine what data elements make it up. This can be done by analyzing existing information systems, interviewing the "creators" of the data, or in some cases, simply identifying the standard accounting or management algorithm which produces that result. What results from this exercise is an expanded list of management control triggers, hierarchically listed, with their component data elements defined. A possible format for this model is shown in Figure 7.11.

Activity 3.3: Identify Data Sources. Identifying data sources is a corporate version of hide and seek. Once the data required to generate the con-

DATA DECOMPOSITION MODEL
Management Control Triggers

Trigger	Description	Data Element	Description
1. ROI	Return on Investment	1a. Capital	Amount of capital invested
		1b. Term of investment	Length of time invested
		1c. End value	Amount of capital at end of term
2. Investment Turns		2a. Average on hand	Average on-hand inventory
		2b. Period	Time span of the observation
		2c. Units remove	Units pulled from inventory during period

Figure 7.11 Data decomposition model

trol triggers are identified, the planner must find which organizational responsibility generates the data. Typically, this can be done by identifying which transformation processes the data are measuring and backing through the production/provider domain to find the responsible organizational entity. As important as finding the source of the data is finding multiple sources of the same data.

>   ***3.4: Develop Data/Organization Matrix.***   Identifying the data required
to make management decisions solves only half of the information requirements problem. In addition to having multiple sources, these data can also have multiple uses. One of the major database-oriented values of undertaking the development of a systems architecture is the ability to specify integrated databases. From this, integrated data-sharing applications can be developed.
>   Any given piece of data can have six states—it can be:

1. Created
2. Generated (calculated)
3. Updated
4. Stored (frequently, but unfortunately, in multiple, unrelated places)
5. Retrieved (for update, incorporation, or reporting)
6. Incorporated (used in the calculation of another data element)

Because of the miracle of modern computing, data can have simultaneous multiple states under the control of multiple users. Since one of the objects of the systems architecture is to preplan the location and states of data, it is necessary to model the states in which data can exist in the existing macrosystem. Data/organization matrices are in fairly common use, and the example shown in Figure 7.12 is from IBM's Business Systems Planning Process. This type of model clearly depicts the usage of data within the organization and provides the foundation on which to identify and define database structures, data flows, and process definitions.

>   *Phase 4: Define process requirements.*   In Phase 4 the planner
began to identify and understand the nature and usage of data within the organization. Now the planner/architect must define the processes that transform data to new states of data, and from data to information.
>   There are essentially four steps to defining the processing requirements for the enterprise:

1. Identify and list the process that occur to transform data.
2. Define the flow of data between the processes.
3. Map the processes into the organizational entities that use/control them.

Data Class/Organization Matrix

Data Class \ Organization	Corporate: President	Corporate: Attorney & Sect.	Corporate: Planning	Corporate: Personnel & PR	Corporate: Financial	Mecca: President	Mecca: General Sales	Mecca: Sales Training	Mecca: Ind. Retail Dev.	Mecca: Product Develop.	Mecca: Market Research	Mecca: Advertising	Mecca: Merchandise Plan	Mecca: Credit	Mecca: Personnel	Mecca: Purchasing	Mecca: Manufacturing	Mecca: Industrial Relations	Mecca: Controller	Mecca: Cost Control	Aladdin: President	Aladdin: Promotion	Aladdin: Merchandising	Aladdin: Finance & Control	Aladdin: Store Operations	Aladdin: Leased Oper.	Aladdin: Facilities Plan	Sultan: President	Sultan: Retail Oper.	Sultan: Advertising	Sultan: Fin. & Admin.	Sultan: Branded Operations
Accounts Payable																X	U		X				U	X	X				X		X	
Accounts Receivable							U							U					X				U	X	X				X		X	
Accounting	U				U	U				U									X	C	U			X	X			U	X		X	C
Legal Requirements	U	X		X		U				U	U	U	U								U	U	U					U	U	U		
Payroll Performance	U	U	U	X	U	U	U	U	U	U	U	U	U	U	X	U	U	U	U	U	U	U	U	U	X	U	U	U	X	U	U	U
Personnel	U					U									X			U	U		U			U	X	X		U	X		U	
Production Inventory						U							U				X		U													
Manufacturing Order						U							U				X		U	U												
Production Capacity						U							U				X															
Purchase Order																X	U		U	U												
Supplier																X	U		U	U												
Raw Material Invent.																U	X		U	U												
Equip. Perf. History																U	X		U	U												
Fac/Equip. Invent.					U	U													X					X							X	
Production Schedule																U	C		U													
Retail Store					U		C							U					U					U	C				C		U	
Sales History	U		U			U	C		U		C		U	U							U		C		U	U		U	X			X
Customer Order							C	U		U	U	U	U												C				C			C
Shipment							U										C						C		U	U			X			
Receipt							C						U			U			U				C	U	X				X		U	
Customer							C		C					U					U				U		C				X			
Promotions						U	U					C	U								U	C			U			U	U	C		
Vendor		U														X	C	U					X						X			
Buy Orders							U						X			U	U								C				C			
Bill of Materials																U	C			U					U							
Product Specs.							U	U	U	C	C	U	U			U	U					U	U		U	U			U	U		
F/G Inventory							U						U				C		U	U					C	C			C		U	C
Financial Statistics	U		U		C														C	U	U			C				U			C	
Marketplace							U	U		U		U	C									U	C		U	U			X	U		
Master Buying Plan							U	U					C										C		U	U			X			
Financial Plans	U		U		C	U													U		U			U				U			U	
Personnel Plans			U	C											X				U					U	C				C		U	
Facilities Plans			U		U				U							U	C	U	U	U				U	C	C	C		C		U	
Master Product Plan							U						U			U	C		U													
Market/Product Plan			C		U		U	U	U	U	C	U	U										C		U	U						U
Con. Bus. Pln	U		C		C	U	U		U	U			U		U		U		U		U			U				U			U	

U – uses

X – both

C – creates

Figure 7.12 Data class/organization matrix. Reprinted by permission from IBM *Mecca International Suits Corporation Business Systems Planning.* © 1980 by International Business Machines.

4. Transform the organizational/process map into application domains, identifying the application systems that must be developed.

These four steps represent the four activities of Phase 4.

Activity 4.1: Identify Processes.   Processes are operations performed on data to transform them from one state to another or to transform them from data to information. Thus far in the architecture development process we have defined the data/information and the organizations that create and use them. The next step is to identify the transformations that must occur and the relationships between the transformations themselves and between the transformations and the organization.

The primary source of input for the identification of processes is the data decomposition model (Figure 7.11), which identifies the management control triggers and their component data elements. The processes that generate the management control triggers are primitive processes—data-to-data transformations. Once all of the primitive processes have been identified, the more complex processes—data-to-information transformations—can be derived.

Elias M. Awad, in his book *Business Data Processing,* describes four types of operations which are performed on data:

1. *Classifying:* grouping data items into categories (e.g., classifying banking transactions into savings deposits, checking deposits, loan payments, etc.)
2. *Sorting:* arranging data or groups of data in alphanumeric sequence
3. *Calculating and recording:* transforming two or more input or primitive data items into a more complex, generated data item(s) and storing the new value or updating the old value for the generated data item
4. *Summarizing:* generating, or extracting from storage, complex and primitive data items and reporting them in a manner that imparts knowledge to the user (i.e., transforming data into information)

From the data decomposition model, these primitive operations can be directly derived. More complex processes generally revolve around the method by which the primitive and generated data items are summarized and reported to the organization. The sources for this information are the data class/organization matrix and interviews with the users of the information.

It is important to note that the key objective in the systems architecture is to identify *what* the processes and algorithms are and *what* data they require, not necessarily *how* the data are to be presented to the user. The *how* issues are primarily the domain of application development at the project level.

Activity 4.2: Identify Data Flows.   Within an application system, there are data and processes. The data must be structured in some format to be accepted by the processes, and the processes themselves must be defined. We have established the framework for data structures and process algorithms in the previous phases of the systems architecture development process. A crucial element, however, in determining how processes should be grouped into application systems is how the various processes must be linked with each other. Understanding these linkages is necessary to identify complex processes composed of primitives and to establish the domains of particular application systems which are groups of complex processes.

One of the operations not defined by Awad is *transmission*—movement of data between one process and another. Transmission is the method by which processes interface. These interfaces can be via file/database interfaces or process-to-process internal communications or telecommunications. Figure 7.13 depicts a method by which interfaces between processes can be depicted graphically.

Activity 4.3: Develop Process/Organization Matrix.   To this point we have defined:

1. The transformation processes that management must monitor and control

2. The information required to stimulate a management action

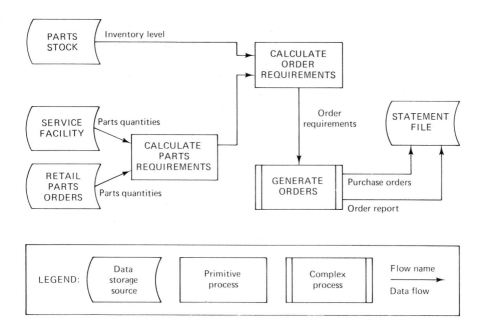

Figure 7.13   Sample data flow analysis

3. The structure of the data needed to generate the information
4. The processes that must be executed to transform the data into valuable information
5. The interfaces between the processes, represented by data flows

The last remaining datum required to identify the applications is that comprising relationships between the processes and the using organizations. Once this has been defined, the processes can then be logically clustered or grouped around the users' need to access the data. These logical process clusters then represent the application systems that must be built.

The easiest way to represent the relationships between processes and organizations is, again, the matrix. Figure 7.14 is an example of one such matrix from IBM's BSP study sample of Mecca International Suits. The processes listed down the left side of the matrix come directly from Activity 5.1—Identify Processes. The organizations across the top represent the organizations identified in Activity 2.1—Develop Corporate Organization Chart.

In addition to simply representing the users of the system, the methodology defined by BSP also identifies organizational process users by level of involvement. An "X" enclosed in a circle represents the owner of the system, the major user/decider/controller of the data. An "X" alone represents a major user of the process, and a "/" represents an organization that has some occasional use of the process (e.g., an organization that supplies input data or requests summarized information).

Activity 4.4: Identify Application System Domains.   Once the processes, organizations, and data have been determined, the application system domains can be identified by using the *rest-state rule.* If the data in the system can be traced into and out of processes, and in the absence of a new input transaction, the system goes to a state of rest, the boundary of the application has been identified. A simple model is shown in Figure 7.15. In this model, process X can have inputs from external A, or process Y. If, in fact, process X ceases after completely processing "input transaction" and producing "output transaction" and "output transaction 2" is not required to completely process "input transaction," then process X is an application unto itself. If, however, "output transaction 2" can occur at random times and is itself required to produce "output transaction" in conjunction with, or independently of "input transaction," "output transaction 2" and its source (process Y) must be included within the application domain. This is true because process X cannot come to rest until completely processing both "input transaction" and "output transaction 2."

Although the rest-state rule is the most complete method of determining the domain of an application, it can be complex to determine. Other methods can be applied as well, reserving the rest state for questionable applications. For example, in an architecture, there may be truly unrelated modules or

Process/Organization Matrix for Mecca

ORGANIZATION		Business Planning	Facilities P & C	Product P & C	Market Analysis	Governmental Compliance	Product Definition	Production Inv. Ctrl.	Buying	F/G Inventory Control	Production Scheduling	Production Order Control	Production	Shipping & Receiving	Order Control	Wholesale Marketing	Advertising & Promotion	Master Production Plng.	Purchasing	R/M Inventory Control	Facilities Acq. & Disp.	Facilities Operations	Retail Store Mgmt.	Personnel P & C	Personnel Hiring & Term.	Personnel Administration	Financial P & C	Cash Receipts & Disbur.	General Accounting
Sultan	Branded Operations	X		X					X	X				X	X	X	X				/	X				X	/		
Sultan	Finance & Admin.	/				X																		X	(X)	X	X	X	(X)
Sultan	Advertising																X									/			
Sultan	Retail Operations	X	X	X	X				X	X				X	X	(X)	X				X	/	(X)	/	/	(X)	/		
Sultan	President	(X)	/	(X)		/																	/	X		/	X		
Aladdin	Facilities Planning	/	X																		X	X	X			/			
Aladdin	Leased Operations	/	/																		X	(X)	(X)		(X)	X	/		
Aladdin	Store Operations	X								X				X	X	(X)										(X)			
Aladdin	Finance & Control	/				X																				X	X	X	(X)
Aladdin	Merchandising	X		X	X				X								X							/		X	/		
Aladdin	Promotion																(X)									/			
Aladdin	President	(X)	X	(X)		/																	/	X		/	X		
Mecca	Cost Control																									X	/		X
Mecca	Controller	/																								X	X	X	(X)
Mecca	Industrial Relations					/																			/	X			
Mecca	Manufacturing	X	(X)				/	X			(X)	X	(X)					X	X	X	X	(X)				X			
Mecca	Purchasing																		(X)							X			
Mecca	Personnel					X																		X	(X)	(X)			
Mecca	Credit																									X	/	X	
Mecca	Mdse Planning	/		X					(X)	(X)		X		X	X	/										X			
Mecca	Advertising			/												/	(X)									X			
Mecca	Market Reserach				X		/																			X			
Mecca	Product Develop.			/	/		(X)																			X			
Mecca	Indept Retail Dev.				/											X							(X)			X			
Mecca	Sales Training																							/	/	X			
Mecca	General Sales	X	/	X	/										X	(X)	X						X			X			
Mecca	President	(X)	/	(X)	/	/							/			/		/						X		/	X		
Corporate	Personnel & PR	X	X			X															X			X	X	(X)	/		
Corporate	Planning	(X)	X	X																				X		X	X		
Corporate	Attorney	/		/	/	(X)																		/		/	/		
Corporate	Finance	(X)	(X)	/		X				/				/										/		X	(X)	X	(X)
Corporate	President	(X)	/	(X)		/																		X		/	X		

(X) Major responsibility/decision maker   X Major involvement   / Some involvement

Figure 7.14 Process/organization matrix for Mecca. Reprinted by permission from IBM *Mecca International Suits Corporation Business Systems Planning* © 1980 by International Business Machines Corporation.

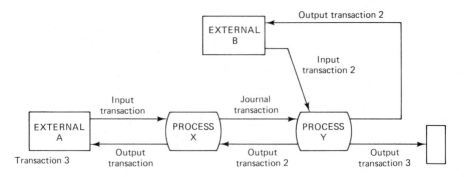

Figure 7.15 System architecture model

applications which share no data and no common processes. In this case, these applications are unrelated and separate. Also, applications that operate on completely different time cycles, although they may be related as externals to each other, can probably be treated as separate in an application sense.

Phase 5: Map the existing MIS.   Although time consuming, Phase 5 is perhaps, the most straightforward of all the systems architecture development phases. The existing processes and databases are mapped against the designed architecture. Variances between the two global models represent the projects to be completed. Nonvariant elements (i.e. those databases and modules common to both architectures) represent either (1) reusable modules that remain intact or (2) externals to the applications defined for development. In case (2), the input and output data to these modules and databases represent design constraints, or requirements, for future development. Even if documentation exists for the existing processes and data, it is probably advisable to convert the form to the matrix form used in the systems architecture so that overlap can easily be identified.

7.3 THE STRATEGIC IMPLEMENTATION PLAN

Role of the Implementation Plan

Once the systems architecture has been developed, the enterprise knows *what* applications need to be developed; however, *when* these applications can be developed is still an open question. The strategic implementation plan is a schedule for implementing the architecture over time, given the variables of the complexity of the architecture and the level of funding or investment allocated to systems development.

Once developed, the strategic implementation plan serves as a guide or baseline against which senior management can make alternative resource allocation decisions. These decisions include not only which applications will be built, but also what level of resource will be channeled into systems development at all (as opposed to capital equipment purchase, advertising, or any other corporate resource consumer). Once systems management has a plan for software development, senior management can begin to make trade-off decisions between various projects and resource assignments.

Objectives

The prime objective of the strategic implementation planning process is to develop a series of scenarios that can be presented to senior corporate management, depicting various alternative methods of implementing the architecture. The basic choices senior management has are:

- Retain the present level of investment in systems development and achieve complete implementation of the architecture in some specified period of time
- Increase the level of investment in systems development resources and reduce the time required to implement the architecture

In addition, management has some choice in the sequence in which various systems and components of the architecture will be implemented. This choice, is, however, somewhat constrained by the physical dependencies between the various modules of the architecture.

The planner must therefore, present to management several alternative implementation plans which vary the level of investment and the completion dates of both the entire architecture and individual components. Each of the alternative plans must advise management of:

- The required investment (in people, hardware, dollars)
- The completion date of the architecture
- The completion dates of each of the projects within the total architecture

Methodology

The methodology or life cycle for strategic implementation planning is fairly straightforward and fundamentally less complex than the methodology for determining the systems architecture. Figure 7.16 summarizes the strategic implementation planning work-breakdown structure.

Identifying Constraints

Since there are a nearly infinite number of investment/completion date scenarios that could be determined for any given systems architecture, any

Strategic Implementation Planning
Work-Breakdown Structure

Phase 1: Determine basic planning constraints

1.1. Determine timing constraints
1.2. Determine budgetary constraints
1.3. Determine implementation priorities

Phase 2: Forecast resource requirements

2.1. Forecast human resources
2.2. Forecast equipment resources

Phase 3: Develop project list

3.1. Determine architectural dependencies
3.2. Identify projects
3.3. Rank projects

Phase 4: Develop implementation plan

4.1. Develop alternative implementation plans
4.2. Review with management
4.3. Revise final plan

Figure 7.16   Strategic implementation planning

reasonable and valuable implementation planning effort must be constrained by the realities of the corporate world. Without such constraints, systems planners could lock themselves up forever, cranking out alternatives while the organization starves itself from a lack of information. The basic data needed by the planner are:

- *Time constraints:* Time constraints imposed by senior management often fall into two categories: "drop-dead dates" and "don't bother dates."
  —*"drop-dead" dates* are those by which each major component of the architecture must be implemented. It is quite conceivable that certain components of the architecture must be implemented to meet legal requirements, new product announcements, or new services to be offered by the enterprise.
  —*"Don't bother" dates* indicate when the usefulness of a particular component has passed. For example, in the early 1980s, banks were allowed, for one year, to offer tax-sheltered savings accounts. If it took 18 months to build the system, why bother?
- *Priorities:* Senior management requires an order of importance for the various architectural components. Order of importance has a direct correlation to the don't bother and drop-dead dates; however, there will be a significant number of components that do not have severe time

constraints. For these applications, it is still necessary to obtain a relatively reasonable ranking of the value of each of these components by senior management. For those without specific data constraints, quite frequently priority is determined by net financial benefit to the organization.

- *Budgetary limitations:* In any organization, there is a finite pool of capital to be allocated among various corporate projects, some of which are related to systems. When the pool is empty no more projects can be started, regardless of the benefit of the project. Any upper-limit budget constraints should be identified in advance, to prevent development of scenarios that will automatically be rejected.

Armed with these constraints, the planner(s) can limit the universe of acceptable scenarios that are developed for senior management.

Forecasting Resource Requirements

To develop a plan or schedule for the implementation of the architecture, it is necessary to estimate the resource requirements to complete each module of the systems architecture. As with any forecasting process, forecasts of resource requirements for system modules defined at only a very high level result in forecasts with low confidence levels. The confidence level can be improved if an organization has a database of estimating guidelines for projects of similar sizes and complexities. If such a database exists, forecasts can be made by evaluating similar projects—those which have processed approximately the same number of data elements, used the same (or similar) application databases, or produced reports approximating the complexity of those which are required by the system architecture.

Unfortunately, few organizations have such a database, or if the data are available, the system to analyze and interpret the data is not automated, resulting in a significant amount of manual effort. In Chapter 15 we describe a process for capturing and using this information.

Even with the improved confidence of historical data, it is nearly impossible to achieve an accuracy better than ±25% (and history and popular opinion tell us that it's almost always +). Therefore, to achieve any scenario approximating reality, without the aid of a heuristic project planning system, all strategic forecasts should be increased by the maximum factor.

Develop Project List

The basic unit of measure of the strategic implementation planning process is the project—a unit of work consisting of a series of steps with a definite beginning and end. At the strategic level of planning, it is projects that are budgeted and scheduled. Therefore, to develop the strategic implementation plan, it is necessary to carve the systems architecture into a number of projects. These projects, once listed, can then be juxtaposed on the schedule to meet timing and budget requirements. Developing the project list is a three-step process, described below.

Step 1: Determine architecture dependencies.   Phase 5 of the systems architecture development life cycle in Chapter 6 isolated the information system requirements for the organization into the following three levels:

1. *New development:* those applications that must be developed from scratch, or those that completely replace existing systems
2. *Enhancement/adaptation:* those application systems that must be revised substantially to meet the enterprise's information requirements
3. *Stable systems:* those that could remain intact throughout the time horizon of the systems architecture

Those application systems classified as new development or as enhancement and adaptation of existing systems represent the work that must be funded and scheduled. In most cases, however, the development process cannot proceed in strictly user-defined priority order. Certain elements of the architecture require that specific data or information be available (from predecessor architecture modules) or that specific application interfaces be in place before further development can occur. For example, if an organization is going to build all its systems using a particular database management system (DBMS), it is necessary to acquire and install the DBMS before the application programs can be coded and tested. A simple network chart [such as one used in critical path method (CPM) scheduling] can aid in determining the prerequisite systems or modules that will constrain the sequence in which the architecture is implemented (see Figure 7.17).

Step 2: Define projects.   Once the nonnegotiable dependencies of the modules in the architecture have been determined, a project list can be developed. Clearly, the application domains determined in the architecture development establish some of the parameters for the project list. Additionally, however, nondependent modules that are within an application boundary can be identified as separate projects.

One of the constraints in identifying projects should be manageability. To determine manageability, let us operate under the following assumptions:

- The span of control of a systems development project manager is six professionals.
- There will be no more than two levels of management (project manager and team leader). The largest project team could therefore be 36 professionals and 7 managers, a total of 43 people.

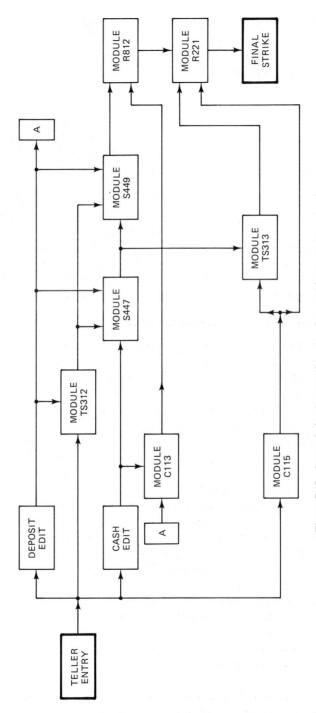

Figure 7.17 Strategic implementation planning: architectural dependencies

- No project will require more than one calendar year to implement at maximum resource loading.
- Administrative overhead, vacations, sick time, and holidays will consume 35% of an employee's time; therefore, one person cannot, without overtime, contribute more than 1350 labor-hours in a year.

We can thus assume that each architecture module that is less than 58,000 labor-hours (43 people × 1300 hours) can be a single project. Within these basic guidelines, the modules of the architecture can be decomposed or combined into individual systems development projects.

Step 3: Rank projects. Once the projects have been identified and listed, they can be ranked by dependencies and priority. This ranking can be accomplished in many ways. Perhaps the easiest is to rank the projects in priority order (by the highest-priority module within the project). Predecessor (or prerequisite projects) that are lower in priority can be inserted on the list directly above the project for which they are required. This accomplishes the objectives of both the users and the systems development organization.

Developing the Implementation Plan

Step 1: Establish preliminary plans. Once the projects have been ranked, implementation scheduling can begin. Projects from the ranking list are mapped onto the calendar using the projected head-count budget from the budgetary constraints. High-priority independent projects and their prerequisites are scheduled first, followed by high-priority dependent projects, followed in rank sequence by the dependent projects.

In scheduling the projects, the number of labor-hours are divided by the number of resources to be assigned to the project. By dividing the labor-hours by an adjusted hours/labor-day, the projects can be mapped onto a calendar. Based on the initial assumption that 35% of the time available is lost to administration, sick time, vacations, and so on, one calandar day (8 labor-hours) yields 5.2 available, productive hours. Hence a 1040-labor-hour project with two assigned team members would required 520 (1040/2) elapsed hours or 100 calendar days (520/5.2). Using this technique, projects can be scheduled concurrently until all resources are used. The end of the implementation of the strategic plan is then the installation date of the last project.

If this initial plan does not yield results that coincide with the constraints established by management, several alternatives (reduction in scope of the architecture or increases in staffing) can be scheduled and proposed. Typically, three or four alternatives can be established which frame the general objectives of senior management.

Step 2: Review with management. Once the preliminary plans have been established, they are reviewed by senior management. After budget and system function negotiations are completed, the planner has enough data to establish the final plan.

Step 3: Review final plan.   The revisions by the senior management team are incorporated into a final strategic implementation plan which is documented and presented to tactical management.

7.4 IMPLEMENTING STRATEGIC PLANNING

The Mission of Strategic Management

The mission of strategic management is to determine the goals and objectives of the organization. This management level established the template or baseline against which organizational subunits will be evaluated. In addition, this level of management controls the purse strings for corporate investment—shepherding and allocating assets to maximize the return. A key asset to the modern corporation is information, commonly referred to as the *information resource.* The information resource of the enterprise is contained within and managed by information systems. Information systems are, in a sense, the keys to the corporate filing cabinet. The ultimate custodians of this information are the senior executives of the enterprise.

As we stated, application systems are the keys to the corporate filing cabinet—the central nervous system of the enterprise—and very costly to develop and operate. The average corporation spends between 1 and 1.5% of revenue on information systems. A $1 billion corporation can easily be spending $10 to $15 million annually on data processing. The number can be substantially higher for information-intensive or information product enterprises such as banks and insurance companies.

This expenditure includes hardware, software, personnel for operations, and personnel for systems development. The independent variable in the equation of information systems cost is the application system itself. The size of the computer required to process data, the cost and complexity of the data communications network, and the number of computer operators employed are all functions of the nature, quality, and efficiency of the application systems they support. In the final analysis, the entire data processing budget is directly and strongly affected by the quality and effectiveness of the information systems.

Decision Making versus Planning

It is important to isolate decision making from planning. *Decision making* is the establishment of objectives, evaluation of alternatives, and selection of a direction or mission. *Planning* is the development of alternatives based on analysis of the objectives and the real environment. Executive management as a group is responsible for the decision making. Systems development management as a group is responsible for planning.

Inoculation against Planning

Information systems, like information itself, are intangible assets. They do not take up much space, they are largely invisible (except for the reports and terminal interactions), and they tend to be viewed as mystical or magical processes that occur on an expensive machine in the basement (or an inexpensive personal computer on a manager's desk). Because of this intangibility, and because the development of these systems seems to be an ill defined and arcane sorcery, many organizations view it as too nebulous to plan seriously. This is reinforced by previous, unsuccessful planning efforts. In a sense, many organizations have been inoculated against planning. They may have had one dose of it, it was painful, and they have become conditioned against systems planning.

Requirements for a Successful Planning Implementation

It is evident why systems planning is important and why it is frequently avoided or glossed over. To optimize systems development, a structured process for making systems development decisions must be imposed. The basic requirements for this decision-making process are:

- Commitment and involvement of senior management in taking an active role in developing the information system architecture requirements
- An organized method of reviewing plans and making decisions
- An efficient method to maintain plans over time as the business environment changes, and to implement those changes

Armed with these requirements, we can define an orderly, functional management decision-making process.

Commitment to Planning

An enterprise would not acquire a new subsidiary without analyzing the objectives of the enterprise, the acquisition's contribution to the overall welfare and profitability of the corporation, and the ability of the acquisition to be synergistic with other divisions of the enterprise. Senior management becomes directly involved in these decisions and evaluations. Every year, the enterprise needs to review its systems architecture and determine its objectives, contribution, and synergy. Senior management needs to invest the time in determining the requirements and constraints on the information system of the enterprise and the application systems that will be terminated or added. Senior management needs to be committed to a successful planning process.

The Committee Approach to Decision Making

The committee approach to decision making can be effective if the committee is well managed and the topics about which decisions are required are well prepared. Typically, an MIS steering committee, composed of top executives and senior operational and financial management, assumes the responsibility of the steering committee—voting on various alternatives which are presented to them by systems management. Using this approach, the time commitment of senior management can be minimized.

The Task Force Approach to Planning

The task force approach is effective for planning—developing alternatives on which decisions can be based. Unlike committees, task forces are not decision makers. Instead, the task force represents a process for the collection of data about the environment in which the systems will be domiciled and the synthesis of various alternatives.

In the task force approach, the actual documentation and compilation of the alternatives is done by the systems development department. Data for the plans are collected from the operating entities of the enterprise through *sponsors,* senior managers who have a vested interest in the development of the applications. By scheduling interviews with sponsors for intensive questioning by the planners, enough data can be gathered to describe the architecture and minimize the time commitment of the senior management team.

Selecting a Planning Methodology

The initial strategic plan is documented as a project. As with any project, methodology for planning must be acquired or developed. The work-breakdown structures in the preceding chapters can provide a basis for an internally developed methodology. Alternatively, an approach such as IBM's Information Systems Planning Process can be adopted.

The important consideration in adopting a methodology is that a detailed listing of tasks and work steps is necessary to control the project, as well as a technique or procedure for defining the architecture. The techniques or procedures for creating and transforming the planning deliverables closely parallel those techniques employed in developing systems. In applying an application system development technique to the process of defining the systems architecture, data structured design techniques (such as those espoused by Jackson, Warnier, and Orr) are much better suited to strategic architecture development (enterprise modeling) than are the process-flow methodologies (such as those of Gane and Sarson, Yourdon, and DeMarco).

The reason for recommending the data structured techniques for representing system architectures centers around the objective of strategic planning—to model the information requirements of the enterprise. The main thrust of architecture development is to determine *what* information is required and *what* data are necessary to generate the information. Architecture development is a *data*-oriented function that results in the definition of processes.

8

Tactical Systems Management

8.1 INTRODUCTION

Once an enterprise has developed a systems architecture and strategic implementation plan, the process of actually developing the applications begins. The tactical manager must marshal and allocate resources within the constraints of the architecture, while balancing short-term adaptation and enhancement (i.e., maintenance) requests and strategic projects. Whereas strategic management focuses on identifying projects and establishing budgets, tactical management focuses on administration of projects and allocation of resources. The strategic planning horizon is generally two to five years, while the tactical planning horizon is rarely greater than one or two years. Tactical management is chartered with operating within a budget; strategic management defines the budget.

Given these relationships between tactical and strategic planning, tactical management can be defined as project queue and resource allocation. Tactics are generally the purview of the systems development manager—one level removed from actual project management.

Objectives

The objectives of tactical management are:

- To allocate resources among projects and adjust resource levels as required to ensure that strategic projects are completed as scheduled

- To evaluate, plan, and implement nonstrategic projects, requested ad hoc by the user community, within the discretionary adaptation and enhancement budget allocated by senior management
- To advise strategic management of required or desired changes to the strategic plan

Whereas strategic management and planning are project processes, tactical management and planning are more administratively oriented—establishing the short-range objectives of operational management, and allocating and adjusting allocations of resources to meet the day-to-day needs of project management and the organization as a whole. Figure 8.1 describes the tactical planning and management process, showing the flow of data and control.

Tactical Management Outputs

This flow depicts the outputs of tactical management:

- *Controls and budgets* to affect the transformation process, issued as plans and directions to operational management, and representing management decisions regarding staffing, budget, and resource allocation
- *Project status* to strategic management, indicating variances against the strategic implementation plan which will affect the strategic management decision-making process
- *Major impacts to the strategic plan,* such as changes in the scope of projects directly related to the systems architecture, user requests for projects that exceed the guidelines for discretionary resource allocation, and technical innovations that could affect the systems architecture either positively or negatively.
- *Productivity and estimating metrics* to reflect the systems development capability of the existing resources and aid strategic management in more accurately forecasting future resource requirements

Information Requirements

By evaluating these outputs, we can identify some of the information required by the tactical manager:

- *The strategic plan:* The tactical manager must have a clear depiction of the strategic implementation plan outlining the projects that must be completed, with their time frames.
- *Budget allocations:* The tactical manager requires budget guidelines for resources to be applied to strategic projects as well as ad hoc tactical-level projects requested by user management. Most frequently, the tacti-

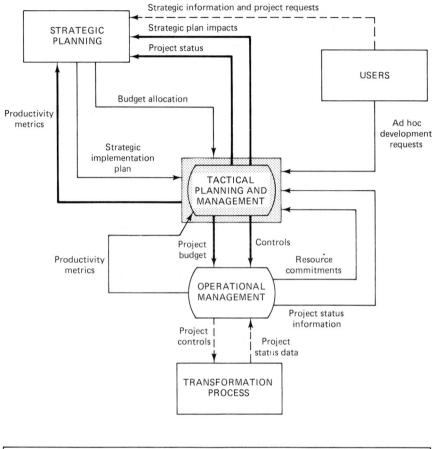

Figure 8.1   Tactical planning and management data flow

cal manager is also responsible for maintaining existing systems and requires a budget of resources to devote to maintenance.

This information is passed to tactical management from strategic management and is an external input to the tactical management and planning process. In addition, the tactical manager requires information from the software engineering transformation process, which is obtained from operational management:

• *Commitment of resources:* The tactical manager must have visibility into the transformation process to identify the quantity and type of resources that are committed to projects, the duration of their commitment, and the time segments when these resources are free to assume new projects.

- *Project status:* The tactical manager must be able to determine whether projects are proceeding as planned and must be able to determine which projects are expanding beyond original estimates (requiring additional resource).

- *Productivity metrics:* Productivity metrics indicate how rapidly systems can be built with a given resource level and quality (defect) constraint. The productivity metrics provide the manager with the data needed to estimate projected resource commitments.

The third source of required information is from the users themselves. On a regular basis, information system users will request projects which are:

- New application systems
- Adaptations of existing systems to meet new opportunities
- Enhancement of existing systems to add new functionality
- Maintenance of existing systems to remove errors

This information allows the tactical manager to assess the validity of the strategic plan as a guide for meeting the enterprise's requirements and enables the manager to plan the allocation of discretionary resources to nonstrategic projects.

8.2 RESOURCE PLANNING

Quantifying Project Resources

The majority of the tactical planning outputs revolve around metrics associated with project resources:

- How they are allocated among projects
- For what duration they are committed
- How the projects are progressing against plan
- How the resource allocation has changed since last reported
- How resources must be reallocated to meet changing requirements

and primarily around the change in metrics between reporting periods. The tactical manager needs a consistent method for documenting resource allocations (planned and actual) and a method for determining the change in the characteristics of the resource allocation.

The Resource Allocation Plan

The starting point for tactical systems planning is the *resource allocation plan*. This plan is basically a distribution matrix of projects across resources. Since most organizations plan at monthly, quarterly, and annual points, the resource allocation would be prepared at a monthly level and summarized for quarterly and annual periods. Typically, the tactical management planning horizon is about 12 months; however, since many systems development organizations operate with large backlogs, the resource allocation plan may extend until all projects are projected complete. In any event, where the backlog of projects exceeds two years, it is advisable to develop a plan that extends for 18 months. Figure 8.2 depicts a very usable resource allocation plan format that has been used successfully in several organizations.

Let's take some time to analyze this report, as a study in the information requirements for tactical planning. The first line of the report contains primarily descriptive information: department, report period, and report date. In addition, it contains the *report level*. The level indicates whether the allocated resource hours are depicted for individuals (the lowest level) or groups of individuals. For example, columns "A" through "L" could be 12 individuals in a project group or section, or they could represent 12 individual departments (such as financial systems, administrative systems, field systems, marketing systems, etc.), each of which would be supported by a lower-level resource allocation.

The descriptive line of the report also contains available labor-hours and committed labor-hours (Note: Labor-hours used to be referred to as man-hours). *Available labor-hours* is the standard number of working hours per day for the enterprise, multiplied by the number of working days in the reporting period. *Total labor-hours* is the number of days in the period that could be worked if necessary (e.g., Saturdays, holidays, etc.) multiplied by the number of hours per day. Days is the number of working days in the period. Hours is the standard hours/workday. The *report period* is month, quarter ending, or annual.

Moving to the next segment of the report, we find the column headings. The *Project* column contains all of the projects, administrative activities, and total breaks for the report. *Total Project Hours* is the total hours for the project, from start to finish. *Remaining Project Hours* is the number of hours remaining on the project at the start of this reporting period. *Not Scheduled* represents hours for the project which are not scheduled for this project in this period or any future period.

Under the *Allocated Resource Hours* heading, columns "A" through "L" represent resource names (by individual or group). The hours allocated for each resource, or resource group, are listed for each project. *Total* represents the total number of hours allocated for the project in this period. *Carry*

XYZ CORPORATION SYSTEMS
DEVELOPMENT RESOURCE ALLOCATION PLAN

DEPARTMENT:	LEVEL:	STAFFING LEVEL:	AVAILABLE LABOR HOURS:	TOTAL LABOR HOURS:	DAYS:	HOURS:	REPORT PERIOD:	REPORT DATE:

PROJECT	TOTAL PROJECT HOURS	REMAINING PROJECT HOURS	NOT SCHEDULED	ALLOCATED RESOURCE HOURS												TOTAL	CARRY
				A	B	C	D	E	F	G	H	I	J	K	L		
TOTAL AVAILABLE																	
ADMINISTRATIVE																	
Vacation																	
Other Days Off/Committed																	
Amortized Time Off																	
Status Reporting/Non-Project																	
SUBTOTAL ADMINISTRATIVE:																	
PROJECT AVAILABLE																	
STRATEGIC AVAILABLE																	
STRATEGIC PROJECTS																	
SUBTOTAL STRATEGIC:																	
TACTICAL AVAILABLE																	
TACTICAL PROJECTS																	
New Requests																	
Subtotal – New Requests																	
Maintenance																	
Subtotal – Maintenance																	
SUBTOTAL TACTICAL:																	
TOTAL PROJECT TIME																	
NET TIME (+/−)																	

Figure 8.2 XYZ Corporation systems development resource allocation plan

represents the balance of the project hours which have been distributed in future periods. (Remaining project hours = not scheduled + total + carry.)

Preparing the Resource Allocation Plan

Starting from "ground zero" (i.e., preparing the first resource allocation plan) is a fairly simple task, given that there has been a strategic planning process which provides the tatical manager with:

- A budget (or head count)
- A project list from the strategic planning process
- Preliminary estimates of resource requirements for strategic projects
- Preliminary target dates
- A discretionary budget (or head count) allocation for ad hoc requests (including maintenance)

Armed with these data, the resource allocation plan is a simple process for a "spreadsheet" personal computer program (unfortunately, few, if any commercially available project control systems provide adequate tactical management reports) or, at worst, a couple of days and a calculator.

The first step is to determine the initial planning horizon (12 to 18 months) and calculate the available hours for the resource allocations (hours available in the month × number of resources) and map out the available hours on a report for each month of the planning horizon. Administrative time can be plotted with known data (such as planned vacations) or listed as *amortized time off* (unscheduled vacation, sick, jury, personal holidays, and other hours amortized over a monthly period). The subtotal of administrative time subtracted from total available time yields the project available time. Project available time can then be allocated between strategic projects and tactical projects by the guidelines provided by senior management.

The second step is to identify all of the *predecessor* projects (i.e., those that must be completed before other projects can be started) and independent projects (those that have no predecessors or dependent projects) from the systems architecture and strategic plan. Map out the resource allocations for the prodecessor projects, followed by the independent projects, on a month-by-month basis. Once all allocations have been made for a month, they can be totaled. The total is deducted from the remaining project hours, giving the remaining project hours for the next month (carry). This process is completed for the entire planning horizon. Once this has been completed, the dependent projects can be scheduled. New requests and maintenance can be planned in the same manner. Preparing monthly, quarterly, and annual summaries is simply a matter of totaling the matrices for the period covered.

Value of the Resource Allocation Plan

The resource allocation plan provides the basis or benchmark for evaluating the impact of:

- New project requests
- Changes in project schedules or estimates
- Maintenance work

With a resource allocation plan in place, adding a new project (or expanding the scope of an existing project) can be analyzed in terms of its impact on the entire project queue. With this information, managers can make trade-off decisions between projects in an informed, quantifiable manner. The resource allocation plan also represents a major contribution on the part of the tactical manager to the strategic planning process.

Maintaining the Resource Allocation Plan

Like any other planning process, tactical planning requires maintenance. If the maintenance process is too burdensome, the plan falls into disuse. If the plan is not maintained on a regular basis, the ability to make management trade-off decisions is impaired and managers are "working in the dark," making uninformed, nonquantified decisions about the allocation of corporate resources. To maintain the resource plan, it is necessary to summarize the project data provided by operational (project) management in a format compatible with the resource allocation plan. The primary data that must be collected and summarized are:

- Actual hours spent on projects during the reporting period
- Breakdown of actual hours between planned and unplanned
- Additions to the project queue
- Changes in project estimates

These data can then be mapped directly against the resource allocation plan for update. A model for this process is the *project queue status report,* depicted in Figure 8.3.

The format of the data represented in the project queue status report is similar to that of the resource allocation plan, to promote easy transference of data from one to the other. The heading information is essentially the same, as are the project, total project hours, and remaining project hours. This report, however, makes provisions for revising the overall project estimate. Under the revisions category, *Revision to Total Project Hours* is the value by which the overall project estimate is to revised. *Revised Total Hours*

XYZ CORPORATION SYSTEMS DEVELOPMENT
PROJECT QUEUE STATUS REPORT

DEPARTMENT:	LEVEL:	STAFFING LEVEL:	AVAILABLE LABOR HOURS:	TOTAL LABOR HOURS:	DAYS:	HOURS:	REPORT PERIOD:	REPORT DATE:

	PLAN		REVISIONS			RESOURCE ALLOCATION									
PROJECT	TOTAL PROJECT HOURS	REMAINING PROJECT HOURS	REVISION TO TOTAL HOURS	REVISED TOTAL HOURS	NEW REMAINING HOURS	Resource A			Resource B			Resource C			TOTAL ACTUAL	TOTAL ADJUSTED
						PLAN	ACTUAL	ADJUSTED	PLAN	ACTUAL	ADJUSTED	PLAN	ACTUAL	ADJUSTED		
TOTAL AVAILABLE																
ADMINISTRATIVE																
Vacation																
Other Days Off/Committed																
Amortized Time Off																
Status Reporting/Non-Project																
SUBTOTAL ADMINISTRATIVE:																
PROJECT AVAILABLE																
STRATEGIC AVAILABLE																
STRATEGIC PROJECTS																
SUBTOTAL STRATEGIC:																
TACTICAL AVAILABLE																
TACTICAL PROJECTS																
New Requests																
Subtotal — New Requests																
Maintenance																
Subtotal — Maintenance																
SUBTOTAL TACTICAL:																
TOTAL PROJECT TIME																
NET TIME (+/−)																

Figure 8.3 XYZ Corporation systems development project queue status report

79

is *Total Project Hours* ± *Revision to Total Hours.* The *New Remaining Hours* is *Revised Total Hours* − *Total Hours* (from the resource allocation section).

In the *resource allocation section,* provisions are still made for individual or groups of resources (indicated by the columns labeled "Resource A" through "Resource C"). Each of these is, however, subdivided into three categories: Plan, Actual, and *Adjusted.* The *Plan* column contains the allocated hours from the resource allocation plan. *Actual* contains the actual hours logged by that resource against the project. *Adjusted* is an adjustments column. Here variances that affect estimates, resulting in modifications to the resource plan, can be entered. For example, if 40 hours were planned for resource A on a project and 40 hours were actually spent, this does not necessarily mean that the project is on time. If there are still 40 hours left to complete this month's work, +40 would be added in the adjustment column, indicating that 40 hours should be added in subsequent monthly plans. In this way the manager has the opportunity to revise the estimate for that project by adding or subtracting hours in the adjustments column. The *Total Actual* column is a total of the hours spent on the project. The *Total Adjusted* represents additions to or subtractions from future planned time.

From time to time, new projects will make their way onto the project queue status report. This will be particularly common in the tactical projects area. To the extent that the projects do not exceed the budgetary allocation for tactical work, there is no impact on the overall tactical plan.

From this report, postings can be made to the resource allocation plan. Again, this can be automated using a spreadsheet package or by manually posting the results.

Advantages of the Project Queue Status

On a day-to-day basis, the project queue represents a mechanism with which management can assess the impact of ad hoc enhancement, adaptation, and corrective maintenance requests on the overall strategic plan. Furthermore, by capturing actual and adjustment data, the tactical plan can become a dynamic management tool with which to make management resource allocation decisions. Because the resource allocation plan and the project queue status reports follow similar data formats, maintenance is relatively easy.

Another advantage of this method of tactical planning is that variances from the anticipated development path can be highlighted. Administrative status information can be driven from an exception reporting process (i.e., only tracking in detail those projects that have unfavorable adjustments).

8.3 APPLICATION PLANNING

Having defined a method by which tactical management can plan and allocate resources, feeding this information back to strategic management, we have examined only half of the tactical systems planning problem. In addition to resources, the tactical manager must also be accountable to strategic management for developing a tactical plan for implementing the strategic systems architecture. Senior management needs to know:

- Changes in system scope or requirements detected at the tactical level that will affect the strategic architecture
- Changes in technology that would have a significant affect on the implementation of the strategic architecture
- Problems or changes in system specifications gained through the systems development process that would affect the sequence or dependencies of elements in the strategic systems architecture

In this role, the tactical manager must collect and filter data gained from the transformation process, editing and summarizing them for senior management.

Identifying Deviations from the Architecture

The first and most immediate source of information regarding deviations from this architecture will come to the tactical manager from the transformation process. Changes in estimates for projects and/or significant delays in projects may signal changes in project scope. Although there are many reasons for alterations to project plans, scope changes can indicate deviations from the systems architecture by the project team. The tactical manager must investigate changes in plans or resource allocations and determine if there are operational problems or if the changes are a result of problems in development.

In the case of true deviations from the architecture, the manager must determine if the deviation is required because of some unforeseen constraint on the development of the system. If this is the case, the required deviation should be documented and presented to senior management. This should be done even for deviations in projects that are not on the critical path of the strategic implementation plan.

Critical path projects are those that cannot slip in their estimates without extending the final implementation of the entire systems architecture. Noncritical projects can slip within defined limits without adversely affecting the ultimate completion date for the architecture. There is a tendency to overlook changes in scope or minor deviations in estimates for noncritical projects because the user ultimately ends up with the desired solution within the overall time frame. However, deviations at the noncritical project level can have the effect of altering the dependencies or interfaces that have been defined for future projects.

Assessing the Impact of Technology

Operational and tactical management are typically much closer to the actual computing technology than are systems planners and senior management. For this reason, a prime responsibility of the tactical manager is to identify new hardware, software, and communications technologies, make a preliminary assessment of their value to the enterprise, and advise senior management (or the system architects).

8.4 SUMMARY

Tactical systems management is the watchdog over the implementation of the strategic systems architecture and implementation plan. In this role, the tactical manager must:

- Allocate resources, within budget guidelines, between strategic projects, ad hoc user requests, and maintenance
- Determine the validity of the strategic implementation plan and feed back to senior management alterations in individual project plans so that this information can be included in strategic plan updates
- Assess the impact of new technology and advise strategic management of promising technologies that should perhaps be included in the strategic systems architecture
- Propose changes, additions, and deletions to the strategic architecture and implementation plan based on "front-line" knowledge of the users' needs and problems and the systems problems or challenges in meeting these needs

To be effective in this role, the tactical manager needs to develop an efficient, organized management information system (either manual or automated) to track the quantifiable resource allocations as well as the less tangible effects of changes in system specifications and technology.

9

Operational Systems Management

9.1 INTRODUCTION

Scope of Operational Systems Management

The operational systems manager is the front-line supervisor, monitoring and controlling the software engineering transformation process. Since software development is a project-oriented process—that is, a management and execution process with a defined beginning, middle, and end—the techniques applied in this environment are project (as opposed to administrative)-oriented management, and operational-level managers are usually referred to as project managers or project leaders.

Project planning and management is the foundation of the systems management macro-system. It is the project manager who ultimately defines the nature of a systems project, plans and schedules the work, and generates the information that drives the strategic and tactical planning and management processes.

The project manager typically has the shortest planning horizon of the planning and management hierarchy, extending only to the end of the assigned project. The planning horizon is usually under two years and decreases as the project progresses. In addition, the project manager has the narrowest planning corridor, dealing with the allocation and management of resources on a specific project, many of whom are dedicated to the project full time. In some respects, this eases the planning process.

In other respects, however, the project manager's task is the most complex planning and scheduling task of all levels of management. While strategic and tactical management are defining units of work measured in "projects," operational managers are dealing with units of work measured in terms of activities, tasks, and work steps. Whereas an organization may have several hundred projects to manage, the project manager usually has no fewer than a couple of hundred discrete units of work, and frequently thousands, to allocate, plan, and schedule.

This level of detail is challenging in and of itself; however, it is complicated by the fact that a significant portion of the work must be performed by resources over which the project manager has no direct control. The project manager's plans must include activities of users, quality reviewers, data administrators, and others who administratively report to other areas of the organization.

Objectives of Operational Systems Planning

The objectives of operational systems planning are twofold:

1. Operational management is responsible for the timely and cost-effective execution of the systems project. To achieve this objective, the project manager must estimate project work to the lowest level of detail, assign resources based on skill and availability, schedule the tasks, and track progress, controlling and adjusting the plan and the resources.
2. The project manager must provide input to the tactical and strategic planning processes. To accomplish this, the project manager must capture performance metrics from the project and report progress status and changes in plans to higher levels of management.

The operational systems development manager must attempt to complete work in concert with the resources budgeted, the constraints defined by the systems architecture, and in the time frame dictated by the strategic implementation plan.

Operational Planning Activities

The operational or project planning process can be decomposed into six major activities:

1. *Project definition:* decomposing projects into discrete units of work (work steps) which can be estimated, scheduled, and assigned
2. *Estimation:* determining the labor-hours required to complete a work step within the project
3. *Scheduling:* assigning work steps to project team members and establishing target start and completion dates, given the dependencies between the work steps

4. *Revision:* altering estimates and recalculating the schedule based on the effectiveness of actual task completion

5. *Architectural validation:* assessing the validity of the strategic systems architecture based on conditions and constraints observed in actual implementation

6. *Interfacing:* providing tactical and strategic management with data about required changes in estimates and schedules and changes in the systems architecture based on actual events in the transformation process

Each of these activities is discussed in detail in the following sections of this chapter.

9.2 PROJECT DEFINITION

Operational systems planning or project management begins when a project has been funded, assigned, and is ready for execution. The project manager begins the process with a limited amount of information, usually consisting of:

- A *project request* defining the project and its scope
- The *systems architecture* or the component of the architecture that identifies this project's module and its known interfaces with other existing systems and modules
- A *project budget* outlining the resources assigned and available to the project
- *Preliminary requirements* defining the desired time frame for completion, database and/or language constraints, target implementation system, and as is the case for software developed on contract or for resale, the documentation requirements, required milestone reviews, and required development techniques (if any)

With this information in hand, the project manager must describe or model the project during project definition.

Functional Decomposition

The project model is essentially an identification of all of the work steps that must be performed in the project. The process for developing the model is known as *functional decomposition.* The result of functional decomposition is a *work-breakdown structure,* a detailed listing of individual work steps required to develop, test, and install the system and a definition of each work step.

Using functional decomposition, the project manager first subdivides the project into major segments or phases, which may include:

Phase 1: Detailed user requirements

Phase 2: Logical or business system design

Phase 3: Physical or computer system design

Phase 4: Programming and unit testing

Phase 5: System testing

Phase 6: Installation

Each phase is then subsequently decomposed or subdivided into smaller units (subphases or activities), and this process continues until the project manager has identified the lowest level of project detail.

The lowest level of detailed decomposition is reached when each unit of work identified represents one tangible result or *deliverable* (such as a data element description, program specification, program source code, or data-flow diagram) which can be completed by a single person. The individual deliverables are generally determined by the specific methodology or design technique to be employed on the project, which specifies the number and format of the specification documentation.

Aids to Functional Decomposition

At the phase and activity levels, virtually all information system projects look alike. Subtle differences occur at the task and work step levels based on the specific development technique employed (e.g., data structured design techniques specify a different set of deliverables from those of process-flow structured analysis and design techniques). Since functional decomposition can be a rather formidable task, especially on large development projects, many organizations have developed a standard *systems development life cycle,* a standard work-breakdown structure which the project manager tailors to meet the needs of a particular project. In addition, there are a number of commercially available, proprietary life cycles which provide the functional decomposition in great detail and include customized versions specifically adapted to the various development techniques. (Life cycles and design/development techniques are discussed in detail in Chapters 12 and 13.)

Tailoring the Work-Breakdown Structure

The first step in tailoring the work-breakdown structure to the project is required when a standard (corporate-developed or purchased) life cycle has been employed. Typically, standard life cycles include tasks and work steps which are mutually exclusive. For example, they may contain tasks for identifying both traditional-file structures and database schema, or tasks for developing and testing batch programs and separate tasks for developing on-line or real-time programs. Given the known parameters describing the project, the project manager must delete the excluded tasks. In addition, any special project-related tasks not included in the life cycle may be added.

Defining Iterations

The initial project decomposition, or work-breakdown structure, usually represents a one-dimensional vector view of work to be completed on the project. For example, the project manager, perhaps using a "canned" life cycle, has determined that a step in the life cycle is "code program," which has been defined as a single work step. Since a project will probably encompass the development or modification of numerous programs, each of which will require differing levels of effort (and time), the project manager must define how many times each code program work step will occur during the project. Each occurrence of a work step represents a single *iteration*. Each iteration of a work step can then be independently estimated, assigned, scheduled, and tracked. Once all of the iterations have been identified and documented, the universe of work encompassed by the project is known and the process of estimating the effort required for the project can begin.

9.3 ESTIMATION

Systems development projects are frequently late. There are three conditions that can cause a late project:

1. External influences over the project which prevent work from being completed on time
2. Inaccurate schedules which do not accurately reflect the dependencies between the iterations of work steps on a project
3. Inaccurate estimates of the effort required to complete the work

External influences are unavoidable, may not be predictable, and are understood and accepted in the business world. Although efforts can be made to plan for contingencies, thereby minimizing the impact on uncontrollable events, they will occur, nevertheless. Inaccurate schedules are problems that can be addressed through most project planning and control systems. Bad estimates, however, are the most insidious and least controlled problem in software development.

Estimating: Predicting the Future

Estimating is literally predicting the future. As yet, there is little evidence to support the contention that human beings are prescient and possess parapsychological powers to predict future events. And certainly (as of this writing) there is no technology to move forward in time, witness an event, and return to document it. Because of these factors, estimates are, and will continue to be, *wrong*. However, business and econometric forecasting are big businesses (even though they too are quite often wrong), and senior management expects estimates to be right. Since estimates cannot be 100% accurate, it is necessary to minimize the margin of error in the process. There are some principles that can be applied to estimating to increase the accuracy.

Human Estimation Capacity

In informally observing literally hundreds of business information systems projects over the course of several years, it seems to the author that the more complex the project, the more likely it was that the estimate for the effort involved in the project was wrong; a position supported by Boehm and Pressman. Closer investigation revealed that the level of detail to which work was decomposed appeared to be related to the accuracy of the estimate. This theory was informally tested while teaching a course in data processing project management at the State University of New York at Buffalo over several semesters. Students were asked to estimate a wide variety of tasks (both systems development related and others which were simply common occurrences). Two methods of estimating were used. First, the students were asked to estimate the time required to execute a group of tasks (such as writing and logging into the check register 50 checks or completing data element descriptions for a system with 300 known data elements). Then they were asked to estimate time required to write and post one check or to complete one data element description. A specific time limit for developing the estimate was established. The final step was to perform the tasks estimated.

The results were fairly consistent across student groups and tasks estimated. Estimates of groups of tasks estimated as a group were usually off by 50% or more. Individual tasks were usually off by no more than 5 to 10%. The larger the number of tasks (number of iterations of tasks), the more error there tended to be in the estimate. Also, the more work steps in the task, the more likely the estimate was to be in error, unless each work step was individually estimated and then summed for the task.

Rules for Estimating Projects

In summary, it seems that the human mind deals fairly well with small numbers of data points which can be combined into larger informational units. This concept is supported by other research, including "Miller's magic number" (Miller, 1956). When applied to estimating, this indicates that:

1. Large tasks are better estimated if broken down into the smallest possible units, each of which are estimated and then summed for a total task estimate

2. Large groups of tasks are estimated individually and then multiplied by the number of times the task must be executed.

Methods for Estimating

There are essentially two methods of estimating which support the estimating rules outlined above: calendar-time estimating and labor-time estimating. In *calendar-time estimating,* the estimator includes in the forecast the skill level of the individual, the complexity of the task, the need for interpersonal communication, and startup/shutdown time. The result of a calendar-time estimate is the actual number of hours for a particular person to complete a task, adjusted for environmental factors.

In contrast, *labor-time estimating* assumes an "average" person, locked in a room, with no interruptions and perfect availability of information needed to complete the task. The result is an unreal estimate that must be adjusted for skill level, information availability, complexity of interpersonal communications required, and so on.

Estimating in the "real world" tends to be a mixture of these two techniques. A labor-hour estimate is created and then "fudge-factored" to account for the environmental influences.

In developing project estimates, the labor-time estimating method is preferable, for two reasons:

1. Estimates are not tied to a specific person or to a specific set of environmental circumstances.
2. More discrete estimating parameters can be evaluated and selected (which is a corollary to estimating rule 1).

In developing labor-time estimates, individual tasks can be estimated without regard for the person who will perform the task. Independent *environmental factors* such as:

- Newness of the development technique being employed
- Familiarity of the development team with the application
- Size of the project team (complexity of interpersonal communications)
- Experience of the project team in systems development
- Experience level of the users in systems development
- Availability of machine time, users, and documentation

can be applied to the individual work step or iteration estimates, applied by phase or activity or applied to the entire project.

By approaching estimating in this manner, two objectives are achieved:

1. The accuracy of the estimates can be improved.

2. An estimating model can be developed (and automated) which allows environmental factors to be adjusted globally without affecting individual labor-hour estimates.

9.4 SCHEDULING

Frequently, estimating and scheduling are perceived to be the same task. In fact, however, the objectives and processes are entirely different. *Estimating* determines task duration. *Scheduling* determines start and end times for tasks. There are essentially four stages in scheduling systems development projects— estimate adjustment, dependency networking, task assignment, and calendaring—which are required to produce a final project schedule.

Estimate Adjustment

Assuming that the labor-hour estimating method is applied (as recommended in Section 10.2), the preliminary project estimates need to be adjusted to reflect the environmental factors that become evident as the project organization is formulated. Issues such as size of the project team, experience of project team members in various phases of the life cycle, experience in the application area, availability of users, and so on, are more defined at the time the project team is organized. This enables the labor-hour adjustments to be refined prior to scheduling the work.

Dependency Networking

To estimate the project, the work is functionally decomposed, yielding discrete work modules (iterations) which can be assigned, scheduled, and monitored. These work modules, cannot, however, be performed in a random sequence. Certain work steps must be completed before others can be started. The need to establish work step/iteration dependencies is two-dimensional.

Types of dependencies.   First, there are *intrinsic dependencies* between the work steps themselves. For example, program specifications must be completed for a given module before programming of the module can begin, and the logical database design must be completed before programming specifications can be developed. There are also work steps that can occur in parallel. For example, detailed test data can be prepared as the programming is in process. User documentation can begin when the detailed user interface specifications are prepared, in parallel with programming. These intrinsic dependencies can be determined from the functional decomposition of the project, regardless of the identification of iterations specific to a particular project.

The second dimension of dependencies consists of *architectural dependencies*. Architectural dependencies are predecessor/successor relationships between iterations of work steps constrained by the design of the system. For example, in the testing area, groups of related program modules may be integrated and tested (such as modules for a particular subsystem), even though program modules for other subsystems are not yet completed. In addition, there may be certain physical designs for various subsystems or interfaces which are dependent on the overall logical design; however, the individual physical designs may be done concurrently. Prior to developing a schedule for the project, the various dependencies must be identified and illustrated to confirm the sequence in which the project work must be completed.

Analyzing dependencies.   The method for identifying and evaluating interrelatedness of various work steps is through *dependency networking*. The two most common dependency networking processes are PERT (program evaluation and review technique) and CPM (critical path method). In both techniques, the objectives are the same—to determine the sequence in which tasks must be performed and to determine how long the project will take, from start to completion, given the task dependencies. The duration of the project will be the longest series of tasks that must be performed sequentially, which is referred to as the *critical path* of the project. This is illustrated in Figure 9.1.

In this example* there are five "paths" to get from 100 (start) to 500 (end):

1. 100–210–310–500
2. 100–210–320–500
3. 100–220–330–410–500

---

*There are several notational methods for dependency. The method used in Figure 9.1 is *event-on-line*. Using this notation, the diagram

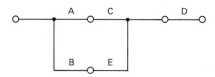

would be interpreted as meaning that events B and C could not be started before event A was completed. Event E is dependent only on the completion of B, and C is dependent only on the completion of event A. Event D is dependent on the completion of both events C and E. This notational method is most commonly employed with the critical path method. The advantage of event-on-line is that if numbers are inserted in the circles, most automated systems will accept the definition of event A as the pair of numbers in the fore and aft nodes (known as IJ task numbering). The disadvantage is that the diagrams are more difficult to evaluate visually.

(*Cont. on p. 92*)

4. 100–220–330–420–500

5. 100–230–500

The duration of each path is determined by adding the hours for each task on the path. In doing so, it is evident that path 2 (100–210–320–500) is the longest, with a duration of 30 units (hours, days, weeks), or the critical path.

This type of dependency network can be developed for the "standard" or preliminary functional decomposition for a project, as indicated in Figure 9.2. The highlighted tasks, 04.00.10—Physical Program Design, 04.05.13—Code Program, and 04.20.66—Unit Test Program will occur multiple times, and therefore the dependency network must be expanded to include each iteration of the three tasks. They may be done in parallel or in some dependent order. For example, if programs A, B, and C are to be developed, and program A contains multiple modules that can or will be used in program B, but program C is independent, then that portion of the dependency chart would look like Figure 9.3. In this type of situation, the parallel tasks can literally be inserted into the network as a repeating group, with only the durations of each iteration varying.

Rules for analyzing dependencies. The easiest way to determine and analyze dependencies for a systems development project is outlined below.

1. Establish the dependency network for the major tasks or activities in the project, without considering iterations
2. Determine which iterations of each task are dependent on each other and map those dependencies
3. Insert the iterations into the initial dependency network for the project

(*Cont. from p. 91*) The other commonly employed notational method is *event-on-node.* The diagram shown below uses *event-on-node* notation.

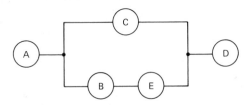

This method, commonly employed with PERT (program or project evaluation and review technique), is easier to comprehend by quick visual analysis. It requires, however, that each task be uniquely numbered. Many of the more simplistic automated network analyzers are not equipped to handle network evaluations that do not use IJ task numbering. Network analyzer programs compatible with this notational method require the user to list the predecessors or followers of each task. Using IJ task numbering, the predecessor relationships can be inferred from the task numbers.

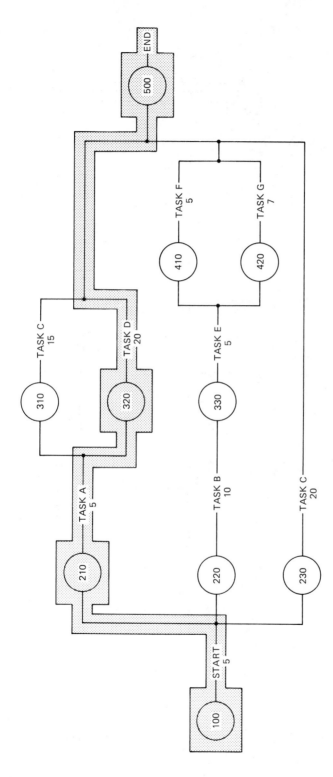

Figure 9.1 Dependency network for Project X. The duration of project X is 30 hours with START, TASK A, TASK D, and END being the Critical Path

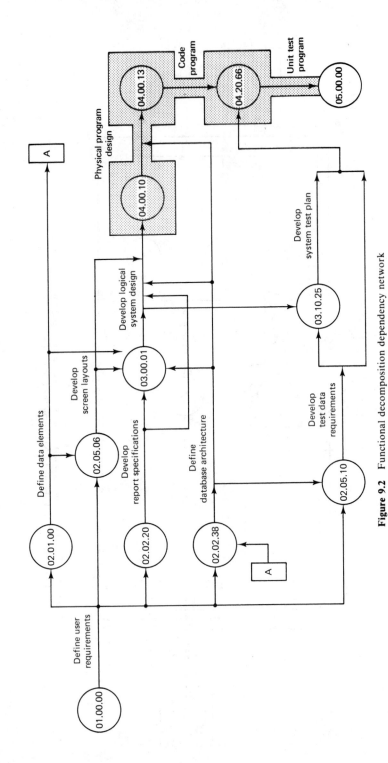

Figure 9.2 Functional decomposition dependency network

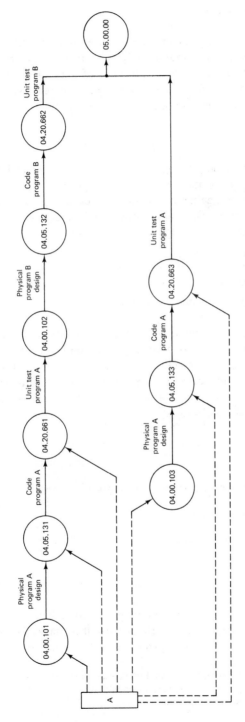

Figure 9.3 Functional decomposition dependency network—including program iterations A-From previous dependency network

Task Assignment

Once the network dependencies have been determined, assignments can be made from the task list to individual project team members. The reason for making assignments after the determination of dependencies is that concurrent tasks can be assigned to different people, whereas while dependent or serial tasks may as well be assigned to a single person.

Calendaring

Once the tasks to be performed, their dependencies and durations (estimates), and the assignments are known, the project manager can map the work to be performed against a calendar, determining start and completion dates for the individual tasks, work steps, and iterations, as well as for the entire project. There are three steps to calendaring:

1. Calculating the duration of a calendar day
2. Scheduling time off
3. Assigning start and completion dates

Calculate the calendar day.   A calendar day is not equivalent to a workday or person-day. A calendar day is a number of productive hours a person can devote to a project, producing deliverables, less time off for breaks, interruptions, meetings, administrative responsibilities, and so on. A calendar day starts at 8 hours (or whatever shift length is standard for the enterprise) and shrinks as follows:

Shift length		8.00 hours
Breaks	0.500	
Lunch	0.500	
Administrative time (time reporting, etc., at 3 hours/week)	0.600	
Phone calls and interruptions	0.500	
Nonproject meetings (4 hours/month)	0.250	
Sick time (5 days/year)	0.200	
Startup/shutdown (15 minutes twice daily)*	0.500	
Total nonproject time		3.05 hours (38.1%)
Net project time available		4.95 hours (61.9%)

Although the nature of the interruptions and their durations may vary from organization to organization, the net result is that only about 62% of the time the person is in the office is project work actually being completed.

---

*Where task breakdown has been so discrete that a number of tasks are to be completed on a given day, or where developers are working on multiple projects simultaneously, the startup/shutdown time must be increased substantially.

Schedule time off.   In the example above, sick time was scheduled on a daily basis. Since sick time generally cannot be scheduled in advance, the average sick time (either corporate average or an individual average) is amortized over the workdays per year. This amortization is not necessary for other time off, such as vacations and holidays, because they, like weekends, can be blocked off on the calendar and scheduled around. Where project plans cover extremely long times (such as a year or more), or where the planning is occurring far in advance of the actual execution of the project, these too can be amortized, yielding an accurate completion date. There are other time-off necessities, such are bereavement time, budgeted education and training time, jury duty, and so on, which can be included or excluded from the calculations, and plotted or amortized, as the project manager requires.

Determine calendar task duration.   Once the net project time available has been calculated, the estimated hours for a task can be divided by the net time available, yielding the number of calendar days required to complete a project. By consulting a calendar, with vacations and other time off noted (if not amortized), start and completion dates for each task and iteration can be determined with a fairly high confidence level.

9.5 REVISION

The major problem with many software development project plans created today is that they are wrong. For this, there are two prime reasons:

1. Estimating and scheduling procedures employed did not yield accurate forecasts of project activity.

This problem can be addressed by following the estimating and scheduling procedures outlined in previous sections of this chapter.

2. Project plans are developed with imperfect knowledge of the scope or nature of the project, or the nature and scope change, for valid business reasons as the project progresses. Revisions to the project plan are not made, and the enterprise assumes that the project is progressing in concert with the original plan.

The need for and methods of revision, as highlighted in problem 2, are addressed in this section.

Imperfect Knowledge

With the exception of a small number of software maintenance projects, it is very likely that little of the information needed to specify and plan a system is known at the time the request is made for the project or at the time it is first included on a strategic systems plan. Yet, to budget for the future and plan resource allocations, initial project requests must have a preliminary project plan. All too frequently, this plan is identified as a commitment on the part of the systems development organization, as a final "bid" for the project.

This is an unrealistic perception. Many projects are efforts to automate new processes or existing manual processes. There may be no basis for knowing the detailed information, such as number of screens, reports programs, or calculations. Even with adaptations and enhancements to existing systems, there may be little or no documentation of the interface requirements, or even a full understanding on the part of development, as to the user's needs. The further a project progresses, the more information is available from which to generate accurate, informed project plans.

Sliding Window Planning

Because of this imperfect knowledge of the systems, and because the information base improves as the project progresses, a method of planning that allows phased plans will give constantly improving insight into the project plan. This concept of phased plans is called *sliding window planning.*

In sliding window planning, the project is segmented into various phases (such as requirements definition, logical and physical design, programming, system testing, and installation). As the project progresses through each phase, the subsequent phases can be planned with an increasingly higher level of confidence. Frequently, at the end of logical design, and certainly at the end of physical design, the entire universe of parameters governing the implementation of the system are known, and a final project plan for the project can be "cast in concrete."

By default, the sliding window planning process means revision—replanning the project. With better information, the work-breakdown structure can be more complete, estimates more precise, and dates more firm. There is, however, a cost associated with this effort, which is why it meets with resistance in implementation.

The Cost of Revision: Span of Control Problems

The project planning effort consumes management resource. Quite often, project managers are also project team members, with assigned project deliverables. In this context, working at planning means not writing code. If the average project manager can supervise four to six team members (on a full-time management basis), then a four- to six-person-year project requires a full-time project manager of four to six people—a project manager not assigned specific deliverables.

Addressing the level of resource required is one method of attacking the problem, the other is to make use of automated tools to aid in planning and controlling software projects. There have been, for some time, project planning and control systems that apply automation to this process, and in the mid-1980s we also see the introduction of computer-aided software engineering (CASE) systems which can make a tremendous contribution to limiting the time spent by valuable and scarce resources. CASE is discussed in more detail in Chapter 16.

In either event, there must be an investment in time or tools to achieve accurate planning, and acceptable levels of management control for systems development projects. The return on this investment is the ability to plan for the future, schedule and select appropriate projects, and execute the systems architecture in a reasonable time frame—all of which hinge on solid operational planning.

Creeping Commitment

If an enterprise adopts the sliding window planning process, there is a necessary management policy that must be adopted: creeping commitment. Using the traditional "plan it one time and execute" method of developing systems results in commiting funds to a project, spending that money, and finding out later that it was not enough—when it is too late to cut your losses. In and of itself, funding blindly is a bad management practice. The solution to this problem is the *creeping commitment* method of funding development projects. Using creeping commitment, the senior management team of the enterprise funds the project only to the extent that detailed, accurate plans, based solely on the known universe of information about the requirements, are available.

Under this scenario, projects are segmented into *funding points* which correspond to the phases in the project where estimates are revised. Upon reaching a funding point, the revised plans are presented to management. The format for these plans is typically two-part: (1) a committed plan for the next phase of the project for which systems development management has a high level of confidence, and (2) a tentative plan for the remaining segments of the project which is based on still imperfect data. Senior management funds only part 1 and parcels out funding at subsequent review points. This is much like the executive branch of the federal government, which budgets funds for various initiatives but releases the funding only on individual justification. In this context, project budgeting is distinct from project funding.

The Advantage of Creeping Commitment

The major advantage of creeping commitment is that it allows management to make informed decisions as to the validity and business sense of spending project money. Budget excesses can be approved and accounted for, or canceled. In 1979, a major New York bank canceled an international money management project after spending $10 million on the project. By the time senior management decided to cancel the project, programming had begun, and it was evident that the project was more massive than previously believed. Creeping commitment could have enabled the bank's management to foresee the problems, segment the project, and implement only the highest-yield components. It would potentially have been possible to get a smaller system for $10 million, rather than scrapping the entire effort.

Management Data Flow

The processes of sliding window planning and creeping commitment funding imply an interface between the corporate decision makers and the operational managers. The data exchange process that accommodates this planning method also provides a vehicle for transmitting virtually all of the administrative data on estimates, plans, and schedules which are required for strategic and tactical planning. Figure 9.4 outlines this data flow.

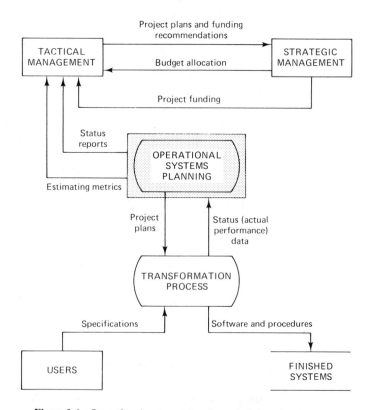

Figure 9.4 Operational systems planning: administrative data flow

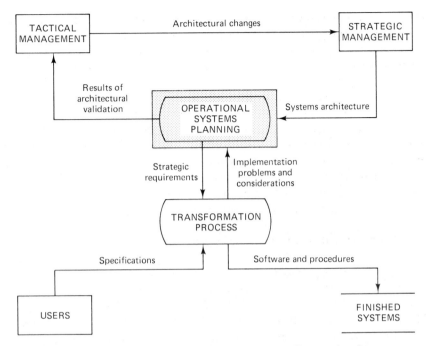

Figure 9.5 Operational systems planning: systems architecture data flow

9.6 ARCHITECTURAL VALIDATION

Up to this point, we have focused on the administrative issues involved in operational systems planning. Another major issue, which is frequently not integrated into the operational management process, is *architectural validation*—the review and revision of the strategic systems architecture. Typically in an enterprise, the systems architecture is developed by different people from those who will actually build the system. As mentioned in Section 9.5, the early phases of a project are plagued with imperfect knowledge about the nature and scope of the system. There is no phase earlier than the development of the systems architecture. The logical result of that is that the first time an architecture is developed, it will be wrong. Unless the knowledge with which the architecture was developed is improved, it will continue to be wrong. An essential element of an overall software engineering macro-system is the need to interface operational and strategic planning. Figure 9.5 outlines the data flow for this interface:

Related Materials

In any systems project, the generation of deliverables requires the input of requirements and specifications and the input of previously completed deliverables. For example, in developing a program, you need the input and knowledge of the programmer (new requirements/specifications) plus the previously completed program specifications. These previously completed deliverables are *related materials*. Related materials are either updated or referenced in the development process.

A related material critical to the success of the systems development effort and required for each software development project is the systems architecture, outlining the boundaries or *domain* of the application and all of its intended application and human interfaces. Presuming that the systems architecture exists, it will serve as the foundation for the definition of the software development project. As such, it should be considered an integral part of the systems documentation to be updated as the need arises during execution of the software engineering transformation process.

Updating the Systems Architecture

In attempting to build a system corresponding to the blueprint, the system developers may encounter errors, inconsistencies, or technical considerations with respect to the systems architecture which necessitate alterations. The operational manager needs to assess the validity of the changes proposed during the transformation process, and pass along to tactical management the recommended or necessitated changes. Tactical management can then assess the immediate impact and the overall tangential impact throughout the entire architecture. Making the changes to a version of the strategic plan, it can then be submitted to strategic management for approval and authorization. This closes the loop between the transformation process and the strategic planning process and ensures that the architecture does not become an outdated, useless document.

10

Systems Planning Metrics

There are essentially two types of metrics that can be applied to the systems development process. Each of these metrics suits a particular purpose. Although they are related to each other, they are not necessarily capable of being substituted.

The first metric class is *productivity metrics,* which deal with the measurement of efficiency (output of system per unit of input) and quality (absence of defect per line of system). Productivity metrics are valuable only when measuring the delta, or change in the metric, between two points in time. The change in productivity metrics indicates whether the development organization is becoming more or less productive. They can be valuable for indicating the effectiveness of productivity improvement programs such as new development tools, new management practices, or new development/project management techniques.

The second class of metrics is *estimating metrics,* which measure the amount of time/resource required to complete a particular unit of systems development work. Like productivity metrics, estimating metrics are determined from data captured by examining the software development transformation process.

10.1 PRODUCTIVITY METRICS

Measuring Both Components

The textbook definition of productivity is "output per unit input." For purposes of measuring systems development productivity, we have labeled this as "efficiency" and are considering it one component of productivity, the other component being quality of the software product. The reason for adding the quality component to the productivity calculation is that low-quality software ultimately necessitates future expenditure of effort (input to the systems development process). Without considering the quality issue, the productivity model is biased toward producing defective systems at a higher rate of speed, deferring the measure of input of effort required to produce the system into future reporting periods.

A Productivity Formula

There are a wide variety of published methods for measuring systems development productivity. Although many are valid, and capable of being performed in the typical organization, few take into account both efficiency and quality. One of the typical (and controversial) methods of measuring productivity is lines of code (LOC) per labor-hour. This measure alone not only ignores the quality (or future resource commitment) issue in the productivity calculation, but also ignores any adjustment for the complexity of the software, or differences in the speed with which programs can be developed in various programming languages.

Rather than simply measuring LOC/labor-hour, a more realistic measure of efficiency is to measure the number of decisions, inputs, outputs, and calculations that are coded in a given period of time, with a realization that decision logic adds to the complexity of the software more than simply adding a data element to a record. By making this complexity adjustment, the relative productivity achieved on dissimilar development projects can be equalized and compared.

Also, by measuring the complexity of the system being developed, and measuring specific system events, rather than lines of code, productivity can be measured for analysis, design, programming, and testing individually. This allows the impact of new techniques and tools, focused on one or more particular aspects of the life cycle, to be measured and assessed. Overall productivity is simply the aggregate of these individual productivity measures.

The formula in Figure 10.1 provides a model for measuring systems development productivity, including the considerations mentioned above. This formula enables the systems development organization to measure both efficiency and quality as elements of productivity and enables management to bias the measure of productivity toward either efficiency or quality (by changing the values of E and Q), if that is desired. This formula produces a numerical value P, which represents a measure of the productivity over the time the observations were made.

The essential elements of the productivity formula are the measure of efficiency:

Software Engineering
Productivity Formula

$$P = \left(E\,\frac{C + U}{T} \right) + \left[Q\,\frac{t}{D/(S + d)} \right]$$

where C = complexity of the software
D = number of defects found in the system after installation
d = number of lines of user/operations documentation
E = management weighting factor for efficiency
P = productivity
Q = management weighting factor for quality
S = lines of source code
T = time required to complete the project
t = time, in hours, to complete the corrections
U = number of deliverables (interim and final) to be completed

(a)

Complexity of software

$$C = \frac{8b + 2i + e}{S}$$

where b = number of decisions (logic branches)
i = number of input/output operations
e = number of data elements
S = lines of source code/documentation

(b)

Figure 10.1   Formula for calculating software development productivity

The complexity of the software [as measured in data elements, decisions (IF-THEN-ELSE or similar constructs), and the number of I/O operations] and the number of deliverables required to document these over time.

and the measure of quality:

The time to complete the system divided by the ratio of number of defects in the system in a given time frame to the amount of source and documentation it took to complete the system.

This formula results in a number, P. As P gets bigger, productivity is increasing; as it gets smaller, productivity is decreasing. Although many organizations may wish to embark on more complex and finite methods of productivity measurement, this basic formula will provide a guideline to ensure that the essential elements are being evaluated.

10.2 METRICS FOR ESTIMATION AND SCHEDULING

The Estimating Problem

The problem of estimating and scheduling systems development work is complex. Typically, the method used is the "expert-person" method, otherwise known as "seat of the pants." A senior person (or group) with lots of experience in building application systems looks at a task or group of tasks and estimates how long it would take him or her to accomplish it. This is then subjectively adjusted to compensate for the experience or efficiency level of the person who is actually doing the work.

This method has distinct disadvantages. It is not scientific and is not based on any empirical evidence. This technique was abandoned long ago by other transformation process managements (such as manufacturing). A steel fabricator certainly would not estimate the time (and materials) required to build a trailer in this manner. Manufacturing has adopted the "standard cost" approach to estimating.

The standard cost approach, however, presumes that the work required to perform the project has been defined and that there are statistics captured from previous iterations of the whole process, or subgroupings of work, which can be used as the basis for estimating future projects. This method of estimating from historical data has not been widely applied in the systems development field for two reasons:

1. Methods for capturing historical data have been cumbersome and the reporting methods have been ineffective.
2. Systems development has been viewed as a craft or artform rather than as a structured, defined engineering process.

Both of these problems have been overcome for some time, but the attitudes toward estimating have not changed.

Capturing Historical Data

In Part III, systems development life cycles and design techniques are discussed. At this time, let us just say that the tasks to be performed in systems development, like strategic planning, can be identified. Although the number of times a given task may need to be executed to complete a project vary, the overall set of tasks and their definitions will not change. Given that we can define the tasks and that all systems developers share the same definition, we

Estimating Guideline Matrix

LIFE-CYCLE TASK:

SKILL LEVEL	Complexity Level			
	1	2	3	4
1				
2				
3				

Figure 10.2

can begin to capture the data necessary to provide more scientific estimating guidelines.

Figure 10.2 is an estimating guideline matrix for summarizing the historical data about the time required to complete various tasks of the life cycle. There needs to be one matrix for each task in the systems development life cycle. The two axes of the matrix are skill level and complexity level. Each system developer is assigned a skill level for each task in the life cycle, indicating the experience at performing and proficiency with which the developer can complete the task. *Complexity level* is a measure of the complexity of the difficulty of the task for a particular assignment. The complexity formula in Figure 10.1 is one method to measure this.

As work is completed in the organization, hours to complete are captured for each task and each cell within the matrix, which are then averaged. What results is a fairly accurate representation of how long it takes to perform certain tasks within an organization. These averages can then serve as the basis for estimating future projects. To achieve higher levels of abstraction, say for estimating an entire project or phase for systems planning purposes, a summation of the task-level averages can be used.

This basic model can also be enhanced to record the highest and lowest (or five highest and lowest) actual times recorded for each cell of the matrix, providing suggested minimum, average, and maximum durations. Of course, it takes time to capture the historical data; however, the larger the organization and the more widely distributed the projects, the more quickly statistically valuable estimates can be derived.

11

An Overview of the Systems Development Transformation Process

In Chapter 7, the systems planning process produced a list of applications that were required to meet the enterprise's information requirements and specified how the work to complete those projects would be categorized and subdivided into systems development projects. In this chapter we define the process by which the architectural design is transformed into working application systems.

11.1 THE SOFTWARE ENGINEERING LIFE CYCLE

The software engineering process is project oriented. A development project has a defined beginning and end and a sequence of activities between those two points, which results in a completed system. The completed system consists not only of executable computer instructions, but also source code; systems specifications to be used in future maintenance and enhancement; user procedures describing how users interface with the system to enter data and retrieve information; operations procedures that describe how the data center starts, operates, and stops the system, including procedures for backup and recovery of data; and for developers of software products that will be sold, product descriptive information. All of these project outputs generated during the development process will be referred to as *final deliverables.*

The final deliverables are produced by a series of transformations performed on *interim deliverables,* or working papers, which are produced at various stages of the process, then added to, updated, and modified until they are ultimately transformed into the final deliverables. An example of an interim deliverable would be a detailed program specification used to develop the source code.

This series of transformations is referred to as the *software engineering life cycle,* sometimes referred to as the systems development life cycle. At the

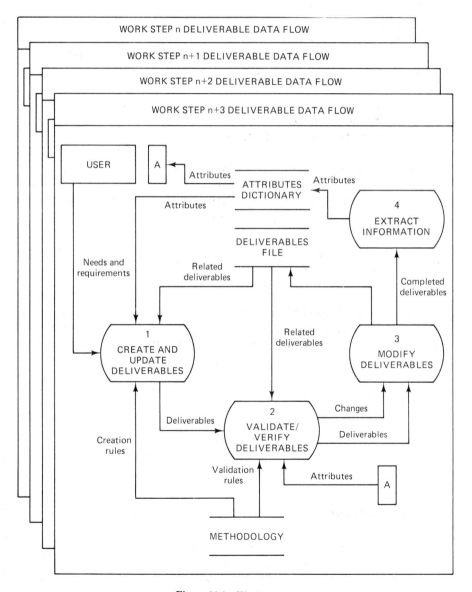

Figure 11.1   Work steps

highest level of abstraction, a software engineering life cycle can be defined in five phases:

1. Requirements definition
2. Logical design specification
3. Physical design specification
4. System implementation
5. Installation

each of which consists of a series of transformations of interim deliverables. Figure 11.1 depicts the data flow for the deliverable transformation.

11.2 LIFE CYCLES AND DEVELOPMENT TECHNIQUES

In Figure 11.1 there is a data store labeled "methodology" which provides rules to the "create/update deliverable" and "validate/verify deliverable" processes. The term "methodology" is complex, frequently misinterpreted, and important to an understanding of the software engineering transformation process.

By definition, a methodology is a "system of methods." Methods are "a regular, orderly arrangement." In software engineering, there are two distinctly different types of methodologies: life cycles and development techniques.

Development techniques provide rules and procedures for creating the deliverables and executing transformations. Development techniques specify the graphics and/or linguistics to be used in developing interim deliverables, the rules for validation, and to a small degree, the sequence in which deliverables must be transformed.

The *life-cycle methodology,* on the other hand, provides the rules for managing development projects, defining the work steps that must be completed and their sequence, guidelines for estimating and selecting project work, and rules for scheduling and assigning tasks. In essence, the life cycle provides rules for determining *what* work (or deliverable transformations) must be performed *when.*

11.3 THE METHODOLOGY THOUGHT PROCESS

In the realm of methodologies there are two distinct schools of thought. The life cycle proponents such as John Toellner, David Katch and, to a lesser extent, Phillip Metzger (see Metzger, 1973), believe that to successfully implement systems within an enterprise, you must have strong management controls, with the firm work-breakdown structures, and some form of quantifiable metrics. In their view, without the necessary management controls, systems reach 99% completion and stay there indefinitely. This school of thought focuses heavily on the issue of project management as a science.

Members of the design technique school, such as Yourdon and Constantine of the "process-data-flow" genre, Orr and Warnier of the "structured data" school, and Dan Teichroew, the father of PSL/PSA (a problem definition language), believe that you must first know how to build systems, construct the specifications, and communicate designs in some comprehensible syntax, in order to implement systems. Their view is that without these techniques, the best management in the world will produce poor quality systems—albeit on time.

Although the positions are described as extreme, most methodologies pay some heed to the issues of the other side of the argument. In point of fact, a work-breakdown structure implies that some deliverables, in some format, will be produced. Life cycle methodologies often specify the deliverable formats (in terms of preprinted forms). Some, such as John Toellner's Spectrum/structured, have gone as far as to incorporate specific design techniques within the life cycle. In the design technique school, Ken Orr's DSSD (Data Structured Systems Design) technique is supported by the DSSD Management library, which provides project management and structure to the development process. Methodologies, then, can be considered to exist along a continuum

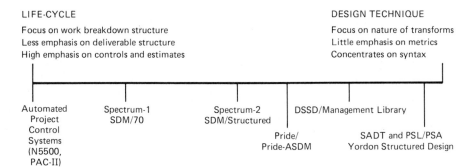

Figure 11.2   Spectrum of methodologies *

*Spectrum-1 and Spectrum-2 are trademarks of Spectrum International, Inc. SDM/70 and SDM/Structured and PAC-II are Trademarks of AGS Management Systems. Pride and Pride-ASDM are trademarks of M. Bryce & Associates, Inc. DSSD is a trademark of Ken Orr & Associates, SADT is a trademark of Softech, Inc. PSL/PSA is a trademark of ISDOS. N5500 is a trademark of Nichols & Associates.

from pure management life cycle to pure design technique. The chart in Figure 11.2 shows how various commercially developed methodologies range across the spectrum of alternatives. At issue in this chapter is the method of selection, implementation, and use of these various methodologies.

11.4 MANAGING THE SOFTWARE ENGINEERING PROCESS

The methodologies discussed above deal with only part of the issue of the software engineering transformation process (albeit a major one). The other issues focus on types of tools required to support and aid software engineers in the development and validation of their systems, techniques for controlling the projects, and methods for implementing systems, which are typically not covered by either the life cycles and design techniques. These issues, too, are addressed in the context of the overall software engineering macro-system.

12

Software Engineering Design Techniques

12.1 INTRODUCTION

Defining the Techniques

The 1970s marked a change in thinking about the way systems were developed. Prior to that time, the technological emphasis was on finding better ways to communicate instructions to the machine (i.e., better languages and compilers). In the 1970s, however, some people (e.g., Constantine, Orr, Yourdon, and DeMarco) began to wonder if both qualitative and quantitative improvements could be made by altering the way in which programmers and analysts built systems, without necessarily improving the compilers and programming languages.

Structured programming (also known as "goto-less programming") was the logical place to start. This concept required that programmers structure their code in a particular manner to gain efficiency in development, spread large programming projects controllably over several people, and reduce the effort required to maintain programs.

It was quickly realized that lack of design led to well-structured garbage programs, so *structured analysis and design techniques* emerged. These techniques focus on logically and systematically identifying the requirements for programming, designing the system, and testing the design before jumping into coding. It quickly became evident that the structured analysis and design techniques paid off even better than the structured programming techniques.

Graphic and Linguistic Techniques

In order to study the software engineering design techniques, it is helpful to categorize them. One way to categorize techniques is by the mechanism used to document the system. A quick look at techniques indicates a recognizable difference between those which focus on words and those which focus on pictures. Some techniques are *linguistic*—that is, they rely on words, structured in a particular format, to describe or specify the system to the programmer. Linguistic techniques (also known as problem definition languages or pseudocode) had historical appeal because machines could deal with words better than with pictures—users of linguistic techniques could use computers to help them write and modify their designs.

The *graphical techniques* focus on updating the traditional flowcharting process in the belief that pictures convey more information with less work and greater understanding than do words. The graphical techniques relied on this factor, rather than the computer, to improve efficiency and productivity. Advances in low-cost computer graphics in the early part of this decade have erased some of the automation advantage of the linguistic techniques (see Chapter 16).

Categorizing Techniques by Method

There are four main schools of thought employed in the application of software engineering development techniques:

1. *Process flow,* also called data flow, concentrates on the flow of data within the system and the processes that modify or transform the data. Process-flow design concentrates on the *input–process–output* method of specifying systems.

2. *Data structured design* concentrates on the nature of the data available to the system and the transformations that must be performed on the data. Data structured design starts with the required outputs, defines their components, and builds the input and process specifications. Data structured design is *output–process–input* oriented.

3. *States and transitions* is a method of specifying real-time systems (such as process control) which do not operate with or require large information databases. States and transition methodologies describe the state of the system and specify how the state will change given a specific outside stimulus (or input). States and transitions will not be discussed much further because they are not well suited to information-oriented systems.

4. *Knowledge-based design* is an artificial-intelligence (AI) approach to specifying systems and requires advanced, sophisticated AI simulation systems to describe the operating environment in which the system will reside, and then generate the appropriate processes to transform the

data. Knowledge-based design is highly experimental and not yet at a point where it can be implemented on a wide scale.

Since states and transitions is used primarily for real-time process or command and control applications, and knowledge-based design is still primarily a theoretical concept with limited commercial history, our discussions of development techniques will focus on process-flow and data structured design—the most practical, proven techniques for the engineering of information systems software.

12.2 PROCESS-FLOW TECHNIQUES

The process-flow development techniques (such as Yourdon and Gane and Sarson), also known as *structured* or *top-down analysis and design,* focus on defining the processes that a system must perform in order to transform input data into output information. Data are treated as flows between the processes. That is, with these techniques data can be represented as flowing into a process, out from a process, or stored between processes. This process orientation is a direct result of the evolution of the process-flow techniques from programming techniques.

Decomposition and Structure

The process-flow techniques operate on the principle of functional decomposition (hence the "top-down" designation). In applying functional decomposition, the developer examines the existing system and describes or documents it in very global terms, using graphic representations for the processes, flows, and data stores. This preliminary document, or *data flow diagram,* is then decomposed process by process until the developer has a series of *primitives,* processes that cannot, or need not, be decomposed further to be understood. Figure 12.1 depicts the functional decomposition of a data flow into its primitives.

Once the existing system has been decomposed, the new or modified system can be designed in much the same way. The highest level of the decomposition can be modified to represent changes in the input and output data flows. The more primitive processes can then be modified to reflect the changes in data content. The bottom level or most primitive processes represent *modules* of software (or manual procedure) that will ultimately be produced in the final system.

Once the flow of the system has been decomposed into its primitive processes (representing modules), the processes must be reconstructed into procedures or programs. The representation of the relationship between modules of a program or procedure is typically done with the use of *a hierarchy.* The

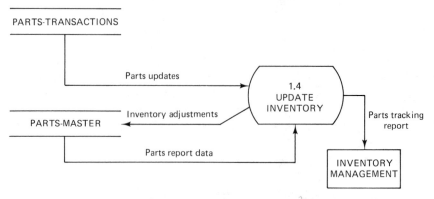

(a) Process-flow design technique: data flow diagram—Level 1

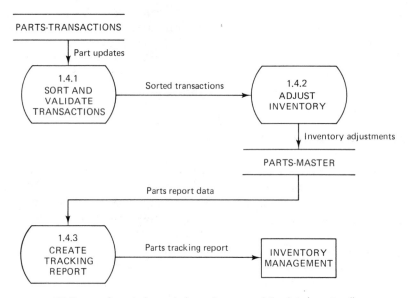

(b) Process-flow design technique: decomposed "update inventory" process

Figure 12.1

hierarchy is essentially an organization chart similar to those found in corporations to represent the relationships between people or departments. At the
top of the hierarchy chart is the program or procedure. This is then followed
by various levels of individual processes which are linked together to form the
program or procedure. Figure 12.2 represents a typical hierarchy chart for a
portion of an application system.

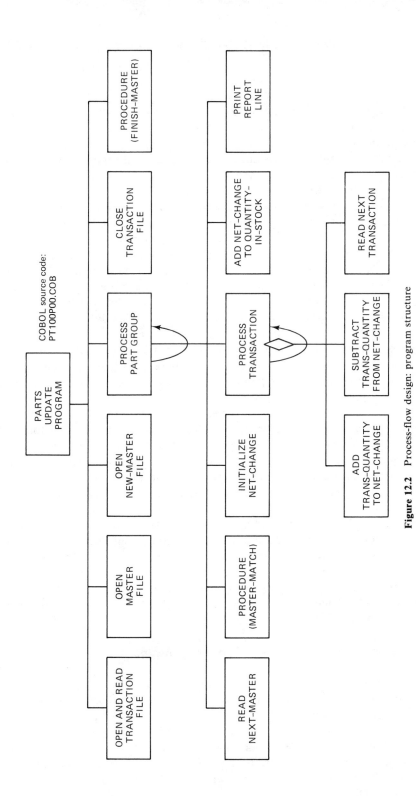

Figure 12.2 Process-flow design: program structure

117

Coupling and Cohesion

Some of the underlying principles for structured design were constructed and defined by Edward Yourdon and Larry Constantine. According to Yourdon and Constantine (1978), the measure of good versus bad systems is coupling and cohesion. The prime reasons for decomposing and structuring systems are to identify small enough modules which can be arranged and structured to minimize coupling and maximize cohesion.

Coupling is, in essence, a measure of how dependent two or more modules are on one another. A system may contain one module for calculating gross pay and another module that computes interest on an employee's cash advance. These modules will probably require few common data and are therefore uncoupled. A module represented by a subroutine in a FORTRAN program which shares a formatted COMMON data storage area with the mainline program cannot operate outside the mainline (or another program that has the same statement in it) and is therefore highly dependent and *tightly coupled*. As Yourdon and Constantine state, tight coupling is bad. Changes in one module of a tightly coupled set will force changes in other modules. *Loosely coupled* modules (such as those which are connected only by sharing access to a file) are good, because they are less dependent on each other and require less maintenance.

Loosely coupled modules are beneficial because they lessen maintenance requirements and may be reusable. An example of reusability of a loosely coupled module is a standardized PRINT-REPORT routine which formats a report based on parameters passed to it by a calling module. Changes in calling modules may not necessitate changes in the report formatting routine, and furthermore, a generalized reporting routine can be used or called by several programs.

Cohesion is an indicator of how modules relate to one another. A high level of cohesion is good and is an indicator of loose coupling. Yourdon and Constantine (1978) identified seven levels of cohesion. At the lowest (least desirable) level, cohesion occurs by a *direct binding* (through a CALL or PERFORM statement) so that the modules are physically linked together. At the highest level, modules are linked indirectly by data transferred between them with a process intervening.

Advantages of Process-Flow Techniques

The principles of process structuring and relatedness identified in the structured techniques is a valid measure of the "goodness" or "badness" of a system design. By applying the principles of coupling and cohesion, developers can improve the adaptability and reusability of their systems, thereby lessening both maintenance and development required for new systems. The continuing research and evolution in process-flow techniques provides rules by which reusable, adaptable systems can be developed.

Since process-flow techniques are action oriented—concentrating on *how* the system will perform its functions—in many of the proprietary and public-domain techniques, "mini-specifications" and pseudocode (structured English or a problem definition language) are attached to the hierarchical and data flow deliverables. Because of this action orientation, the thought process required to use the techniques more closely represents programming. Since programming is basic to most system designers, they are comfortable with the techniques. This comfort level undoubtedly has attributed to the rapid growth of these techniques from the early 1970s to the mid-1980s.

Another advantage of the process-flow techniques is the simplicity of the graphical representation. The old adage says that "a picture is worth a thousand words," and this is certainly true with structured design graphics. Data flows and structure charts allow software developers to visualize and identify complex module relationships that would be buried or nearly unintelligible in a linguistic context.

Disadvantages of Process-Flow Techniques

With the growth of computer-aided software engineering systems, one measure of the value of a technique is the ability to automate it. Although process-flow techniques have distinct advantages, there are some drawbacks.

First, although the deliverables are clearly identified, as well as some relationships between the deliverables, there are few provable rules for transforming preliminary deliverables into final deliverables. The process-flow techniques improve the performance of good developers, but not necessarily junior ones, for much of the transformation from specification to code is still left up to the discretion of the analyst or programmer, outside the scope of the technique.

Second, many systems use or access large, complex databases that must be managed by the systems. The process-flow techniques do little to generate optimized data structures.

Another major disadvantage with the process-flow techniques is that they presume that requirements have been defined, yet they provide no grammar, symbology, or procedures for the capturing and documenting of requirements on a specific deliverable. Typically, data flows are described as requirements documents, but from where were the constraints and initial identification of data-flow content derived? These procedures are not particularly well defined in the process-flow techniques.

12.3 DATA STRUCTURED TECHNIQUES

Jean Dominique Warnier and Kenneth T. Orr are perhaps the most identifiable parents of the data structured techniques for developing systems; however,

Michael Jackson, the British systems consultant, may in fact be the earliest proponent of data structured development.

Unlike process-flow techniques, which evolved by applying programming or instruction specification thought processes to design, prior to coding, the data structured techniques grew out of research into ways to define more efficient systems (and programs) that would ultimately be coded. Process-oriented programming principles were not the underlying logic on which data structured design was developed.

The Jackson design technique still focuses on the programming issue, but approaches the definition of a large program by first defining the data to be processed and their relationships. The Orr technique, on the other hand, takes a systems approach to the problem of design.

Orr, in his DSSD approach, begins by identifying the *outputs* of the computer system. These outputs are then decomposed into various levels of data, until *atomistic,* or most primitive data elements, and their logical relations are defined. These are then reconstructed (bottom-up) into databases, processing modules, and computer systems. (See Orr, 1981).

Assembly Technique

As the process-flow techniques are referred to as "top down" because of the way they decompose higher-level structures to lower-level structures, the data structured techniques are frequently referred to as "bottom up," a designation that is somewhat inaccurate. Jackson, (1983, p. 370) states that "Top-down is a reasonable way of describing things which are already fully understood. . . . But top-down is not a reasonable way of developing, designing or discovering anything."

The data structured techniques focus on the *data* that the system will transform into *information.* The processes that must ultimately be coded are derived from a process of decomposing output information (or output intermediate data). Contrary to Jackson's opinion, data structured design is also "top down" in a sense, using definitional data decomposition rather than functional decomposition. Data structured techniques begin with the outputs and determine the inputs. Therefore, a more appropriate label for these techniques may be "right to left" based on the basic system model *input* → *process* → *output.*

The first question asked by the developer using a data structured technique is: "What output information do you want to see?" Hence data structured development is a much more requirements-oriented process. (Although this orientation is a distinct advantage, it also represents an implementation disadvantage, as we shall see later).

Data Structured Development Procedures

The data structured approach begins by defining the system domain—identifying objects (or entities) which accept and transmit data and information. The relationships between objects (represented by transmission of data) are referred to as *transactions*. While object/transaction graphic representations closely resemble the data flows depicted by process-flow techniques, their applications are considerably different.

The object-transaction diagram deals with tangible or organizational objects as opposed to processes. The diagram depicts the transmission and transformation of data through the transactions. In essence the diagram represents the movement of data and information between information users. This is consistent with Jackson's belief that the process-flow techniques are valuable for defining things that are known. The users of data and the nature of the data are known.

The other objective of the object-transaction diagram is to identify the boundary of the system. Warnier–Orr techniques indicate the boundary by drawing a dashed line around the objects which are contained within the target system to be automated or modified. Transactions that cross the boundary represent a set of requirements, in that the format of those transactions cannot be modified without altering objects external to the system.

Rather than proceeding from this point to identifying and decomposing processes, the data structured techniques examine the data/information contained within the transactions and decompose it. In the process of decomposing data, the procedures required to assemble the higher-level data from more primitive elements gives rise to the definition of processes or modules. The series of charts in Figure 12.3 are examples of a sequence of data structured specifications.

Advantages of Data Structured Systems Development

In many respects, data structured development is a superior approach to specifying *information systems* software and procedures. The prime objective of building an information system is the construction of information from data. It is logical, therefore, to construct the processes from an analysis of the data rather than defining the data requirements from the processes. In any information processing system, the data are known and the processes are to be defined. In the process-flow techniques, it is assumed that the processes are known (or can arbitrarily be assigned) and that the data are unknown.

Since the data structured techniques are a search for the processes, the definition of processes from a logical analysis of the data yields systems with higher levels of cohesion and lower coupling. Processes are automatically defined around the data. Logical cohesion [the second highest level of cohesion identified by Yourdon and Constantine (1978, pp. 118–120)] is an automatic by-product of data structured development. Lower levels of cohesion must be directly specified by the designer in the assembly of complex processes from the primitives.

Another distinct advantage of the data structured approach is its finite nature. Since the number of objects, transactions, and data elements in a sys-

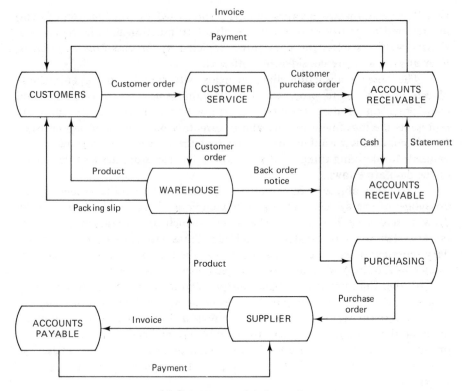

(a) Data structured design: entity

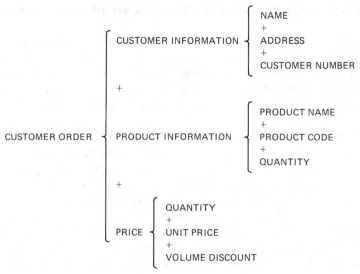

(b) Data structured design: assembly line

Figure 12.3 Data structured design

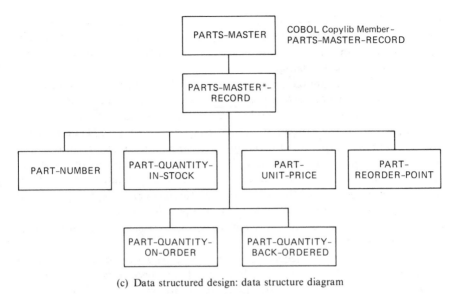

(c) Data structured design: data structure diagram

Figure 12.3   (Continued)

tem is finite, the "end" of the design process in data structured approaches is known. The bottom of the data/information hierarchy is the smallest unit of data uniquely identified to the system and stored in a field. These low-level primitives are assembled using well defined rules until the desired information required by the user or the external object is produced. This is in direct contrast to the process-flow techniques, which specify no "end" to the decomposition process, leaving it up to the developer. Identifying the "most primitive" process is a difficult and often arbitrary search, as was John Gilbreth's search for the "therblig," the smallest unit of mechanical motion, or the mathematician's search for the physical geometric point. Because of the finite nature of data structured design, it is theoretically (and perhaps in the near future actually) capable of being automated.

Disadvantages of Data Structured Approaches

In a conversation with Ken Orr at the 1984 Federal Computer Conference, the author asked him why process-flow techniques were presently more prevalent than data structured techniques. The answer confirmed my own observations. Essentially, system developers are more comfortable thinking in terms of processes rather than data. System developers grew up writing code to specify processes and drawing logic diagrams to specify processes—data were merely objects to be manipulated by the processes. Data structured development is a different approach requiring a different perspective or mind set to be assumed by the developer, inducing change (and some level of trauma) into their work environment. Also, the data structured approach is newer and has not had as long to become entrenched in the data processing culture. This cultural change means that there is a required investment in training and startup in an organization and occasionally some minor resistance from people adverse to change.

Another disadvantage frequently perceived is the graphical representation used by some data structured techniques. Process-flow techniques use symbols that more closely resemble traditional flowchart methods but are more simplified. Data structured techniques (particularly DSSD) make use of *bracket diagrams,* also called *assembly line diagrams* which are purely data oriented decomposition schematics. Because the information on these diagrams is spatially dependent (rather than graphically related), some developers consider them to be difficult to follow. Interestingly, graphic representation (which is easy to modify), rather than the process versus data issue (which is fundamental to the technique), seems to be the barrier to wide-spread adoption of the data structured techniques.

Another barrier to acceptance is the perceived difficulty in specifying interactive or real-time system modules which are becoming more common elements of application systems. Developers are reluctant to require two design techniques (one for batch applications and one for interactive modules), regardless of the considerable productivity benefit of the data structured technique.

In the final analysis, however, there are tremendous advantages in productivity, reusability, and adaptability to be gained from the use of data structured techniques.

12.4 LINGUISTIC TECHNIQUES

Methods

The linguistic approaches to designing and specifying information systems tend to be methods or procedures for preparing specific deliverables rather than methodologies or integrated sets of procedures for producing systems. Linguistic techniques can be divided into two major categories: structured English/problem definition languages and documentation methods.

Since the linguistic approaches tend to be support procedures for various aspects of specifying systems, they represent excellent opportunities to augment other structured approaches (process-flow or data structured). Frequently, the graphical approaches require further definition or explanation of specific constraints, user requirements, or processes to be reviewed with users or to augment the graphics given to programmers. These requirements for additional documentation, usually referred to as *mini-specifications* or *process specifications,* can be supported with linguistics more efficiently than with completely free-form text. In essence, the linguistic approaches provide a template to be filled in with words—the template serving as a memory jogger to ensure that all the salient points have been covered, in much the same way that a preprinted form ensures that the user has provided all of the necessary information.

Structured English

Structured English and problem definition languages (PDLs) such as the ISDOS PSL (Problem Statement Language)* or Backus–Nauer form focus on a very narrow issue within systems development—the specification of processes prior to developing code. Since they pose a less rigid syntactical structure, they can be generated faster than a compiled or interpreted programming language. Also, they tend to be more easily understood by nontechnical personnel.

Because of these characteristics, structured English techniques provide an additional level of documentation that system designers can employ to describe and explain procedures for end users and modules to be developed by programmers. These techniques can be superimposed over other techniques and employed as additional steps in the development process.

12.5 SUMMARY

Weighing the Techniques

The primary focus of this book is on the engineering of information processing systems, as opposed to real-time systems. Information systems, such as financial systems, inventory control, and order-entry systems, typically have large databases with comparatively few data types, however, these systems process many values for each data type. Also, information systems have comparatively few transactions per unit of time. Real-time systems, such as flight avionics, data communications networks, and missile guidance systems, however, have many data types but relatively few values are stored and retrieved. Real-time systems tend to have small databases with simple data structures and access paths, but process enormous quantities of data (hundreds of transactions per second).

Because of the characteristics of these types of systems, the data structured approaches tend to be more supportive of the database design process (traditional file structures or DBMS) than do the process-flow techniques. Since data sharability and integrity are major concerns in information processing systems, the data structured approaches tend to provide more benefit in this area. This is perhaps why most of the systems architecture, strategic sys-

---

*PSL and PSL/PSA are trademarks for ISDOS, Inc. PSL is a proprietary, commercial problem definition language, accompanied by PSA, Problem Statement Analyzer. PSL/PSA was originally developed by the Univerity of Michigan, Ann Arbor, under the direction of Dr. Daniel Teichroew.

tems planning, and enterprise modeling methodologies embody data structured transformations.*

Conversely, real-time system development is much more oriented toward the process, with the data being merely a stimulus to some process that must respond and take some action. Real-time system development is therefore much more conducive to process-flow or state and transition design techniques.

Selecting an Approach

Even though the data structured design techniques offer some advantages over the process-flow techniques, that fact alone is not sufficient to make a decision. For example, because of the cognitive disadvantages of data structured approaches, some of the graphic representations of process-flow design can be superimposed over data structured design. The techniques can be mixed and matched to optimize performance, as is evidenced in some recent publications in the process-flow school which apply some data structured concepts represented in data-flow form. This approach is particularly useful in organizations that may already have made a significant investment in process-flow techniques and education.

Another possibility to consider is applying a particular technique to the segment of the life cycle to which it is most appropriate. As Jackson noted, process flow is an excellent tool for modeling a known environment. If this is the case, then perhaps those techniques should be used in the discovery, or requirements and systems analysis phases, where the current environment is being modeled. Data structured or process-flow techniques can be applied to decompose the model, and data structured techniques can then be used to design the new system, by recomposing the appropriate data and operations into processes. However there is little published documentation on this combined approach.

Of course, to effectively select a specific methodology for use within your organization, it is necessary to examine the alternatives. Individual vendors can be polled, but a good place to start may be with *Software Design: Methods and Techniques* by Lawrence J. Peters (1981). This book provides an analysis and comparison of a number of different techniques, both public domain and proprietary. Although it should not be viewed as providing the answer, it can provide sufficient data to begin your evaluation.

---

*The process of identifying objects and transactions and then identifying application boundaries or domains is similar to the approach used in IBM's Business Systems Planning (BSP) process—a data structured approach to developing a systems architecture for an entire organization.

Management Considerations

Any change in technique will result in some organizational trauma. This may tend to affect the net productivity of early projects using new techniques. It is important to recognize that this is temporary and a result of the learning curve. Another serious consideration is the financial aspect of acquiring a proprietary methodology and training the staff. This investment can conceivably exceed $100,000 for a sizable organization.

Benefits

Almost universally, the investment in implementing a methodology is well worth the return. In general, the benefits of applying a methodology to software engineering are:

- Fewer defects in installed systems, resulting in lower maintenance and an increased level of resource available to complete projects with positive financial impact on the organization.
- Improved efficiency with which developers specify systems, resulting in shorter development times and earlier realization of new system benefits.
- Reduced programming and testing effort. System defects are identified prior to coding or more extensive design, resulting in less redesign and reprogramming. Also, because of improved coupling and cohesion, modules are more reusable. Programming and detailed design effort can actually be eliminated by reusing previous design and code modules. These modules are easier to identify because documentation is more complete.

Higher-quality software. Formal software engineering analysis and design techniques contribute directly to improvement in the quality, or absence of defects, in the final product. There are several reasons for this, which are discussed below.

At a minimum, the software engineering development technique acts as a checklist for the software engineer, identifying all of the deliverables that must be completed to specify the resulting software programs. This ensures that no steps have been omitted. Also, the techniques specify how to produce the deliverables: what questions must be asked and what procedures must be followed to transform the answers to those questions into specifications for the solution to the problem.

In supplying the "how to" instructions for specifying systems, they employ rules that must be followed—a graphic or linguistic syntax for describing the problem and the solution. The syntax, although less complex or rigid than the syntax for writing a COBOL or FORTRAN program, nevertheless provides a measure of provability for checking the solution. For example, Constantine and Yourdon provide methods or rules for measuring coupling and cohesion of systems described using their notations. By following the procedures and evaluating design deliverables against the rules, certain qualitative deficiencies can be identified in the design before they make their way into the code, to be found at test time or worse yet, after the software is in use.

Improved Efficiency.   Efficiency is the most paradoxical of the benefits of formal development techniques. The reason for this is that projects using development techniques occasionally take longer than projects using conventional "code and go" and so-called fourth-generation methods. Why? Because the developers are forced to do more preparatory work before coding begins, work that may not be done at all using less formal methods.

How can doing more work increase efficiency? Well, the answer is that you are doing more work within the confines of a specific project, making that project take longer. However, many projects end prematurely. A project should end when error-free software, meeting the users' needs, is installed and functional. All too often, projects end, only to have work begin again on an enhancements and corrections list for the system, or fixing bugs the users find after they work with the system for a period of time.

We established in Part 1 that the longer it takes to find a bug, the more time consuming and costly the repair is. By ending projects prematurely, software engineers are giving the illusion of greater productivity; however, they are only adding to, and deferring, the work that remains to be done on the project.

By employing formal development techniques, the illusion of rapid completion evaporates. This is distressing to many developers and managers who prefer the illusion—the ability to say "I'm done." But by removing the illusion and developing high-quality software, the future maintenance (to fix bugs) or enhancements (to add features the developers left out or failed to identify in the first go-round) are in the system—designed in, programmed in, and tested in, where the costs are lower than postinstallation modification. This represents a true improvement in efficiency.*

Reusability.   One of the major factors that can contribute to improved systems development productivity is *reusability*—taking working, preexisting modules and incorporating them into present designs or programs. T. Capers Jones, a software engineering consultant, with Nolan Norton, quotes productivity increases of tenfold in Japanese firms employing reusability (Jones, 1984).

---

*A satirical, but enlightening dissertation on the subject of self-delusion by systems development professionals and corporate management can be found in *The One Minute Methodology* by E. Z. Systems as Told To Ken Orr, written by Orr (1984). This short book is highly recommended reading.

These improvements, however, cannot be achieved without thinking through the design before implementing the system. Formal development techniques provide the opportunity to examine a design and identify processes or functions that are candidates for employing reusable modules rather than building from scratch. The documentation resulting from development performed using formal methods also provides a description of the modules, their interfaces to other systems, and input/output requirements which are necessary attributes or criteria for selecting a module as being reusable.

In the same article, Jones likens stocking your reusable code library from existing software to building a new car from junkyard parts, stating that reusable modules should be designed as such. Designing reusable modules means building modules with the characteristics of low coupling and high cohesion—the object of the formal development techniques.

With such dramatic productivity increases available through the application of reusability, one wonders why it is not more prevalent in practice. The reasons for this are two-fold. First, building reusable modules requires a level of consistency which has been difficult to achieve using traditional software engineering tools. The task of assuring consistent usage, format, and names of procedures, subprograms, and data elements was a tedious, time-consuming job. On complex system designs with large numbers of these objects to verify, without the use of automated tools, the need seemed to be outweighed by the cost. This is most likely a problem of perception rather than reality.

The second problem associated with reusability is the difficulty experienced by the developer in identifying and locating reusable modules. In the "olden days" of computing, programmers kept card decks of routines in their desk drawers (today they're kept in on-line, but individual, disk libraries). These card decks contained frequently used program fragments which the programmer scavenged, because they could be incorporated into new programs. These fragments included such things as date routines, report shells and frequently used calculations. The programmer accessed this library through sheer memory power (recalling that a particular fragment was contained in the drawer or file), or through a time-consuming sequential search of all the card decks. Reusability in this environment is limited by the practicality of remembering the existence and location of a particular fragment or polling co-workers within ear-shot to see if they had, or knew of, a particular fragment. This method of locating reusable code is highly inefficient. Successful practice of reusability depends on allowing free and easy access to the reusable fragment library, coupled with an easy-to-use index to locate the module needed.

These two problems can now be overcome (as we shall see in more detail in Chapter 16) by the use of computer-aided software engineering (CASE) environments which provide tools such as design dictionaries and design analyzers that significantly improve the ability to locate modules, and provide automatic (or at least computer-supported) consistency checks of designs. The first such CASE environment was DesignAid, released by Nastec Corporation in 1984. The DesignAid GraphiText editor allows analysts and programmers to interrupt their design or programming session to directly access the Design Dictionary to search an on-line, relational library of reusable modules, and returns a list of potential candidates to the software engineer. These reusable modules can then be inserted into the program or specification being created. DesignAid's Design Analyzer automatically creates "where-used" entries into the dictionary to aid in creating the index to the reusable library.

Given that CASE tools are becoming widely available to system developers, we must also examine Jones' analysis of reusability. While he describes "ideal" reusability, there may, in fact, be lesser levels of reusability which can still reap significant productivity gains. For example, if one could have perfect knowledge of the existing base of system documentation and code, one could most likely find modules that were similar in structure and/or function to the module under development. Simply finding the module, examining it, and using it as a template for a new module can save a lot of time in developing the new module. We call this level 1, or *referential reusability*. Level 2, or *operative reusability*, occurs when a similar module is located and can be copied (in whole, or in part), modified to fit a new purpose or to fit within a new construct, and then incorporated into a new program or system design. Jones identifies level 3 or *identical reusability*, which means a module or fragment of a design or program can be retrieved from a library and directly inserted into the new program or design. Identical reusability is common in the computer-hardware and electronics design arena where electronic components such as transistors, diodes and gates are designed, placed in catalogs, and then simply rearranged into differing configurations to create new products and/or sub-assemblies.

Without argument, identical reusability is the most desirable; however, the readers of this book could all be retired before an organization had all of its existing library identically reusable. Referential and operative reusability are admirable interim targets for any software development organization.

Redundancy elimination. Since the design techniques provide rules for identifying objects (processes, data, etc.) contained within programs and higher-level designs which use a standard syntax or grammar, it is possible to examine the designs for redundancy. For example, if a data flow diagram contains a process *Print Report* which takes, as input, data elements *part-number, customer-number, quantity,* and *back-order* and outputs data records *heading-line, detail-line* and *totals,* then any other process in the same or related data flow diagrams containing the same inputs and outputs should be labelled *Print Report.* If other names for processes with the same inputs and outputs are listed, then there is a high probability that duplicate modules are being specified.

This duplication of modules can be quite costly. Every duplicate label on a data flow diagram can cause duplicate detail design, programming, testing, and maintenance. Rigorous adherence to a methodology can substantially reduce this redundancy. As the size of the project team grows, the probability that an identical module will be created increases geometrically. Some of the methodologies (such as data structured design techniques) bias against this, while others, such as structured analysis and design permit the creation, but provide easy-to-read, consistent graphical documentation which can be reviewed for redundancy.*

Redundancy elimination, as we shall see in Chapter 16, is another prime candidate for CASE technology.

---

*DesignAid and GraphicText are registered trademarks of Nastec Corporation.

13

Software Engineering Life Cycles

13.1 INTRODUCTION

Phillip Metzger (1973, p. 5) defines a *development life cycle* as "a series of orderly, interrelated activities leading to the successful completion of a set of programs." By referring to "programs," the definition is somewhat restrictive. A rephrasing more suitable to software engineering principles would be

> A series of orderly, interrelated activities resulting in the successful completion delivery and support of an information system—including programs, operating procedures, and documentation.

Also in his book, Metzger indicates that "purists" often take issue with the term "life cycle" because it refers to an ongoing, cyclic process. Typically, a discussion of development life cycles focuses on the project process—from requirements definition through installation. From this perspective it is questionable whether life cycle is an appropriate term. However, when examining the entire software engineering process from strategic planning through implementation, it truly is cyclic, with the development of a new project being simply a stage through which the enterprise's management information systems pass.

In reality, the entire software engineering life cycle is composed of smaller stages:

- Strategic planning
- System development

- Plan maintenance
- System support (maintenance)

It is through these stages that the software engineering process constantly cycles. Strategic planning and plan maintenance were covered in Part II. In this chapter we deal primarily with system development and system support.

Development and Support

Pure new system development is a rare occurrence in the software development environment. Pure development can occur only when an entirely new application system is being developed—typically, the automation of a manual process or the development of an entirely new system to support a new product, service, or function within the enterprise. The vast majority of development performed today is support or maintenance.

The term *support* is probably preferable, since *maintenance* usually means bringing some system, machine, or process back into compliance with the original specification. Computer hardware maintenance is applied when the machine goes down or produces erroneous results. In computer hardware, *engineering changes* are applied to enhance the functionality of the machine. In the software world, maintenance is performed when a system has a bug or does not operate to the original specification. This typically happens early after installation or when rarely used modules (such as year-end accumulations) are executed for the first time.

Most often, the support performed on software is not fixing bugs, but rather *enhancing* the functionality of the system—processing additional data types, generating additional reports, or performing new calculations on existing data within the system. Another type of support performed is *adaptation,* modifying an existing system to solve problems other than those for which the system was originally specified. For example, a banking "checking account" system may also be adapted to be a "line-of-credit checking" system.

Even if the system is truly not operating to specifications, the documentation may not have to be changed. In this circumstance, it may be safe for a programmer to go directly to the program and fix the problem. However, with other forms of support, the actual purpose and functionality of the system are being altered. In these cases it is essential to define the problem and objectives, define the requirements, design the changes, implement, and test. These functions are almost identical to those performed in new development.

Why a Formal Life Cycle

The basic premise behind a formal, documented life cycle is that there is a defined series of processes that transform knowledge and organizational information into information systems. The life cycle identifies these processes and the sequence in which they occur. In its simplest form, the life cycle serves as a checklist or memory jogger to the project manager of all the transformations of data that must occur in order to have sufficient information to generate computer programs. In this sense, the life cycle is a timesaver in that the project manager does not have to go through the process of identifying all the steps that must be completed each time a project is undertaken.

A more advanced formal life cycle further serves to set the format and standards by which deliverables are developed. By providing a standard format, the life cycle establishes "rules," or *performance standards,* by which effective completion of the work can be judged or evaluated. This provides a better communications environment for all the team members. Systems are well defined and documented, so subsequent support can be undertaken with a clear understanding of what needs to be done to the system to adapt or modify it.

Also, formal life cycle provides a standard nomenclature for describing systems projects. This is absolutely essential to the management process. Life cycles yield better estimates, greater conformance to expectations, and ultimately, better systems at lower costs. The development life cycle uniformly defines all the work steps in a project. In a manner very similar to the manufacturing process of standard costing, the life cycle enables identical units of work to be measured from project to project. If metrics are established and captured consistently, estimating and planning become much more accurate, and management controls can be applied more consistently.

Finally, formal life cycles ultimately reduce software development costs. Boehm (1981) indicates that "bugs" in the system can be fixed for 1 to 10% of the cost if detected in the early stages of the project rather than after implementation. Studies performed by the IBM System Science Institute (Ellsworth and Burrill, 1979) indicated that implementing a formal software development life cycle caused significantly earlier detection of system bugs—reducing postimplementation bugs from 20% of the total to 1% of the total. This is primarily because of the accuracy in work resulting from operating in a structured environment.

Finally, technology is moving at a rapid pace. Historically, software developers were like the cobbler's children who had no shoes. They spent all of their time and resources providing automated tools to aid the enterprise's transformation processes and developing none for themselves. Traditionally, programmers were cheaper than equipment. As that trend changes, programmers, analysts, designers, and project managers become considerably more costly, and technologies to aid them in performing their work become more attractive financially. Most of these aids, however, presume that the software development (or at least major portions of it) are well defined and consistent. The life cycle provides this consistency. In fact, the life cycle provides the framework or blueprint for the "software factory"—the highly automated process of providing specifications as input to the factory, and getting operational, well-documented systems out.

In the scenario of rising software costs, the well-defined life cycle is a prerequisite to "software solvency." Organizations that cannot afford systems will become information bankrupt and hence not competitive.

13.2 THE LIFE-CYCLE ARCHITECTURE

The software engineering transformation process depicted in Figure 13.1 is essentially a nonelectronic counterpart to the von Neumann machine. The computer components are replaced by software engineers. The software program is replaced by the software development life cycle. The data to be processed are the requirements, constraints, and specifications for the end product or system. In this sense the life cycle is the program for the software development process, which yields different application systems based on varying input data.

Components of the Life-Cycle Methodology

Since the life cycle is a software program (for people), it has a defined structure and content. The basic components of the life cycle are:

1. *Work-breakdown structure:* The phases, activities, tasks, and work steps that comprise all the events or transformation which must take place to convert the requirements and specifications into software and supporting documentation.

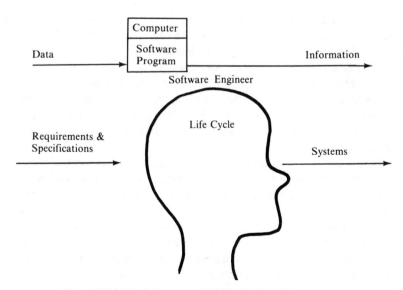

Figure 13.1   The software engineering transformation process

2. *Precedence structure:* The sequencing that must be applied to the work steps to result in a completed information system at the end of the process. This precedence structure is usually represented graphically as a PERT, CPM, or other network diagram.

3. *Development procedures:* The description of the steps that must be executed to transform interim deliverables into final deliverables. In this context, procedures are governed by rules established by the development technique(s) applied to individual deliverable transformations.

4. *Standard deliverable formats:* Structures and layouts for specific deliverables (such as file/schema definitions, data element definitions, source code language rules, manual formats).

5. *Design tips:* Tutorial information for each work step which offers guidance to team members, who may require more detailed, educational assistance in the completion of a particular work step.

6. *Performance standards:* Rules by which completed deliverables can be evaluated for quality and accuracy.

7. *Management procedures:* Steps and activities that must be performed to estimate, schedule, track, and control projects, including reporting formats and mechanisms.

8. *Estimating guidelines:* Minimum average and maximum time allocations typically required for each work step in the life cycle.

9. *Feedback procedures:* Rules and specifications for data to be passed from the software development process to systems planning and other processes external to a project.

The optimum life cycle would contain all of these components. There are, however, a number of life cycles that contain only some of these elements and, as a result, deliver only a portion of the benefits.

Virtually all contain a work-breakdown structure, although the level of detail, or depth, may vary. Also, most contain some management procedures and deliverable formats. One element commonly missed by most life cycles are the feedback procedures—the mechanism to transfer accumulated management-oriented data and information back into the tactical and strategic management processes.

Most often, the proprietary or commercial life-cycle methodologies are the most complete and detailed, often including detailed task and work step procedures based on a specific development technique, such as structured analysis. Frequently, in-house developed life cycles do not provide this detail, either because it is too costly to develop (proprietary product vendors have spent hundreds of thousands to millions of dollars in development) or because the programmers and analysts assigned to the development effort lack the knowledge and experience in defining work-breakdown structures—a process more closely related to industrial engineering than data processing.

The Work-Breakdown Structure

Perhaps the single most important component of the life cycle is the work-breakdown structure (WBS), which defines all of the work that must occur to develop or enhance an application system. A typical software engineering project can contain 1000 or more individual work steps which must be executed to generate a system. As discrete components, the sheer size of the task of identifying the work can be overwhelming. The WBS provides an order to the work which can be comprehended and manipulated by the project participants.

Most commercially available life-cycle methodologies have a hierarchical work-breakdown structure similar to the one depicted in Figure 13.2. At the highest level of the hierarchy is the *project*. It is important to note that the evolution of a particular application or MIS environment is typically a series

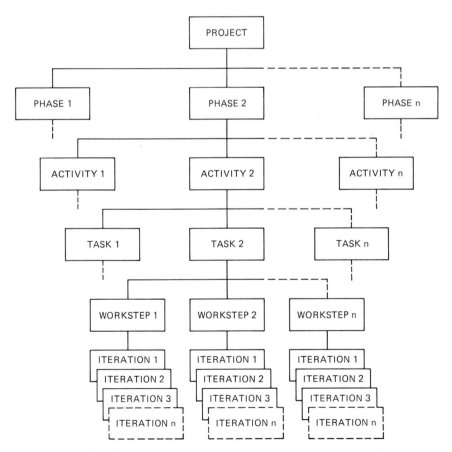

Figure 13.2   Hierarchical work-breakdown structure for life-cycle methodologies

of individual projects. For example, the initial definition of the systems architecture of an enterprise is a project, followed by an implementation planning project, followed by a series of new development, enhancement, or adaptation projects, which result in a project to modify the architecture based on new data—repeating the cycle to continually evolve the MIS environment. The enterprise-wide software engineering process is a series or network of interrelated projects.

Phases, Activities, and Tasks

As mentioned earlier, projects consist of a series of interrelated work steps that produce the final result. There can be literally thousands of these work steps in a project, entirely too many for a person to conceptualize at one time. For this reason, the project is decomposed into a series of lower *levels* of work description: phases, activities, and tasks. The *phases* and *activities* (sometimes referred to as *subphases*) are essentially arbitrary, management-oriented segmentations of project work, designed to ease communication and statistical reporting about the project. Another purpose of the phases and activities is to indicate management control points within the project—checkpoints where quality is reviewed, estimates are reevaluated, and funding levels are altered or confirmed.

Also, interim deliverables may be clustered into specific documentation manuals at each level so that the entire system, as it exists at a particular point in time, can be reviewed in context. Phases and activities can also indicate major changes in responsibility within a project; for example, a business systems analyst may, at the end of Phase 1 (requirements definition), turn over the requirements definition to a designer, who will subsequently turn over a logical or physical system design to the programming team at the implementation phase.

Tasks usually represent a more discrete definition of the work to be performed on the project. For example:

- Develop overall data flow for the system
- Write detailed program specification
- Develop program (module)

might represent typical project tasks. At this level of the hierarchy, even the tasks may be independent of the specific development technique being employed on the project.

Generally speaking, a task is a unit of work that can be defined and executed by a single person working on the project. Frequently, tasks are organized according to the "8 and 80 rules," which states that a task should be no shorter than 8 hours or longer than 80 hours in duration. The logic behind this rule is that in a nonautomated software engineering process, units of work smaller than 1 calendar-day (8 hours) are too difficult and time consuming to track and measure, and tasks larger than 2 calendar-weeks (80 hours) can get out of control and can probably be decomposed into two or more tasks between 8 and 80 hours. As we shall see in subsequent chapters, computer-aided software engineering (CASE) systems allow much more management control of tasks below the 8-hour level and permit much more accurate and controlled project management.

Work Steps and Iterations

The next level down in the hierarchy is the *work step*. Again, a work step is an individual unit of work to be performed by a person. The work step does not necessarily follow the 8 and 80 rule and may not be specifically tracked by the project manager.

Each work step in the life cycle results in the production of an individual *interim deliverable* or assembly of a *final deliverable*. A specific, tangible, measurable result occurs from each work step, which is the output of the deliverable transformation process, depicted in Figure 13.1.

Unlike tasks, work steps are directly tied to a specific development technique. For example, a task might indicate "develop system flow." For this task, the work steps will vary depending on whether Yourdon/DeMarco or Gane & Sarson techniques are applied, since the rules for performing the transformation differ between the two techniques. Another example of the impact of differences in techniques is programming. In coding a program, a specific development technique (or language) is employed, resulting in entirely different appearances between FORTRAN, COBOL, PL/1, and Pascal deliverables (source code).

The final level of the hierarchy is the *iteration*. Iterations have a somewhat different characteristic from other life-cycle levels. An iteration is a discrete unit of work (a work step) assigned to a person, but is *not* unique in terms of its execution procedure.

Life cycles are constructed linearly; that is, if each work step in the life cycle were executed once, you would get a system with one subsystem, one screen, one report, one program, one data element, and so on. The work step "code program," for example, appears in the life cycle only once. In live projects, however, a variety of programs, screens, modules, and reports need to be developed. *Code program A100* and *code program A101* are iterations of the work step *code program*. A major pitfall of many automated project control systems and project management techniques is the inability to recognize, estimate, and track various iterations, which is essential to improving estimating and management techniques and applying metrics to software engineering management, as we shall see in Section 5.5.

Management Tasks

The tasks and work steps discussed above revolved around the deliverables transformation process, which yields applications systems as an output. The other tasks outlined by the life cycle pertain to the management of the life cycle itself and are executed by both project management and team members. These tasks can generally be categorized as:

- Estimating and scheduling tasks which result in initial project plans and assignments as well as periodic revisions to the overall project plan
- Quality assurance tasks executed by the project manager, team members, and users which continually compare the progress on the project to the original requirements for the application
- Project reporting and measurement tasks to be executed by project managers and team members to provide input to the operational management decision-making process to control the project
- Project reporting and measurement tasks executed by project managers which provide historical data and requirements changes in the tactical and strategic management processes

These tasks are interwoven within the hierarchy and are executed in concert with the deliverables transformation tasks.

Precedence Structure

An important term in Metzger's definition (1973, p. 5) is "interrelated." The work steps defined in the hierarchy are interrelated with one another such that previously created interim deliverables provide input to subsequently developed interim or final deliverables, or may actually be modified or updated by some subsequent task or work step.

For example, a logical program or module design deliverable is required to execute the process "develop physical program design" (which may also be referred to as "develop detailed program/module specification"). Similarly, the physical program design, file or database definitions, sample report layouts, and screen layouts must be used by the developer as input to write the program or module source code. These interim deliverables which must be used in subsequent work steps are called *related materials*.

A complete life-cycle methodology will include a precedence network of the tasks and work steps. A partial (and simplistic) precedence network based on related materials is shown in Figure 13.3. This type of network assures that all the data necessary to complete a particular work step has been accumulated or generated prior to execution. In addition, it serves as a basis or developing PERT (program evaluation and review technique) or CPM (critical path method) scheduling and planning networks.

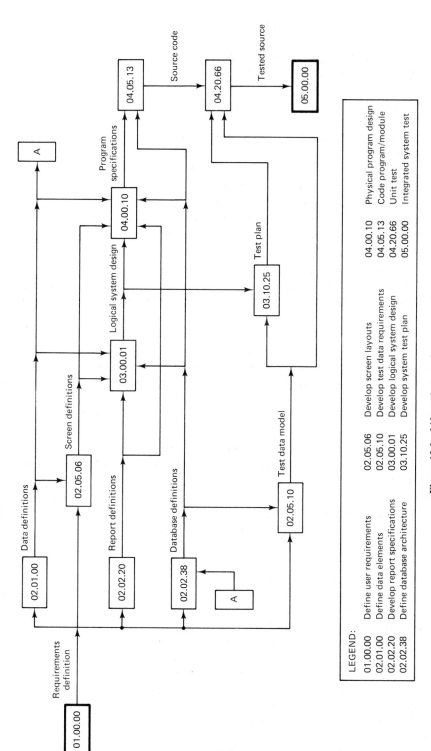

Figure 13.3 Life-cycle precedence network

LEGEND:

01.00.00	Define user requirements	02.05.06	Develop screen layouts	04.00.10	Physical program design
02.01.00	Define data elements	02.05.10	Develop test data requirements	04.05.13	Code program/module
02.02.20	Develop report specifications	03.00.01	Develop logical system design	04.20.66	Unit test
02.02.38	Define database architecture	03.10.25	Develop system test plan	05.00.00	Integrated system test

13.3 CONTROVERSY OVER THE LIFE-CYCLE APPROACH

Implementation Objectives

The primary objectives of a software development life cycle are:

1. To provide a set of management procedures by which projects can be estimated, planned, and controlled
2. To provide a set of technical procedures for software developers to execute which place the various deliverable transformation procedures (development/design techniques) into the context of the overall systems development process
3. To provide a *baseline,* or template, for the project against which progress can be measured. A baseline is a fundamental requirement of management and essential to the project manager's ability to keep the software project under control.

If these three objectives are met, there will be a corresponding reduction in the number of errors detected in systems after installation and conversion. In addition, time can be saved during the development process by:

- Reducing the time spent by project managers in developing initial project estimates and assignments
- Reducing time spent by team members on spurious activities and tasks that do not produce deliverables directly related to the objectives of the project
- Catching errors earlier in the development process (during requirements definition or logical and physical design), where the time and effort required to make the corrections is significantly less than during coding, system testing, or installation

Changes in Project Profile

Applying a life-cycle methodology to the software development project changes the project profile. The three graphs in Figure 13.4 depict typical project profiles and the impact on total project effort of implementing a development life cycle. From these charts, several observations can be made. First, the model project is more heavily front-loaded in a defined life-cycle methodology. More time and more effort is spent in requirements definition and logical and physical design. Since this effort reduces the number of decisions that must be made in programming, the time and effort for programming and unit testing are reduced substantially. Since one of the objectives of front loading the project is to identify and correct errors before implementing the code, there is a

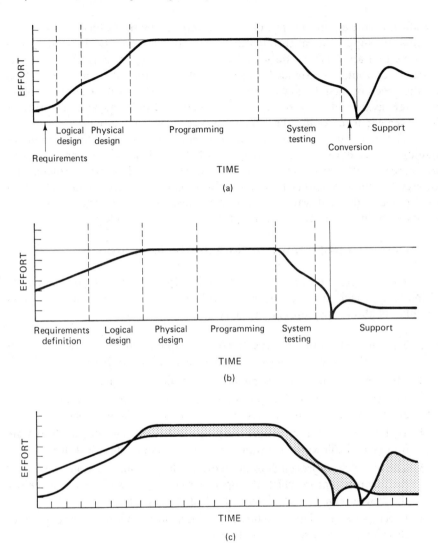

Figure 13.4   Impact of the software development life cycle

substantial reduction in the costs and resource required for system testing and support. In both scenarios, conversion was conservatively left unchanged. In the example given, the improvement in productivity is approximately 40%.

Impact on Staffing and Completion Times

In the examples above, project B beat project A's completion time. This is not always the case when using a software development life cycle. Quite a significant portion of the productivity improvement is yielded in the post-installation support area, through improved software quality. It is quite conceivable that an organization with a high "bug-fixing," or corrective, maintenance level would see extended project completion dates but a substantial drop in the level of maintenance effort required. Overall, this results in more resource availability, in more projects being completed, and a resultant improvement in attaining the benefits projected by the systems.

The maintenance efforts on projects completed using a life-cycle methodology typically gain an additional benefit. Not only are there fewer errors to be corrected after installation, but the effort required to find, isolate, and correct the bugs is reduced. Systems thoroughly documented in a standard format mean that software engineers can trace the systems logic and isolate errors without having to read through reams of source code.

Common Objections to the Life-Cycle Approach

The life-cycle approach to developing software, although considered the ultimate approach in the 1970s, is not without its detractors today. The chief complaints about this approach to developing systems are:

1. The life-cycle approach to software development is time consuming and frequently results in longer overall project completion times.
2. The life-cycle approach is paper/documentation intensive.
3. The life-cycle approach requires a significant investment in training and is extremely difficult to enforce at the programmer/analyst level.
4. Techniques such as rapid prototyping yield usable systems in short time frames and allow for constant changes in system specifications.
5. The life-cycle approach does not work for large, complex systems because the environment in which the operational system resides changes before the system can be completely specified or implemented.
6. Process-flow or data structured development techniques are being used; therefore, a life cycle is not needed.

Let's examine each of these objections more closely.

Time Consuming and Paper Intensive

There is no doubt that the life-cycle approach to developing information systems requires more work, in the form of documentation and specification, to be done before the code is developed. As discussed earlier, the effort level shifts to earlier phases of the life cycle, into requirements and design. However, with the life-cycle approach, there is the efficiency/quality trade-off which must be decided by management. Typically, in non-life-cycle-oriented development, many of the bugs in the system are found after installation. These bugs are the most costly to repair [as indicated by the work of Boehm (1981)]. In organizations such as these, while projects may take somewhat longer, the result is substantially reduced maintenance after project installation. Another common problem is that although estimates in a non-life-cycle approach are often lower, they are also frequently missed. The most common reason for late projects is bad estimating.

In those rare organizations that approach zero-defect software without a life-cycle approach, there is a high probability that the increase in productivity will occur on the efficiency side of the equation. If this is not the case, I would encourage those developers using such a technique to publish it.

Difficult to Enforce

There is no doubt that any procedure is difficult to monitor and enforce. To achieve the benefits of a life-cycle approach, it is *essential* that the project manager manage the work of the project team. Too often in today's development organizations, the project manager is the chief designer. The absolute span of control for a project manager is about six software development professionals. A project of six person-years of effort will require one person-year of management to be completed. We cannot expect projects greater than or equal to six person-years to be managed and controlled if the project manager is also doing implementation tasks.

Computer-Aided Software Engineering

Although the arguments above support the life-cycle approach in its present form, the mid-1980s has also seen the birth of a new software/systems development technology—CASE (computer-aided software engineering). Founded on the concepts of structured development techniques within a life-cycle framework of management controls, CASE provides automated tools that significantly improve the efficiency side of the productivity equation.

CASE systems recognize the limitations of the unaided developer in producing software deliverables and provide tools to complete deliverables faster and more accurately, decreasing the effort level in the requirements through programming life-cycle phases. In addition, CASE systems link the work of the developer with the work of the manager, providing greater control over the development process. A more complete description of CASE is presented in Chapter 16.

Prototyping

The issue of prototyping as a software development technique is thoroughly discussed in Chapter 14. However, gains on the side of efficiency

usually result in losses on the side of quality. Techniques such as rapid prototyping and evolutionary development have three significant drawbacks:

1. Management control over the process suffers significantly. Prototyping
   and evolutionary development are iterative processes. Successive refined
   versions of the system are delivered to the user. Although the users get
   something faster, the ultimate delivery of the final product is unpredicta-
   ble, and may, in fact, take significantly longer than if the user had waited
   for a system built using the life-cycle approach.
2. Evolutionary development approaches run counter to planning, the prime
   element in sound management. Management trade-off decisions on new
   applications are nearly impossible to make or track. It is simply bad business to commit to development where the cost is unknown. There is no
   financial basis on which to evaluate the return on the investment.
3. These approaches do not take into account sharability of data and make
   no effort to normalize the organizations' databases. They can frequently
   result in loss of data integrity.

Problems such as these have been clearly identified by users of this
approach. Gillin (1984) describes these types of problems as encountered by a
major New York bank. The bottom line is that these approaches are unman-
ageable. Pure prototyping or evolutionary development without prior design
merely gets poorly designed systems implemented faster. Maintenance on a
particular bug can be done much faster, but again, there are more iterations.

Large Complex Systems

In the early 1970s, the global corporate MIS was seen as the panacea for
all information problems. By the mid-1970s, it became apparent that a corporate MIS was simply too large a project to attempt to implement. The author
personally witnessed the scrapping of a $10 million software development proj-
ect in 1979 at a major New York bank. It was simply too large a problem to
attack. The key to solving this problem is the ability to decompose the system
project into smaller components that can be managed.

Another problem frequently found with the life-cycle approach is its
inability to produce a system that cannot be defined or conceptualized. This is
a common argument of the artificial-intelligence folks, who berate information
systems developers for their approach.

Fact: Production information systems in commercial or public-sector
　　　use are typically requested by users with a specific need.
Fact: The developers of these particular systems are required to deliver
　　　a working product (or seek employment elsewhere).

Given these two facts, information systems built by the vast majority of the readers of this book are not incomprehensible systems which are primarily research efforts. For pure research projects, application of new generations of development techniques should be encouraged, but not at the expense of present-day systems developers with deadlines and budgets to meet.

Conflicts Between Life Cycles and Development Techniques

Frequently, users of a particular in-house or proprietary commercial development technique (process-flow, data structured, PDL, etc.) assume that the technique is a complete solution. Nothing could be further from the truth. The development techniques address the specific deliverables that must be produced and to a minor extent, the sequence. These techniques provide a nomenclature for the professional to use to specify a system. They do not necessarily provide a hierarchical work-breakdown structure or process-control function to manage the completion of the deliverables or management of the project. This has been evidenced by the fact that proprietary methodologies such as Spectrum/Structured, a product of Spectrum International, Inc., and SDM/Structured from AGS Management Systems, Inc., have been developed which incorporate process-flow design techniques into the management life cycle. Both of these products represent an evolution of the traditional life cycle into a process-control system which incorporates a specific design technique.

In Figure 13.5 we can see the true relationship between the life cycle and the design technique. As you can see, the life cycle drives the completion of the deliverables and encompasses all the management planning and control procedures, including identification of the deliverables which are tied to each step in the work-breakdown structure. The design or development technique, however, specifies the format of the individual deliverable.

Given this relationship, virtually any design technique can be incorporated into a life cycle, with minor revisions to the sequence and definition of specific deliverables. This is, in fact, what some of the proprietary life-cycle methodologies have done, and it is the method advocated here to incorporate both the management process control and the professional procedures into the organization.

Although some view it as arbitrary whether the organization chooses the technique or the life cycle first, there is an advantage in the former. First, the life cycle is more adaptable, requiring less revision, and having less impact on the quality of the final system. Modifying the life cycle usually entails a minor resequencing of tasks, and occasional referencing to a design technique procedure, rather than the procedure included in the life cycle for completing a particular deliverable. Modifying the design technique to fit the life cycle can significantly damage the technique. The reverse is not necessarily true.

Furthermore, organizations may choose to supplement a design technique with a PDL or the use of prototyping. This is easy to do by adding the

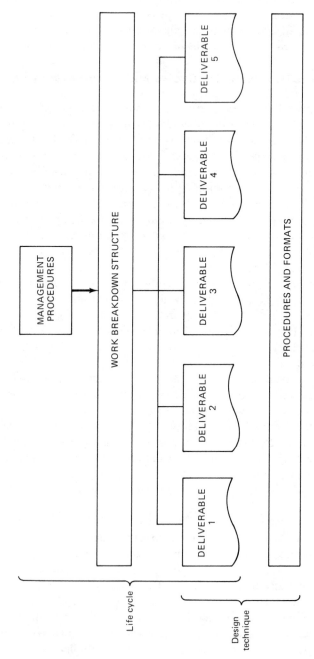

Figure 13.5 Relationship between the life cycle and the design technique

PDL or prototype deliverables into the life cycle as additional deliverables. This puts the prototype or PDL deliverable in context with the other deliverables of the project. Where there is clear duplication of intent or data, the technique specified deliverable can be deleted. Without the context of the life cycle in which to compare the techniques and methods, the impact of changing deliverables on the validity of the process often cannot be determined.

Attendance of life-cycle user groups, or any experience with implementing life cycles within organizations, gives a ready indication that life cycles are frequently modified in this fashion to accommodate the needs of the organization. Many vendors of proprietary life cycles even provide consulting services to aid in this effort.

13.4 SUMMARY

Effect of the Life-Cycle Methodology

Successful implementation of the life-cycle methodology will result in an improvement in the productivity of the software development organization. However, the improvements in productivity may be manifested in three ways: (1) through increased efficiency in software development, evidenced by a reduction in the time to implement software systems; (2) through increased software system quality, as evidenced by a reduction in the number of corrections that must be made to the system after implementation; or (3) a combination of both.

Effective Application of the Methodology

Life cycles are not necessarily advocated for research efforts to produce systems that are not defined or definable.

Emphasis on Management

To be effective, the life cycle requires attention to project management as a specific, measurable element of the project and discourages the role of the project manager as active analyst/designer/programmer. The life-cycle approach to developing systems requires a work-breakdown structure which can be mapped into a number of software development techniques.

Implementation Requirements

To be successful, the life-cycle approach must be endorsed by senior management and project management. It requires an investment in training and education to be effective. Buying a life-cycle methodology and having developers read the manuals are not sufficient to achieve success with this approach.

14

Fourth-Generation
Development
Techniques

Fourth-generation languages and prototyping techniques were considered in the early-to-mid 1980s to be the leading edge in application software development technologies. However, these tools and processes are often misunderstood and frequently misapplied in practice. The most commonly identified fourth-generation techniques are prototyping and evolutionary systems development. The most widely identified fourth-generation tool is the *fourth-generation language* (4GL), also known as the nonprocedural language.

Frequently, fourth-generation languages are referred to as *prototyping tools,* and the term "prototyping" is interchanged with software development using fourth-generation languages. This can be somewhat confusing, especially when evolutionary development enters the conversation. To set the stage for the rest of the discussion, let's define the fourth-generation concepts.

14.1 WHAT THE FOURTH GENERATION IS

For those of us who share in the fourth-generation confusion, let's back up a step and look at software genealogy:

> *First generation:* First-generation information system development was application development by plugboard. Jumper wires on the plugboard were the programmer's means to give instructions to the computer on how to process the data. Program changes were effected by altering the wiring configurations.

Second generation: The second generation was the advent of the stored program concept, pioneered by John von Neumann. The stored program concept dictates that programs (instructions) can be stored in the machine as data. Second-generation programming was done in machine-level octal or hexidecimal coding. Later second-generation programming was made easier by the use of assembly languages that contained mnemonic instructions which mapped essentially one to one with the octal or hex operation codes (program instructions).

Third generation: Higher-level languages (such as COBOL, FORTRAN, Pascal, PL/1, APL, and Algol) are introduced. One programmer instruction yields multiple machine instructions. Programming is done faster. People begin to think about and develop procedures for designing programs and systems, resulting in structured programming, structured design, data structured system design, and life-cycle methodologies. Database management systems enter the scene and prime the industry for the fourth generation.

Fourth generation: Significant confusion caused by magic using smoke and mirrors.

Admittedly, that definition of the fourth generation is tongue in cheek. In reality, the *fourth generation* is characterized primarily by program/system generators (early fourth generation) which translate specifications into a third-generation language and nonprocedural languages. Nonprocedural languages arrived on the scene as a result of users becoming increasingly frustrated over the inability of software development to build application systems for them. The early fourth generation was characterized by a large movement to end-user systems development.

A debate over end-user system development appeared in *Today's Office* in 1982. In the April issue of the magazine, a commentary by Dave Lockwood stated: "Only when the control of electronic processing systems moves into the hands of the real users will the cost effectiveness of these advanced systems be fully realized." Lockwood strongly advocated end-user system development. In the September issue, "Commentary: Don't Fight DP, Join 'em," by Albert F. Case, Jr., appeared. The basic premise of this article was that nonresponsive DP departments should be controlled through management channels by the users as a service organization. Having end users develop applications diverted them from their primary missions.

In any intellectual debate, the end result is usually positive. As a result of the end-user development movement, software developers became aware of the new, higher-level languages, which permit development of programs in substantially less time. Generators and nonprocedural programming languages moved into software development, and database query languages remained popular with end users.

However, because programming could be done so much faster, new techniques such as prototyping and evolutionary development evolved. The concept behind these techniques is that since programming is so fast, you can skip design, make mistakes, and fix them in less time than it previously took to design the systems in the first place—a position backed up with little empirical evidence. But like all new ideas, these concepts, too, spur debate and yield refined, valuable ideas. Prototyping and evolutionary development, in a managed context, can be valuable software engineering tools. Let's examine the fourth-generation concepts and put them in a software engineering context.

14.2 FOURTH-GENERATION LANGUAGES

Fourth-generation languages are simply higher-level programming languages that provide the programmer (who may be an end user) with the ability to execute complex functions with few commands. Therefore, using fourth-generation languages, programmers can more rapidly program operational code. In many instances, the set of commands for fourth-generation languages is significantly smaller, which substantially reduces learning time for the system. Also, fourth-generation languages tend to be supported by *syntax-directed editors,* interactive development systems which edit user (programmer) input before the commands are processed. This makes finding syntax errors much easier, but adds another editor to the set of tools that needs to be learned.

Fourth-generation languages, like any other language, can be compiled or interpreted. These languages require that the "programs" or language parameters be entered, validated, and then executed. Others, such as IBM's SQL, STAIRS, and other database query languages, are interactive. That is, commands are entered into the system individually and then executed instantly. Most query languages provide *macros,* or the ability to store commands and command strings for future use.

Some of the reasons that all programming is not done with fourth-generation languages are: high machine resource requirements, database incompatibility, high investments in non-4GL-installed systems which need to be maintained, and limited functionality. With respect to limited functionality, as languages become more abstract or, "higher level" (i.e., farther from machine code), the ability to internally manipulate the function of the machine is lost. The trade-off is more machine instructions per programmer instruction versus more ability to customize the machine instructions. With these constraints in mind, however, fourth-generation languages can be replacements for languages like FORTRAN and COBOL, for those applications where they provide the desired functionality.

Advantages and Disadvantages of Fourth-Generation Languages

Fourth-generation languages provide speed, flexibility, and ease of use. Because they are higher-level languages, significantly fewer programmer-written instructions are required than with traditional languages. Because of the development speed advantage of fourth-generation languages, programs can be created, modified, and enhanced much faster. Because fourth-generation languages are easier to use, they can be placed in the hands of end users with little learning curves. Also, since fourth-generation languages substantially reduce the complexity of developing on-line and database inquiry programs, the level of programming expertise is substantially reduced, making all software developers more productive.

There are, however, some disadvantages associated with fourth-generation languages. First, many fourth-generation languages operate with their own database management software. Applications developed using these languages must work with their own database, or extract information from corporate databases, copy it into the fourth-generation languages database, and reverse the process to update corporate databases. This causes problems with database integrity and system responsiveness. There is a high probability the 4GL database and the corporate database can get out of sync.

The second problem associated with fourth-generation languages is machine utilization. In addition to the burden of moving data from corporate databases to 4GL databases and back, there is the response-time problem associated with volume users. Systems such as UFO, SQL, and MARK/IV are interpretive. Interpretive systems require overhead to translate the program commands each time the program is executed. This limits their applicability to low-volume inquiry and update systems.

Finally, proliferation of applications can occur in organizations allowing end-user access to fourth-generation languages. Although this is not necessarily a problem of self-contained applications, it is a problem with applications that update corporate databases. Uncontrolled proliferation of applications can compromise the integrity of the corporate database. Even worse, the information from the systems, while highly trusted, can be highly suspect.

Fourth-Generation Language Summary

It is important to recognize fourth-generation languages for what they truly are, programming languages. As such they can have a valuable place in the software engineering tool kit. Fourth-generation languages are:

- easy to learn
- fast to program

These are highly desirable attributes; however, they also have limitations in that they:

- can be difficult to maintain
- are often slow in execution
- can be incompatible with standard database/file techniques
- may not be readily integrated into existing systems which use conventional programming languages

Since they are primarily programming tools, they must be examined for their applicability and value within the context of the software development life cycle. Fourth generation languages:

- reduce programming time

That is their single benefit. They do not aid in the analysis or design of computer systems. Therefore, their productivity gains apply to only about 20% of the overall resource expenditure, and are applicable only to the efficiency (output) component of the productivity equation.

Disenchantment with fourth-generation languages can be avoided if these considerations are weighed when evaluating or using this technology. These languages are valuable tools, but not cure-alls.

14.3 THE PROTOTYPING PROCESS

Prototyping is a language-independent process for building functional and semifunctional models of application systems during the development process. While prototyping may use a fourth-generation language, such languages are not necessary to the prototyping process. It is accurate to characterize prototyping as one of many *fourth-generation techniques*. This technique would be in contrast to such development techniques as structured analysis and design techniques based on data-flow or data-structure principles. The structured techniques have been characterized as third-generation system design.

Prototyping allows software developers to review system models with end users to verify format and functionality of system functions and input/output formats. In some instances, prototyping is used as a conversational requirements definition tool. Historically, prototyping was used for hardware system and engineered products (embedded software) systems. Since prototypes were relatively expensive to build, they were applied to systems projects where the prototyping costs could be amortized over a large number of installed systems. Because in-house business applications were not widely distributed, prototyping costs were extremely high. COBOL and other third-generation languages from which applications were developed made development of a prototype as costly as the operational system.

With the advent of fourth-generation languages, the actual programming or design implementation time was substantially reduced. A fourth-generation language prototype of a CICS system could be developed in a fraction of the time of an actual, interactive application system written in command-level CICS. Fourth-generation languages therefore opened up the prototyping process to the majority of application software developers.

The prototyping process can clearly be segmented into two different types of prototypes, each of which is described below.

1. *Requirements or user-view prototyping:* User-view prototyping is a method of translating system requirements into a system prototype which simulates the screens, screen traversal, source input documents, and reports, but does not perform calculations or database updates. User-view prototyping enables the developer to rapidly develop a system prototype for the purpose of verifying and validating requirements and providing a baseline for subsequent design. Since user-view prototypes allow screen traversal, they may simulate calculations from screen to screen but will not function as an application.

2. *Functional prototyping:* Functional prototyping is basically system development, except that a 4GL is used because it is faster than writing in a traditional language, using a conventional or database file access/update technique. In a functional prototype, the requirements are translated into an operational system that simulates the production environment.

Advantages and Disadvantages of Prototyping

Rapid prototyping, using fourth-generation languages, allows software developers to build models of screens and reports quickly, and in some cases interactively. This enables the software developer and the user to see easily what an application system will look like. Rather than drawing report and screen layouts, they can be done on the system. Users can quickly decide what other fields, calculations, and displays are required. This helps nail down software requirements definition. Additionally, prototyping improves the quality of specification communications among software development team members. Building an operational system from a visible model is easier than building one from paper specifications.

One of the major problems associated with prototyping is the tendency to substitute prototyping for systems design and requirements definition. Many users of the prototyping process skip a structured requirements definition and design process and go straight to prototyping (translate—programming) the software. For self-contained systems this may not be a significant problem; however, for systems that must interface with other corporate systems and databases, this can be troublesome. Software developers may miss required interfaces in the prototyping process. In addition, in the absence of true design and analysis, there is little probability of capitalizing on existing design and code modules which may already exist. This causes significant duplication of effort.

Another problem is phantom systems. Prototypes may find their way into the user environment before development is completed. In addition to the interface problems this may represent, it also places a high maintenance burden on the software developers. Frequently, in addition to trying to get the production system out, they also get wrapped up in maintaining the prototype. Phantom systems, however, can be eliminated by using only user view prototyping, since the prototype cannot operate in a user environment.

Evolutionary Development

A real problem, disguised as a blessing, with the prototyping process is the speed with which simulated systems can be developed. Many prototyping aficianados believe that it is okay to build prototypes (actually end-user systems coded in fourth-generation languages) with bugs, because using fourth-generation languages, the bugs can be fixed quickly. The problem is that in many instances, the number of iterations required to finally fix the problems can easily exceed the time required to perform a detailed analysis and design. "Prototyping acrobats," infatuated with the technologies employed in prototyping, can easily waste valuable time playing with the system.

14.4 COMPATIBILITY OF SOFTWARE ENGINEERING AND PROTOTYPING

The software engineering process is a macro-system whose purpose is to improve the productivity of the application development organization through:

- *Increased efficiency:* less resource, hence less cost to build applications
- *Increased quality:* fewer "bugs" in applications, resulting in reduced software maintenance and improved performance

In the sense that both prototyping and fourth-generation languages are individual tools that can contribute to the required end result of the software engineering process, they are beneficial and complementary. Problems arise, however, when these tools are used out of context.

A historical problem within the application development process has been the tendency to focus on programming aids as the solution to development productivity problems. The vast majority of the dollars spent on tools are for programming aids. However, without proper analysis, poorly designed programs are still poorly designed programs, regardless of how rapidly they were developed. Fourth-generation languages do nothing to improve program design.

Prototyping, on the other hand, can significantly improve software design. Here the problem is in knowing what needs to be built. A fabulously functional prototype of a system, which performs all of the calculations and permutations required by the user, is of no value if the final implementation has no data integrity or if it does not integrate with other major application systems.

In summary, prototyping and fourth-generation languages are tremendous tools to support analysis, design, and programming, but they are not substitutes. These tools need to be invoked in the context of the software development life cycle to validate design concepts. Prototypes are simply *additional* or *replacement project deliverables* in the life cycle which serve to aid in the final system implementation. If the ultimate system is conducive to use of a fourth-generation language, so much the better, because programming can be substantially reduced.

14.5 ALTERNATIVE SYSTEM IMPLEMENTATION APPROACHES

The combination of the software engineering life cycle, design techniques, and overall development strategy for designing and implementing applications constitutes the implementation approach. As we have seen, there are various implementation approaches in practice today, some of which have been outgrowths of the "end-user development" and the fourth generation. The adoption of a software implementation approach or policy is key to the successful implementation of software engineering. Since different implementation approaches are better suited to different types of applications, let's examine the types of applications that are built.

14.6 CLASSIFICATIONS OF SYSTEMS

At the May 1984 workshop of the Batelle Memorial Institute (Columbus, Ohio) there was a discussion of prototyping and software implementation approaches. One of the conference attendees, a user of both traditional and prototyping-oriented application development processes, divided applications into two categories: front-office and back-office. Each system classification lends itself to a different design implementation approach.

Front-office systems are those which support day-to-day operating needs of users. These tend to be decision-support-type systems which can operate with localized databases, which can be created and maintained by the users. Typically, they do not need to interface with corporate databases, or if they do, they merely extract information and do not update corporate data. Front-office systems usually have low transaction volumes and support few users.

Back-office systems are the more traditional software development applications which require interfaces to many existing databases and applications, update corporate data, and have high transaction volumes and large numbers of users. Since these applications share databases, information integrity is important. Since they are large-volume systems, performance is significant. Back-office systems also tend to be larger projects, with large development outlays that need to be more tightly controlled.

To support these categories of systems, there are two broad classifications of implementation approaches:

1. Those implementation techniques that do not involve prototyping

2. Those techniques that use prototyping

Non-prototyping Techniques

There are three common software implementation approaches in wide use today: life cycle, traditional, and incremental.

1. The *life-cycle* approach to developing software dictates that there is a standard work-breakdown structure (WBS) which serves as a model for all software implementation projects. The WBS provides the procedures necessary to execute the steps. In addition, the life cycle specifies the standard deliverables that must be produced at each step in the WBS. Deliverables are any tangible objects, such as data-flow diagrams, structure charts, source code, JCL, and so on.

   In the life-cycle approach, several disciplines may be established which are used selectively on projects based on the type of project. For example, there can be work steps associated with packaged software implementation, database design, on-line systems, or specific design techniques (Yourdon versus Gane and Sarson). Segments of the life cycle can be eliminated or added based on discipline.

2. *Traditional software development* may apply specific design techniques and methods but does not follow a rigorous WBS. The work breakdown for a particular project is established by the project manager when the project is planned, and may vary based on the design techniques employed on a particular project.

Both the life-cycle and traditional approaches assume that the system will not be installed until it is completed. Incremental implementation is a contrasting approach.

3. *Incremental implementation* is an implementation approach in which a determination that certain modules, functions, or features can be implemented without requiring the entire system to be developed. This approach gets functionality to the user without having to wait through the entire development life cycle. Incremental implementation, in practice, may be used in conjunction with either the life-cycle or traditional techniques, varying only the project structure and work breakdown.

All three of these approaches take a view that some requirements definition must take place, followed by a design (which is at least partly validated) that drives the coding or implementation process. Once the system is coded and tested, it goes through user-acceptance test and finally operation. The major advantage of these approaches is that they all ensure that an analysis of system interfaces, database considerations, and performance issues are addressed prior to expending the effort to code the system. They all allow a strategic systems plan or architecture to be considered in the implementation of an application system. The disadvantages are (1) there is the potential for loss of information between specification and implementation; (2) the user sees nothing operational until the acceptance test; and (3) there are few design validation tools which help to validate the accuracy of the design before it is tested after coding. This last problem makes the cost of correcting defects higher.

Prototyping Implementation Techniques

There are three schools of thought on implementing systems using prototyping techniques:

1. *Pure prototyping:* A prototype of the operational system is built to serve as a model, replacing screen and report layouts. The model is reviewed with the user, and possibly even interactively updated. Once the user approves the model, it is then submitted for actual development. In a stand-alone mode, pure prototyping is the method for requirements definition and design. Pure prototyping may result in the operational system being developed in a different language from the prototype.

2. *Evolutionary implementation:* A prototype such as the one developed in pure prototyping is constructed and modified by the developer based on user input. Under evolutionary implementation, the operational system is the prototype. Again, the prototyping process is a substitute for analysis and design.

3. *Prototyping/life cycle:* In this approach, a standard development life cycle is used; however, a prototyping discipline is assigned within the work-breakdown structure or exits in the life-cycle point to prototyping

tasks. In this type of approach, the required design, analysis, and requirements tasks can be retained, but traditional tasks, obviated by prototyping, can be eliminated. This approach can eliminate many of the problems associated with prototyping implementation techniques. This approach is also consistent with the ability to develop systems using incremental implementation if that technique is desirable on a particular project.

In looking at these three prototyping-based implementation techniques, some conclusions can be drawn:

1. The life-cycle implementation approach is the foundation on which software engineering is built. To build systems, one must, in fact, execute a series of ordered steps. Establishing a standard set of steps with defined performance criteria is the only way to manage the application development process that ensures management control.

2. Prototyping/life cycle and pure prototyping are not inconsistent with software engineering principles. By having a tailorable life cycle surrounding the prototyping tasks, the prototype can replace many specific project deliverables.

3. Evolutionary implementation may be an excellent way to develop front-office systems which have little corporate database impact, integration requirement, and which are small projects with little outlay required to implement. Evolutionary implementation may be a way to satisfy the needs of some software development customers who may otherwise have to live without the applications they need, for significant periods of time.

    The source language implication of evolutionary implementation is not a problem in the prototyping/life cycle approach. If the 4GL is the appropriate source language, simply delete life-cycle tasks that deal with translating the software to a third-generation language.

15

An Overview of the Software Engineering MIS

15.1 INTRODUCTION

Integrating the Software Engineering Macro-system

In the previous chapters we discussed the various elements of the software engineering approach to systems development, which included:

- Systems architecture development
- Strategic, tactical, and operational systems management
- Software engineering development techniques
- Software engineering life cycles

In Chapter 3 it was indicated that the primary difference between the software engineering approach to information systems development and other approaches is that software engineering presumes that each of these components is integrated into a cohesive systems development macro-system. Software engineering is not a technique (such as Yourdon's structured systems design) but rather a management and technical approach for *selecting* the most appropriate "methodologies" to meet the specific systems planning or implementation problem, and *integrating* them into a single, cohesive system. The mechanism to achieve this integration is the software engineering management information system (SE/MIS).

Systems Development: An Enterprise Microcosm

The systems development organization has been charged with producing a product (computer systems) for its customer base (the data processing user community). In a sense, systems development is a microcosm of the enterprise as a whole—a software engineering macro-system—and must be managed in the same fashion. The process of allocating resources and making decisions at the strategic, tactical, and operational levels does not differ substantially from the process required to manage the design, engineering, and production of widgets, golf balls, or microprocessors.

The manager in any of these engineering/production environments (systems development included) must allocate resources among different variants of a product, or in some cases multiple products being produced at one plant. The manager must maintain inventory levels and equipment capacities and be able to project the engineering/production resource requirements over time to prevent resource shortages, backlogs, and excesses throughout the product development life cycle.

Types of Management Information Systems

Virtually all enterprises employ management information systems (MIS) to aid management in planning, allocating, tracking, and controlling functions. In some instances, these management information systems are manual procedures to capture and organize data and report information. In other cases, they are computerized management information systems that support the management process by tracking the transformation process through manual data entry and machine information reporting, which report information to management, which subsequently provides direct control over the transformation process. In still other cases, the systems are process-control systems which accept direct sensor input from the transformation process and provide direct control over the transformation process without human intervention.

Regardless of whether the MIS is manual, computerized, or process controlled, all of these management information systems have one thing in common: they are planned, organized, and proceduralized. The capture of data and their transformation into information is "programmed" via manual procedures or machine-executable code. The system, which collected, integrated, and organized a set of procedures that performs the information transform, can be identified.

Just as enterprise macro-systems require management information systems, so does software engineering. Throughout this book the software engineering transformation process and the mechanisms for planning and managing have been discussed. What remains is to design the system of procedures for collecting data from the various software engineering development and management processes and integrate them into a definable management information system for software engineering.

Once the system has been designed, it can be implemented either with a manual software engineering management information system or with varying degrees of automation—from simple data reduction and reporting aids for budgeting, resource allocation, and tracking to sophisticated systems that provide process-control-like mechanisms to aid in managing the software engineering transformation process.

15.2 INFORMATION SYSTEM REQUIREMENTS

Rationale

Most organizations building information systems have not defined the requirements of their own information system. Traditional (non-software-engineering) approaches tend to view the information needs of senior management, middle management, project managers, and individual system developers as discrete universes of information that have minimal data interfaces. In searching to improve systems development productivity, tools, processes, consulting services, and methodologies to support each level of the hierarchy are evaluated, selected, and implemented in a piecemeal manner, without focusing on the overall *system for building systems*. Without the perspective of the software engineering approach, organizations find themselves with project control systems, design techniques, planning techniques, and reporting procedures which lack integration.

The net result of this approach is that the productivity benefits of these partial solutions are not realized, and the constant search for the panacea continues. How many times have you heard the comment: "If we realized the benefits of all of the productivity aids we purchased in the past, we'd have systems done before they were requested and they'd be perfect systems"?

There are at least two reasons for this syndrome:

1. Benefits of solutions to productivity and management problems are not cumulative. It's like the thirsty frog who jumps toward a well. With each jump he travels half the distance of his previous jump and ultimately dies of thirst, for he never reaches the well. A set of tools and/or procedures to improve systems development productivity, implemented serially, provide smaller and smaller returns, because there is less and less "overhead" to eliminate.

2. Most purchased solutions are designed to operate in a stand-alone environment or in concert with related partial solutions which are packaged together. The lack of integration between piecemeal solutions reduces the overall effectiveness of the software engineering macro-system. Histori-

cally, there have been no integrated solutions which have addressed both the management and technical issues of the entire software development process. There have been few organizations which have consciously defined the requirements for, or designed, their systems development macro-system. This reduces the probability that total solutions can be implemented or that they can meet all the systems development needs.

The first step toward meeting all of the organization's needs is to define the nature of and requirements for a software engineering management information system for the enterprise.

Software Engineering Information Flow

To develop the specifications for the software engineering management information system (SE/MIS),* there must be a requirements definition. Figure 15.1 depicts an information flow among the various systems management levels.

Information Requirements

Having defined the information flow for the SE/MIS, we can now determine the requirements for a system (manual or automated) which will support the software engineering management process. The SE/MIS must provide the following information:

- A nomenclature or language structure for describing software engineering projects. This language must be standard among projects and understood among all levels of management and personnel within the organization to facilitate communications.
- A set of performance standards for the management, execution, and quality review of software engineering tasks so that the quality of the product can be evaluated.
- The level of resource used on a project and a comparison of that usage against a predetermined plan.
- A queue of outstanding and in-process projects. A measure of the level of resource allocated at present and in the foreseeable future.
- Historical information about the level of resource required to build projects of varying complexity and to aid in the estimation of future projects.
- Correlation between systems projects based on the enterprise's information needs to assess future resource requirements.

---

*I believe that as the use of acronyms increases, the understandability of the text decreases; however, in the interest of saving time, ink, and paper, I shall henceforth abbreviate the "software engineering management information system" as SE/MIS.

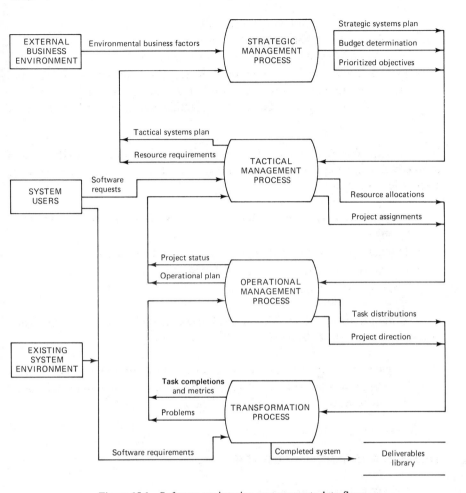

Figure 15.1   Software engineering management: data flow

Process Requirements

In addition, a software engineering management information system must:

- Collect the data required from the software engineering transformation process and the business environment; producing information in a format suitable for the various perspectives of strategic, tactical, and operational software engineering management

- Manage the deliverables (such as specifications, data flows, data structures and data definitions, prototypes, data structures, user procedures, and code) created during the software engineering transformation processes, including:

—Logging and tracking deliverables

—Channeling deliverables for review

—Assembling deliverables into documentation

- Provide a method for system developers and quality reviewers (developers or end users) to easily locate and access previously completed deliverables which must be referenced to complete the deliverable or review at hand

It is also an objective of the SE/MIS to provide methods, procedures, and tools which can be applied in both system architecture development and during a specific project for:

- Identification, cataloging, and access of reusable design and program fragments
- Tracing requirements through design and implementation
- Validation of design prior to implementation
- Identification of redundant design

A management information system meeting these general requirements provides a mechanism by which:

- Management can manage and control the software engineering process
- Relevant information about designs, constraints, and requirements can be shared between planners and developers

15.3 SE/MIS ARCHITECTURE

Architecture Overview

Having defined the requirements for the software engineering management information system, it is now possible to develop a systems architecture that supports these requirements. Figure 15.2 illustrates the basic architecture of a SE/MIS. The SE/MIS can be divided into three subsystems:

1. *Administration:* the process of defining software engineering projects, determining productivity statistics, developing and revising estimating guidelines, managing the content and implementation of the work-breakdown structure and design techniques, and providing project queue and resource allocation information to planning process
2. *Management:* the process of managing the tasks required to develop the strategic implementation, tactical project administration, and project plans in a logical, structured manner

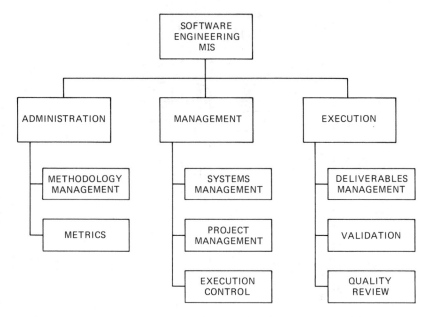

Figure 15.2   Systems architecture: software engineering management information system

3. *Execution:* the process of creating, validating, and managing systems architecture and project deliverables

These subsystems provide software engineering management with the information required to make decisions affecting the implementation of applications and a mechanism for management to influence the software engineering transformation process. In addition, developers are provided with an orderly process for creating software development deliverables.

SE/MIS Data Flow

To see how we achieved the architecture for the SE/MIS described above, let's examine a data flow of the SE/MIS depicted in Figure 15.3. In this diagram we can see more detailed relationships between the management and control functions in the context of the overall software engineering macro-system:

- Strategic implementation planning
- Project initiation
- Project planning
- Project management and control

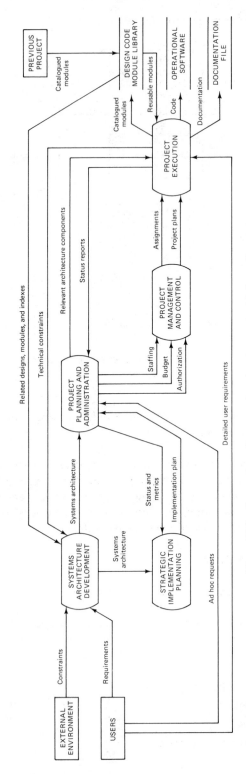

Figure 15.3 Composite software engineering management information system

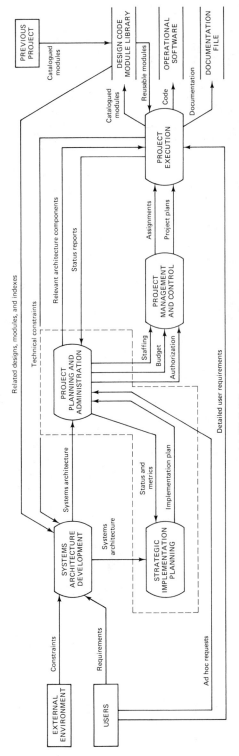

(a) SE/MIS administration subsystem

Figure 15.4

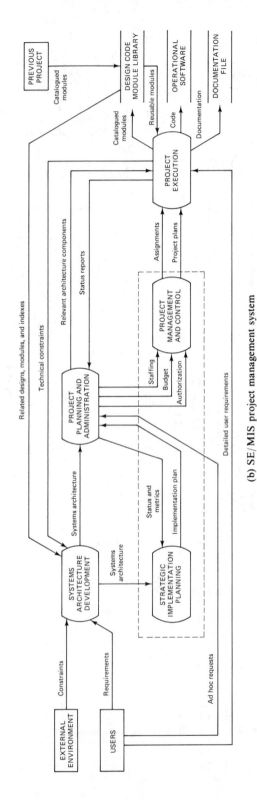

(b) SE/MIS project management system

Figure 15.4 (Continued)

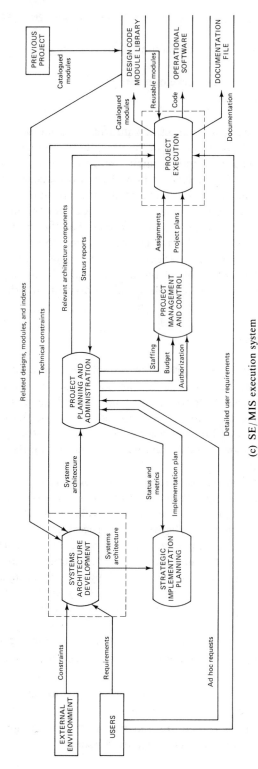

(c) SE/MIS execution system

Figure 15.4 (Continued)

171

and the actual development functions:

- Systems architecture development
- Project execution

This model does not present new information, but rather, summarizes the processes that we have discussed in the previous chapters and depicts the integration of these processes into a single, integrated macro-system for building systems. In Figure 15.4 we can see how these processes relate to the SE/MIS subsystems of administration, management, and execution. The software engineering approach to systems development recognizes the integration of these systems within the organization and requires that the interfaces between the various elements of the software engineering macro-system be defined and implemented in a consistent manner. Other, less global approaches to systems development focus on certain of the processes and frequently do not provide procedures and/or tools to establish and enforce the interfaces.

15.4 SUMMARY

The software engineering approach to systems development addresses the systems development function as a microcosm of the enterprise which it supports—a business itself which must be planned, managed, and executed. Other approaches to systems development focus on individual processes within the systems development macro-system, such as strategic planning, project control, or design methodology, without considering the processes outside their own domain.

The mechanism that differentiates the software engineering approach is the *software engineering management information system* (SE/MIS), which identifies all of the processes involved in building information systems and identifies all of the interfaces between the processes.

A SE/MIS can be implemented for a particular organization—building on existing components and acquiring or developing components and interfaces that are missing. The key to successfully implementing a SE/MIS, however, is in designing the *system to build systems,* just as you would design and implement a management information system for your users:

- Identify information requirements specific to your organization
- Analyze your existing software development environment and compare it to the requirements
- Determine information and/or processes that are missing, or that are not providing the information required
- Develop a plan to acquire and implement, or design and develop internally, the components which are missing

This process will prevent the fragmentary acquisition of non-integrated methods, procedures and tools and result in an optimized software engineering organization.

Automating the Software Engineering MIS

Of course, like any other system, once it has been defined, the SE/MIS can be automated. A new breed of tools—the *computer-aided software engineering* or *CASE* system—is evolving which provides a completely integrated SE/MIS. Rather than buying individual software engineering/development tools and defining and implementing the interfaces individually, these systems can be purchased, installed, and customized to your organization's specific needs.

Systems developers are like the cobbler's children. The cobbler was so busy making shoes for the entire village that his children went unshod. Systems developers have been so busy automating the users' systems that they have not built their own. Identifying and describing the software engineering management information is the necessary prerequisite to implementing a CASE system. Of course, like any other system, it is wise to clean up the manual system before automating the inefficient one that is in place.

16

CASE: Automating the Software Engineering MIS

16.1 INTRODUCTION

What Computer-Aided Software Engineering Is

As stated in Chapter 1, software engineering is the application of the engineering process to the development of computer software:

- To improve the productivity of the software developers (engineers)
- To increase the quality of the software product
- To achieve greater management control over the process

Computer-aided software engineering (CASE) is the application of automated technologies to the software engineering procedures. CASE is, in essence, the automation of the processes defined by the software engineering MIS.

Pre-case Development Automation

The pioneers of structured techniques, such as Warnier, Orr, Yourdon, Constantine, DeMarco, and Jackson, identified analysis and design techniques for transforming information about data and processes into working computer programs. These techniques, however, took the form of manual procedures. Similarly, Toellner, Bryce, and Katch identified procedures to manage the execution of these techniques (life cycles). These, too, were in the form of books and procedures to be followed by developers and managers.

Lack of design tools. Through the 1970s, there were few automated tools to aid developers in the execution of the procedures which were identified by the life cycles and design techniques. Certainly, there were source editors, compilers, and data dictionaries, but there were no tools to support the development of nonprogram deliverables such as data flows, data structures, decision tables, and other text and graphics devices required by the various design techniques. Programming tools such as compilers and syntax checkers are effective in identifying errors in programs because programs can be analyzed in relation to predefined rules or grammars defined by the programming language's syntax. Once the move is made to create non-program deliverables on-line and store them electronically, then programs can be developed which will analyze these deliverables for conformity to the rules of the design technique, much like a compiler analyzes a program for conformity to the grammar or syntax. These objective, nondeterministic analyses of deliverables by the computer result in a much more accurate evaluation of the deliverable in much less time than could previously be achieved by a manual audit.

By their nature, methodologies require additional deliverables to be developed during the software development process. Methodologies enforce discipline and improve quality—frequently at the expense of increasing the time required to build a new system. Without automated tools, methodologies can be difficult to implement and enforce. Therefore many of the benefits may not be fully realized. The historic lack of tools has resulted in sporadic, and sometimes ineffective, implementation of the methodologies.

An example of a methodology which is very difficult to implement and administer without an automated support system is *reusability*. Jones (1984) has wisely and repeatedly recommended that systems development departments embark on a program of building reusable system modules. The difficulty in the procedures outlined thus far is the complexity of cataloging reusable modules and finding them in the design phases when they can be reused. It is even more complex, if not impossible, to manually identify and catalog the existing base of potentially reusable software which has already been developed.

Absence of management tools. The lack of tools is not limited to support for analysis and design methods. There also has been limited availability of tools to support the management and control aspects of the life cycle methodology, or the procedures governing planning, assignment, review, and coordination of the tasks to be performed and deliverables to be completed.

The tools most frequently associated with software engineering management are *planning and tracking systems* which focus on scheduling the tasks to be completed, usually using PERT or CPM scheduling algorithms, and tracking time and costs as completion of the project progresses. This leaves a whole universe of processes surrounding the management of software engineering which have been left unautomated:

- *Tailoring* the life cycle to meet the needs of a particular project which includes definition of iterations of various work steps, elimination of unnecessary work steps, and addition of new deliverables
- *Estimating* task durations which includes access to historical information on times to complete tasks adjusted for various environmental factors
- *Revising* the project work breakdown structure and estimates for a project based upon problems, opportunities, and contingencies arising during development
- *Reviewing and evaluating* deliverables for accuracy, completeness, and conformity to specifications and requirements
- *Tracking the earned value* or percentage of actual work completed, rather than time expended, against a particular task
- *Controlling* the actual work steps completed by individual project team members and the sequence in which tasks are executed

Strategies for implementing CASE environments need to address these processes as well as the more traditional planning and tracking processes.

The Integration Issue.   Even though there has been a limited set of management and development tools, integration between the development of the systems architecture and the development of a project has been lacking. Similarly, planning the enterprise's project queue is often not directly related to the planning of an individual project. Estimating is done largely by a "seat-of-the-pants" method, and metrics from individual project completions were not easy to access for the development of subsequent estimates.

Individual project deliverables may represent the biggest problem in developing an integrated software engineering process. How do you determine from a data-flow or assembly-line (Warnier–Orr) diagram what reusable modules are available. How do you ensure that every project team member has access to the data structures developed or the interfaces defined in the systems architecture? For that matter, how do you ensure that a programmer, working on a particular module, has all of the previously prepared deliverables that completely specify that module? Historically, these have been unanswered questions.

The answers to these questions and the solutions to these problems do not lie in the "traditional" methodologies and tools for systems development. They lie in the new generation of computer-aided software engineering environments, integrated CASE systems designed to resolve these specific issues.

Elements of a CASE System

The essential elements of CASE are:

- Procedures—a disciplined, life-cycle methodology for the development of software
- Methods—standard design techniques and procedures for producing project deliverables
- Integration—automated tools for:
  —Estimating and planning projects
  —Tracking project progress
  —Creating and modifying project deliverables
  —Managing design information
  —Reusing design and code modules
  —Analyzing and verifying design
  —Reviewing deliverables for quality
  —Tracing system requirements through system implementation

Although processes and tools in all of these categories are available today, the difference between a loosely coupled collection of procedures and tools and CASE is integration, flexibility, and user friendliness in the development environment.

Genesis of CASE Systems

CASE environments are actually computer systems for building automated systems. CASE systems address the issues of project management and design and implementation of the system—providing tools for management and analysts, designers, and programmers. CASE systems view the software engineering process as an integrated software engineering management information system which begins with strategic systems planning and continues through maintenance of operational application systems.

It is safe to say that there are no complete, fully implemented CASE systems which cover all of the requirements of the software engineering process. The original CASE system (although never labeled in that manner) is probably *Pride/ASDM* (Automated System Development Methodology),* developed by M. Bryce and Associates, Inc. Pride/ASDM was originally brought to market in the late 1970s as an extension to the PRIDE (Profitable Information by DEsign) methodology (encompassing both design technique and life cycle) developed by the same company. Pride/ASDM essentially automates the PRIDE methodology, providing host-based tools for project management and control and deliverable creation with an integrated data dictionary. In its present form, Pride/ASDM presumes (in fact, requires) that the PRIDE design techniques and life cycles be used. The major drawback to Pride/ASDM is its inability to support multiple, integrated techniques for the development of systems—its an all-or-nothing proposition to which many organizations cannot totally commit.

*Pride/ASDM is a trademark of M. Bryce and Associates, Inc., Cincinnati, Ohio.

The State of the Art in CASE Systems

Since the introduction of Pride/ASDM, there have been many advances in technology. Higher Order Software's (Ann Arbor, Michigan) *USE.IT* system uses "mathematically provable" (their words) techniques to build systems, employing graphics and text. *Excellerator* from Index Technologies Corporation (Cambridge, Massachusetts) provides some data dictionary capabilities integrated with a line editor for flowcharting graphics. *TAGS/IORL* from Teledyne Brown Engineering (Huntsville, Alabama) provides complete graphics support and automation for the Teledyne Brown Input/Output Requirements Language (IORL).

Although these systems represent the movement in the state of the art in tools for systems developers, they are not true CASE systems because they do not address the management aspect of software engineering. On the flip side of the coin are the new *life-cycle management systems,* such as Arthur Anderson's DESIGN/1 and AGS Management System's automated SDM/70 and SDM/Structured systems, which aid in the management of the work-breakdown structure, providing a "front end" to the project control systems, helping to eliminate some of the manual burden of estimating and planning projects. But these systems, too, attack only a slice of the total software engineering management information system.

At present, only one firm, Nastec Corporation (Southfield, Michigan) provides an integrated CASE system, *NASTEC CASE 2000* which supports multiple life cycles and development techniques and addresses both the management and development tools issues. The CASE 2000 system provides the *DesignAid* Tool kit which integrates text and graphics in the *GraphiText* full-screen editor, provides a *Design Dictionary* which catalogs the typical information found in data dictionaries, and in addition, allows any deliverable field or object on a deliverable to be assigned an object type and stored in the dictionary. DesignAid also includes a scanner (called *Design Analyzer*) which "looks at" graphic design documents, validates them, and automatically makes dictionary entries. The DesignAid tools can be overlaid with a life-cycle management system *LifeCycle Manager* which can automate any life-cycle methodology with up to a five-level work-breakdown structure. LifeCycle Manager provides project-level customization and expansion of the life cycle and on-line estimating, planning, and task assignment. LifeCycle Manager also controls the software engineers development, invoking DesignAid tools automatically where required in development and quality review.

16.2 CASE SYSTEM REQUIREMENTS

Responding to the Problems

Having defined and analyzed the basic problems in the software development process—limited, expensive resource, volatility of installed software, and lack of process control—it is possible to define solutions to those problems which serve as the foundation for a requirements definition. Globally, the requirements of a computer-aided software engineering environment are:

- Improved productivity to reduce the volume and cost of development resources
- Improved software quality resulting in a reduced maintenance work load and corresponding improved user satisfaction
- Increased management control over the software development process

In addition, any system or process must be less of a burden than the problem it is trying to solve; therefore, the last requirement is

- Flexibility and ease of use

Based on these general requirements, we can develop the detailed requirements for a CASE system.

Detailed Requirements

If the demand for software development resources outstrips supply, making those resources either unavailable or unaffordable, then there are two options: increase the supply of resource or improve the productivity of existing resource. Since the supply of people is finite, improving productivity is the sole alternative. Therefore, the first requirement of a process to automate software engineering is to improve development productivity:

1. Decrease the time required by developers to create and modify project deliverables
2. Decrease the time required by project managers to develop and modify project plans

The volatility of the software base presently installed increases the maintenance demand on the development organization. This volatility results from poor requirements definition, weak or inaccurate initial design, or loss of design integrity through repeated maintenance. As we have seen, the term *maintenance* is applied to error correction, adaptation, and enhancement. Since maintenance tends to be less structured and disciplined than development, maintenance can, in fact, deteriorate software by weakening the design, thus geometrically increasing the maintenance load. Additional requirements of a system to automate the project management process are those related to decreasing the volatility of installed software:

3. Treat enhancement, adaptation, and error correction as controlled activities, like development

4. Drive maintenance programming from design to maintain design integrity through multiple maintenance projects

5. Provide facilities to create and validate design prior to implementation to ensure that designs are complete and accurate

6. A mechanism to review design and software quality and drive the actions necessary to ensure that quality is built-in rather than tested-in

The last set of requirements are those that deal with increasing control over the development environment. These requirements are to provide:

7. Standard software development life cycle with a patterned work-breakdown structure which can be used to govern projects and as a basis for a standard costing/estimating process

8. Standard methods and techniques for software analysis and design which are directly related to the life cycle

9. An easy means to access the life cycle, standards, and procedures so that their use is an advantage rather than an encumbrance

10. An easy means to tailor the life cycle to a particular project

11. Estimating guidelines, based on historical data, which track with the life cycle

12. Tools to quickly and easily develop and revise project estimates and plans

13. A means to drive the project execution process directly from the project planning process

14. A mechanism to track progress against the plan

In responding to the basic problems, these requirements enable us to define an environment or process that will have the effect of meeting the software challenge. However, to optimize functionality, a CASE system must

15. Provide a mechanism to integrate the project management, execution, and quality review tools

The problem of integration may, in fact, be the single biggest reason that software development organizations today are not operating in a completely automated environment.

Evolution of Solutions: Piecemeal Tools

The idea of automating systems development has not gone unaddressed, and there have been a number of solutions focusing on resolving the problems outlined in problem definition. The majority of existing solutions fall into three categories (see Figure 16.1): programming solutions, design solutions, and management solutions.

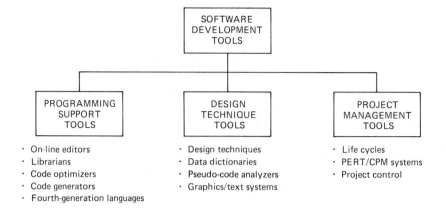

Figure 16.1   Evolution of solutions

As recently as 10 years ago, coding sheets and Hollerith cards were a way of life for many programmers. Decks were punched and read into card readers, listings were printed, and cards corrected and read in again. Today, automated techniques such as on-line source editors and librarians coupled with interactive compilers have made life much easier. Fourth-generation languages are becoming commonplace, reducing the number of instructions required to manipulate data. Code generators, while still in their infancy, hold promise for going from specification to software without the coding step. The vast majority of tool dollars spent in software development today go for programming solutions. The flaw with making this the only automation strategy, however, is that programming is only 20% of the development effort. Furthermore, programming tools presume good design.

In the 1970s, there was a recognition that programming tools alone could not solve all of the problems associated with software quality and development productivity. Because programs required good design, a number of organizations began developing, publishing, and training in design techniques. IBM's HIPO technique, Yourdon/DeMarco and Constantine's structured programming and structured design, and Warnier/Orr data structured systems design became popular logical process tools (i.e., methodologies for design without automated aids). Today, as we have seen, there are a number of methodologies available for design, but only a severely limited number of automated tools to support them. These automated tools initially focused on development and analysis of text-oriented software specifications. Data dictionaries analyze, record, and report data structures to aid in the design process. Problem statement languages and analyzers process pseudocode-type text specifications. The rapid proliferation of microcomputer-based workstations has spawned new workstation/graphics products that focus on developing and maintaining graphics/text-oriented design documents such as data-flow diagrams, structure charts, and flowcharts. These tools, however, address only specific portions of design techniques and often do not interface with development tools.

At the same time that the design technique school was growing, there was another school of thought, the project management school, which believed that regardless of how sophisticated a design technique was employed, if the project was not well managed, software would not be of high quality. Furthermore, if projects were too late or too expensive, the benefits of implementing the software could be outweighed by its cost. In the early 1980s, life-cycle tools were developed. The life-cycle logical process tools consist of software development methodologies which concentrate on defining a work-breakdown structure (WBS) for a software development project with standard work steps and standard deliverables from each work step (e.g., specifications, flowcharts, data flows, source code). By developing a standard WBS, standard estimating techniques could be applied and discrete units of work could be managed and quality reviewed.

The life-cycle concept grew out of the construction and aerospace engineering disciplines, which made use of such techniques as the program (project) evaluation and review technique (PERT) and the critical path method (CPM), which modeled projects in terms of numbered work steps which were assigned resources, durations, and dependencies (predecessor and successor relationships between other work steps in the process). By reducing projects to PERT and CPM networks, they could be better estimated and better managed. PERT/CPM network analysis tools evolved and have been implemented in the software engineering environment. Since these original PERT/CPM projects employed job costing techniques and systems, these were also applied to software. This resulted in a growth in project control software, or software that could schedule and track software development projects using automated tools. The marriage between life-cycle methodologies and project control software is a natural one. The life cycle provides the WBS, standards, and deliverables, and the project control software manipulates and manages the information in support of the project management process.

Problems with the Tool Kit

With all of these tools available, why are there still problems? The main reason is lack of integration. The design techniques may not map into the WBS of the life cycle or be compatible with the input required by a code generator or fourth-generation language. The project control systems provide information but do not provide process control over development. This lack of integration also makes tool selection and implementation difficult—to effect implementation, integration becomes the responsibility of the purchaser of the systems. As we have seen, this can be quite difficult. With the wide array of methodologies and tools, selection is a time-consuming and tedious process. At what point are the returns offered by the individual tools diminished in their marginal value? How do they interface (if at all)? What is the long-range outlook for a tool that supports a particular methodology? How flexible or adaptable is the tool?

The second major problem with automating software engineering is the difficulty in implementing logical process tools—the design techniques and life-cycle methodologies. By and large, these methodologies are labor-intensive, paper-driven processes which require large amounts of support and training. For this reason, methodologies are rarely implemented as designed. Although they are essential to automating the project management process and frequently provide an above-average return on their investment, in practice, without automation they do not achieve the original level of benefit hoped for.

16.3 CASE SYSTEM ARCHITECTURE

A true CASE system is one that meets the requirements outlined in one integrated system. The architecture depicted in Figure 16.2 achieves this objective. The CASE system is implemented on a standard delivery vehicle which provides a common user interface to all functions and features of the system. All function keys, commands, and other human-engineering factors can be standardized across all software features of a CASE system. If the CASE system is implemented in a microprocessor-based workstation environment, quick response time and powerful intelligence at the workstation level can be invoked, and advanced graphics capabilities can be implemented. In addition, through telecommunications, a CASE system can interface to a host database environment.

Within a CASE system, there are two major components: life-cycle management software and life-cycle tools. The *life-cycle management software* controls the planning, management, and execution of the software project. The *life-cycle tools* support each management or technical step of the development life cycle. Because of the common user interface intrinsic to true CASE environments, the appropriate tools can be automatically invoked during execution by the CASE system and the transition from tool to tool is transparent to the system user.

Life-Cycle Management Software:
The Development Database Manager

Engineering computer software is a knowledge-oriented process based on acquiring and transforming data—both data about the project and data about the design. In the management process, project managers acquire data about the characteristics of the project, development standards, and procedures and transform these data into project estimates, project plans, and work

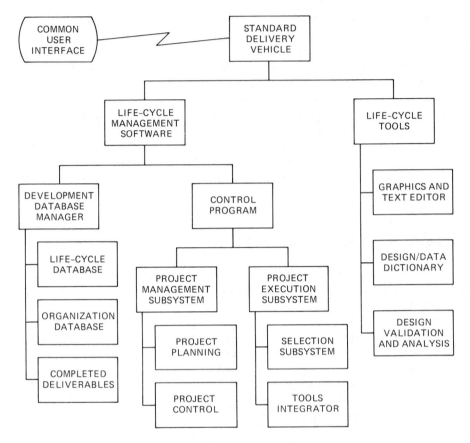

Figure 16.2   CASE system architecture

assignments. During the execution of the project, data are collected from the software engineering development process and transformed into controls and schedule change information. The data required for software engineering can be broadly categorized into three databases (see Figure 16.3): life-cycle database, organization database, and the completed deliverables database.

The *life-cycle database* contains all of the information about the software engineering methodology:

- Work-breakdown structure
- Task relationships
- Estimating guidelines
- Development procedures
- Deliverable formats

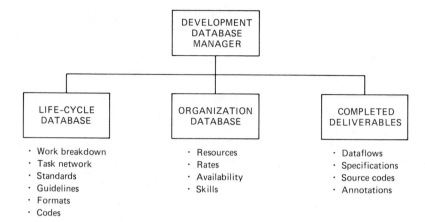

Figure 16.3   The development database manager

- Performance standards and quality review guidelines
- Design tips

In addition, this database contains various codes and their definitions, such as:

- Quality review codes
- Estimating units
- Skill codes
- Discipline codes

which simplify the access to information within the database and allow database processing at higher levels of abstraction. These data can then be provided to the project manager in an on-line environment. Once the knowledge contents of a methodology have been captured in a database, tailoring, manipulation, estimating, and related task linkages can be automated rather than performed manually. In addition, since the information is stored and accessed via a standard delivery vehicle with a common user interface, this information can be available to the developers (software engineers) as well. Life-cycle information can be accessed directly during the development process, on-line, without the need to find a manual and locate the relevant information.

The *organization database* contains all of the data about the development resources, their ID, skill code, availability, department assignments, and budget/billing rates.

Whereas the organization and life-cycle databases contain data and information about the project, the *completed deliverables database* contains information about the design and the application software itself. All of the project deliverables—specifications, data element descriptions, data-flow diagrams, structure charts, source code, and so on—are stored in the completed deliverables database. By storing deliverables electronically, they can be processed by additional life-cycle tools. A data-flow diagram drawn by hand can be reviewed by people. The same diagram, created on-line and stored in a database, can be reviewed by people and/or processed by a design analyzer. The analyzer can check graphics syntax, validate process, data-store and data-flow definitions, balance multiple diagram levels, and extract occurrences. Occurrences can be automatically loaded to a host data dictionary. These validation and extraction processes can be completed faster and more accurately by a machine than ever can be achieved by human processing alone.

In addition, when deliverables are stored in a database, they can be locked after the quality assurance process. Through the database management system, software engineers can be assured of access to the latest approved versions of completed deliverables. They do not have to track down folders containing deliverables, make copies, or search for missing documentation. The development database manager is the nerve center of a CASE system and provides a mechanism to integrate the various automated tools and processes that automate the project management process.

Life-Cycle Management Software: The Control Program

The *control program* acts as the driver to the project execution process. By providing project management functions and integrating CASE tools, the control program allows project plans to control the sequence and execution of project tasks. This is accomplished by generating task menus (as opposed to paper task lists) for project team members from the project plan entered by the project manager. To work on the project, a software engineer selects a task from the menu, and the control program transparently invokes the tool required to complete the deliverable. Since the execution process is now on-line and since it is driven by the project planning process, the control program can record the status of task completions automatically and control the quality review process.

The project management subsystem. The *project management subsystem* (Figure 16.4) provides the functions and features required to create project plans and control the sequence of project task execution and software quality. Through the project planning functions, the project manager can tailor the life cycle to the needs of the project, estimate the resource requirements, perform "what-if" analysis on various plan options, and schedule the project work.

One of the elements of a CASE system is the life-cycle methodology containing the procedures and work-breakdown structure for the project. The

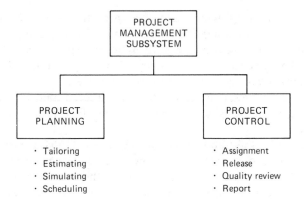

Figure 16.4   Project management subsystem

tailoring functions of the project management subsystem allow the project manager to step through the life-cycle database, select tasks appropriate to the project, eliminate tasks that are not relevant, and if necessary, add tasks unique to an individual project. In a non-CASE environment, this is accomplished by poring over methodology manuals, filling out project planning forms, and consuming many labor-hours in the process. The CASE system substantially reduces the time required for this process. By the use of discipline codes, large groups of tasks related to specific disciplines (such as telecommunications, database, package selection, etc.) can be selected or rejected with a single command. Since some tasks in the life cycle must be executed multiple times, a CASE system provides a mechanism to input a "number of occurrences" indicator to automatically generate and uniquely identify the occurrences of a task.

Once the life cycle has been tailored, a CASE system permits the project manager to step through the life cycle, tailored to the project, and sequentially estimate the project. As each task is displayed, minimum, average, and maximum estimating guidelines appear to aid in the estimating process. These guidelines are heuristically developed from past project performance. Estimating can occur at the detailed work step level, the phase level, or on any level between. As estimates are made at various levels, the system automatically recalculates higher- and lower-level estimates.

Some systems permit the use of par estimating, adjusted by *environmental factors* such as project complexity, team size, newness of design techniques, and overall project team experience. The various adjustment factors and their guidelines are stored in the life-cycle database. Once the factors have been selected, the system will recalculate adjusted estimates automatically. The project database resulting from this process can then be used as input to project scheduling and tracking programs, rather than preparing the input by hand.

When starting a software engineering project, and frequently during its execution, points occur where the estimates must be readjusted. If a project is late, one may wish to add resource. If the scope changes, it may affect completion or cost. To make trade-off decisions, a CASE system provides an interactive *project simulation* function to perform what-if analysis on various project alternatives. This allows contingencies to be explored quickly and easily and allows management decisions to be based on fact rather than educated assumptions.

Project scheduling can be accomplished in the CASE environment using PERT- and CPM-type techniques. The task dependencies are contained within the life-cycle database, together with the structure, estimates, and resource assignments for a given project. Once the tailoring and estimating have been completed on system, the data can be submitted to a scheduling system for translation to calendar time.

The project control subsystem.   Once the plan and schedule have been constructed, the automated project management process of the CASE environment permits tracking of project progress and interactive imposition of project control. Since execution also occurs within the CASE environment, a CASE system is "aware" of the status (planned, in process, in review, passed/failed review) of all work contained within the schedule. Using this information, the project manager can adjust assignments, estimates, and schedules—automatically communicating these controlling adjustments through the menu process. For additional control, tasks can be released for work independently of assignment. Project managers can include work on a menu through assignment but not release the task until the predecessor tasks have passed quality review.

To aid in the quality assurance process, a CASE system, through the development database manager, can automatically schedule completed deliverables for quality review. Quality review menus for individual quality reviewers can be generated and reviewers can access the deliverables from the menu. Once deliverables pass review, they can be locked. If a reviewer fails the deliverable, it automatically appears on the project manager's menu for further action. Quality review types and their associated deliverables can be stored in the life-cycle database. Reviews can be scheduled serially or concurrently. To maintain auditability of the development process, quality review comments can be stored independently of the deliverable, and the original deliverable can be locked from quality reviewer update.

The project execution subsystem.   In a completely automated project management process, project execution is to be controlled by the CASE system. By creating a project plan on-line, a CASE system generates menus of assignments by individual, in much the same way that a traditional project control system generates assignment sheets. The difference is that the actual creation, modification, and review of deliverables occurs on the same vehicle that generated the menu. By accessing the menu, software engineers can see the assignments, estimates, and due dates. By selecting a menu item, a CASE system will:

- Provide access to the guidelines, design tips, performance standards, and example of completed deliverables which pertain to that particular task
- Collect and display the *related deliverables,* completed earlier in the project life cycle, which contain information required to complete the task selected
- Copy previously completed deliverables which must be updated by this task
- Invoke graphics/text processing tools to create and modify deliverables
- Invoke validation tools to check the syntax and validity of specifications
- Invoke synthesis tools to transform data, perhaps even generating code from specifications
- Access tools such as data dictionaries and module libraries to copy/ modify reusable design components or code

(see Figure 16.5). In a completely integrated CASE environment, all of these tools are human-engineered with the same interface to simplify operation. In addition, existing tools, previously not integrated, can be linked through the CASE system. For example, a host-based code generator could be accessed from the CASE system via communications, or while graphics and text deliverables could be prepared within the CASE system, code could be created and stored using mainframe tools.

Finally, a CASE execution system can assemble the final product. Since all of the project deliverables have been created on the system and stored in

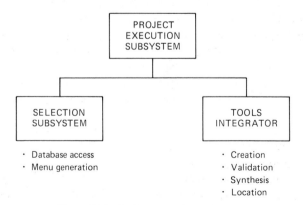

Figure 16.5 Project execution subsystem

the completed deliverables database, all of the necessary ingredients of the user manual, operations manual, and maintenance manual (or others) are contained on the system, as are all the source programs. Since all of the deliverables are predefined, their final destination(s) can be coded into the life-cycle database. At the end of the project, the deliverables can be automatically assembled and indexed for final editing.

Life-Cycle Tools

The number and variety of life-cycle support tools that can be integrated within a CASE system are virtually limitless. A few of the major tools are described here, but the list will surely grow as more specific applications of technology are developed to support new software engineering design and implementation techniques are developed.

Graphics/text editors. As the saying goes, a picture is worth a thousand words. Most of the advanced systems development techniques make extensive use of graphic representations of designs (such as Yourdon, Orr, Jackson, etc.). Virtually all of these representations mix text and graphics. The old source editors do not have the horsepower to handle graphics, yet the new breed of editors (such as the Nastec DesignAid/GraphiText editor) can handle source, data flows, structure diagrams, and such with single-key-stroke symbol generation, wordwrap within graphics boundaries, and facilities to program the editor to automatically perform routine or repetitive text/graphics functions.

Some of the advanced software engineering editors employ unique file management systems which enable deliverables to be embedded within one another with a single keystroke, for example, to "explode" a process bubble to its lower level of detail (another data flow or the actual source code, for example) and display on the workstation.

Some of these advanced editors can accept existing files such as specifications prepared on host-based editors (such as TSO) or source code stored in a host library. These advanced editors are typically easy to learn and use and can reduce the time required to create new deliverables by 15 or 20%. Since the bulk of the life cycle is devoted to updating, enhancing, or revising deliverables, the savings in this area can be enormous—with efficiency increases of 50 to 80% being reported by some organizations in the document revision process.

Some of the new Graphics/Text editors are user-view prototyping (see Chapter 14). With these systems, screens and reports can be "painted" without programming and linked together to emulate the live system. These prototypes require no compilation, no "execution," and the individual screens and reports become part of the documentation set for the system. Some user-view prototype files can be input directly into program generation systems.

Dictionaries. Data dictionaries have been around for some time; however, some of the advanced CASE systems now have design dictionaries with substantially improved functionality for systems developers. Dictionaries store *information* about *objects.* Typically, data dictionaries store attributes (such as length, value, description, COBOL picture) about data elements. Data dictionaries also contain "where used" information such as the programs, files, records, and so on, that contain or use these elements. *Design dictionaries,* on the other hand, are far more powerful. Design dictionary objects are not limited to *data elements;* they allow items such as data elements, files, program modules, and the deliverables that contain these objects, such as programs, data flows, and documentation of all sorts, to be cataloged as objects, too. In addition, they allow the recording of *relations*—relationships between objects. For example, a type of relation could be *data flow-process-data flow (DPD).* All objects of type data flow and process would be cataloged in all of the DPD relations in which they occur. Other relations could be process-diagram (PD). The dictionary could relate all processes to all data-flow diagrams in which the process occurred, or relate a data-flow diagram with all the processes (or data flows or externals) that it contained.

This capability enables the developer or designer to have tremendous power to do redundancy checking to consolidate duplicate modules into one module before the code is written, or to access reusable modules by indicating the input and output data and asking for the process(es) that meet those criteria. If a process, data flow, file, program module, or other design component is changed, a design dictionary enables the developer to quickly identify *all* the places the object is referenced or used. Used in conjunction with the new editors, developers using a design dictionary can mass-update all occurrences of a change, whether they appear in source code or documentation.

Scanners and analyzers. Sitting on the leading edge of CASE technology are the scanner and analyzer products. These systems accept deliverables (graphics, text, source) as input, validate the graphic syntax according to the rules of the design technique used, and ensure that all elements of the deliverable are included in the dictionary. Undefined objects, illegal relations, and other errors are automatically highlighted and can be corrected on-line by the user. Some even split the screen—display the deliverable on top and the error messages on the bottom. Once the deliverable passes the analysis, the scanning functions automatically catalog the "where used" information (objects *and* relations) into the dictionary in a fraction of the time that would be required to make manual entries. Some analyzers, such as DesignAid, can even process multiple deliverables, such as balancing data flows for parent and child data flow diagrams. The area of scanners and analyzers is probably the fastest-growing class of tools with specialized systems for validating real-time system design, supporting new development techniques, and scanning more types of deliverables.

16.4 OPERATIONAL CASE SYSTEMS

As mentioned earlier, integrated computer-aided software engineering (CASE) systems are available commercially. Two "complete systems" in the sense that they provide engineering tools for development deliverables preparation *and* management tools for planning and controlling systems development are Pride/ASDM from M. Bryce and Associates, Inc., of Cincinnati, Ohio, and NASTEC CASE 2000 from Nastec Corporation in Southfield, Michigan.

Delivery Vehicle

One of the key issues is the delivery vehicle of the CASE system—the computer on which it runs, on which its database(s) is(are) stored, and the method by which the manager or developer accesses the system. There are essentially two options: microcomputer-based workstations and mainframes.

Distributed microcomputer-based systems. Many CASE systems are implemented using distributed technology and microbased systems with data/communications links to mainframe systems. This is so for several reasons:

- Flexibility of graphics/text
- Fast response time for analytical and graphic/character manipulation
- More raw "compute power" through the aggregate of multiple systems processing planning, design, and programming information in parallel
- The ability of microcomputer-based systems to share data among workstations via high-speed local-area networks and/or mainframe computer telecommunications networks

The microcomputer-based workstation approach has been well proven as a delivery vehicle in both the computer-aided design (CAD mechanical engineering) and computer-aided engineering (CAE electronics engineering) systems which have been implemented successfully on "industrial-grade" or high-powered, high-memory microcomputer-based systems from hardware companies such as Apollo and Convergent Technologies. The NASTEC CASE 2000 system is such a system, implemented on the Convergent Technologies micro-systems as well as the high-end IBM personal computer XT, AT, and 3270 PC systems.

Some of the disadvantages of adopting a system of this type are more matters of perception than fact. One of the major perceptions of detractors of the approach is the fact that microcomputers are expensive and require a major capital expenditure or lease commitment to acquire the necessary hardware. While this is true to some extent, it overlooks the fact that very few host-computer systems have sufficient idle processing power to absorb the added work load of automating the systems development functions, which will be competing with other data processing functions during peak daytime hours.* While software and equipment acquisition for mainframe-based solutions is initially less capital intensive, the resulting bottleneck at the mainframe can result in significant host-computer upgrade requirements, or significant degradation of system response time. When response time degrades, systems development is usually the first user booted off the system or given a lower processing priority.

This fact has been seen readily in the office automation computer aided design and computer aided engineering efforts. Microcomputer-based distributed systems have proliferated because of the parallel processing needs to support highly interactive, real-time processing requirements of text processing, graphics, and other decision-support system activities. In the late 1970s, a major New York bank evaluated the possibility of performing all word processing and text storage/retrieval systems using IBM's ATMS/DCF and STAIRS systems operating on IBM 3033 computer systems. Although certain application environments were well supported by this endeavor, widespread use would bury their mainframe terminal network. Therefore, most of these computation-intensive, real-time functions were off-loaded to specialized word processing and personal computer–based systems with mainframes acting as large database repositories and wide-area network (WAN) processors. Even with these lessons learned, many data processing and senior corporate managers insist on attempting to automate tens or hundreds of programmers doing real-time, computation-intensive work on mainframe-based systems.

Centralized host-based systems.   Other systems, such as Pride/ ASDM, are implemented on centralized, host-based systems accessed through dumb terminals. These implementations can frequently lead to a lower "entry price" to CASE technology. For small systems development organizations (20 or fewer software engineers), they may even be supportable on existing hardware. There are also some organizations that rely on the availability of redundant, backup mainframe systems which make idle computer time available. In these instances, host-based systems may, in fact, be cost-effective.

---

*At present, only programming functions require access to corporate computing facilities with rare, occasional access for simple text editing. Even at this level of access, many organizations have adopted separate mainframe computer systems to handle the processing load. Others are at or near capacity on systems shared with production. If these systems are at or near saturation, supporting only programming activities, and if programs represent only 15% to 20% of the deliverables created during the systems development life cycle, it is evident that moving all deliverable creation and modification to the same computer resource will cause severe constraints on availability. Simple deliverable preparation and modification can require more than four times the current resource allocated to program preparation. To this must be added the additional processing resource for analysis, design dictionary reporting, and additional project management functions beyond project scheduling and time accounting.

While technology is advancing at a rapid pace, one of the possible limitations that can be found with host-based systems is that they tend to be "linguistic" in their approach to providing automated support for systems development methodologies. That is, host-based systems tend to support the entry of text and parameters and do not support well the automation of the development of graphic deliverables such as structure charts, data flow diagrams, data models, matrices, and other symbol-based development techniques.

Systems Architecture

Presently, at least one vendor, Nastec Corporation, is adhering to the computer-aided systems engineering system architecture outlined earlier in this chapter and indicates the feasibility of an implementation of this architecture. Figure 16.6 maps the NASTEC CASE 2000 System to the architecture diagram depicted in Figure 16.2. With the NASTEC CASE 2000 System, the life-cycle management functions are performed by *LifeCycle Manager,** a program product that allows project managers to tailor and expand a work-breakdown structure to meet the needs of a particular project. Iterations of work steps (Occurrences in LifeCycle Manager) can be generated automatically by specifying tailoring parameters (estimating units), such as the number of programs, number of data elements, number of subsystems, and so on, to the system. LifeCycle Manager then automatically generates all of the unique tasks that must be performed. LifeCycle Manager allows what-if analysis of various project scenarios through its Project Simulation feature, and allows the project manager to absolutely control the sequence of activities for all of the work on the project. LifeCycle Manager is much like a manufacturing process control system geared to supporting a "people" process rather than a mechanical process. Once project assignments are made, LifeCycle Manager generates "menus" of assignments for team members. When a menu item is selected, the appropriate form (blank or partially completed), related deliverables, procedures for completion, and a host of other information can be displayed on the screen. All of the CASE support tools can be invoked once menu selection has been made. LifeCycle Manager also automatically assembles final documentation and specifications from the deliverables database that it controls, and channels completed deliverables to other users on the LifeCycle Manager network who are reviewing the deliverables for quality.

Nastec's *DesignAid* Tool kit within CASE 2000 supports all of the functions performed by systems architects, planners, analysts, and programmers. GraphiText is an excellent example of the new type of graphics and text

---

*LifeCycle Manager, DesignAid, Graphitext and NASTEC CASE 2000 are registered trademarks of Nastec Corporation. IBM, ATMS, DCF and STAIRS are trademarks of IBM Corporation.

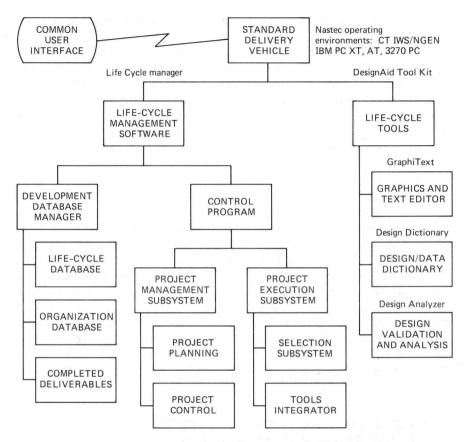

Figure 16.6   NASTEC CASE 2000 system

editors, providing word processing/source editing capabilities and treating graphic symbols and text equally. GraphiText also allows the rapid creation of user-view prototypes of new or modified systems. The Design Dictionary and Design Analyzer perform the consistency, redundancy checking, validation balancing, and reusability requirements previously.

Nastec's Design Dictionary highlights the difference between design and data dictionaries. In addition to storing and cross-referencing various levels of data elements with the programs that use them, Nastec's dictionary allows programs, modules, systems, subsystems, data classes, external entities, and even deliverables to be cataloged and cross-referenced in the dictionary. In addition, Design Dictionary provides a relational catalog. *Relations* between various objects in the dictionary can be established, such that input–process–output relations can be established. By looking for specific inputs and outputs, various reusable processes can be identified, including their related documentation, specifications, and source. Both object and relation types can also be user defined, greatly expanding the use of the system in the development process.

The Design Analyzer automatically feeds the "where-used" information for objects and relations to the dictionary by scanning documentation and source code, reducing this effort from person-days to minutes for certain types of deliverables. Since only valid objects and relations should be entered, the analyzer validates the graphic syntax of documentation and the validity of objects (by scanning the dictionary) in both source and documentation, prior to updating the dictionary.

Summary

The commercial success of CASE 2000, Pride/ASDM, and related systems is proving the feasibility of the computer-aided software engineering process. A page one article in the November 12, 1984, issue of *Computerworld,* "Chronic DP Shortcomings on the Wane?", confirms this, referencing a study by the Diebold Group, which cites the labor intensity of systems development as a major flaw in the systems development process. The report, however, sees the solution evolving and focusing on better "software engineering methods," concentration on design instead of just programming, and application of better management techniques. These efforts will change systems development from a "craft" to a profession—to the benefit of both the professionals and their enterprises.

16.5 CASE AND THE FIFTH GENERATION: SYSTEMS THAT BUILD SYSTEMS

Artificial intelligence (AI) conjures up images of Japanese supercomputers running high-powered "inference engines," "knowledge-based" AI applications, and "expert systems." The contemporary view of AI seems to be one of an application world where complex business, engineering, and scientific problems are resolved by end users using these advanced systems. Like any other new technology, AI is growing and evolving.

If systems development is truly a microcosm of the enterprise, as we have stated earlier, and in fact systems development has its own set of business and engineering problems like any other product-oriented transformation process, then perhaps AI can play a role in software engineering as well. Robert Kowalski of the Imperial College in London supports this view (Kowalski, 1984), stating that software engineering, artificial intelligence, and new systems development technologies relate to each other in a matrixed fashion and are complementary related technologies rather than mutually exclusive. In Kowalski's model (Figure 16.7) AI is not the object of the engineering effort. In point of fact, the information systems that get developed must solve a business problem. The application of AI to the problem is irrele-

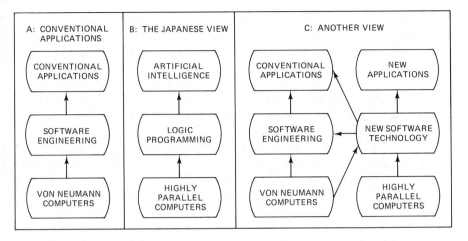

Figure 16.7   AI and computer-aided software engineering. From Robert Kowalski, "AI & Software Engineering," *DATAMATION*, (Nov. 1, 1984). Reprinted with permission of DATAMATION Magazine, © copyright by Technical Publishing Company, a Dun & Bradstreet Company, 1984—all rights reserved.

vant in so far as traditional techniques will produce the desired result. What is really needed is a methodology for engineering systems that suits both conventional problems and problems that require AI solutions and enables what Kowalski labels "new applications" to be developed which may be purely conventional, AI, or some hybrid.

The valuable perspective to be gained from this is that software engineering is a process that can benefit from today's level of achieved technology in AI by marrying present computer-aided software engineering systems (such as NASTEC CASE 2000) with AI, evolving CASE into a hybrid "new application" ("CAISE"?).

Where AI Fits in CASE

For our purposes it is not sufficient simply to state, as Kowalski has, that AI has a place in software engineering. By our definition, software engineering is an *integrated approach* to building application systems, and if the "software engineering approach" is to embody AI technology, we must recognize where it fits and how it can be integrated. Using computer-aided software engineering as the engine for the software engineering approach, then, let's see where AI technology can be inserted into the CASE framework.

AI and Life-Cycle Management

One of the subsystems of computer-aided software engineering is the life-cycle management process, which, in addition to simply scheduling and tracking the project, also encompasses the development of the project work-breakdown structure. This process of the functional decomposition of work could be significantly enhanced by the application of AI technology.

During project definition, the current level of CASE technology simply records the standard methodology as a template within the system and allows the project manager to create "iterations" of work steps based on the project managers quantification of certain events or deliverables, such as number of programs, screens, data elements, or subsystems. An AI-based expert system could potentially offer the opportunity to have the system examine the written definition of the project and make some determinations as to the complexity of the problem, the analysis or design approach that best suits the problem, and generates the task network from this.

AI techniques could also aid substantially in estimating and planning projects. AI-based expert systems could evaluate the complexity of various tasks, look up the skill level of various team members assigned to the project, and develop estimates of the work—even going so far as to assign the work to the "best" person, selecting the "best" based on availability of people and a precedence network for the work to be performed. One of the major problems in systems development today is that projects change but the plans remain constant. That is, events that change the scope of the project or amount or duration of work occur, but the task of redefining the project precedence network, reestimating all of the related tasks, and developing a new project schedule is so complex and time consuming that it simply does not get done. CASE systems significantly reduce the paperwork associated with the development of new project plans but do not necessarily make the need to change the plan visible. An AI system could evaluate the work being performed and raise a "red flag" indicating that the project scope was being exceeded.

AI and the Software Engineering Transformation Process

Within the domain of actually producing software through a series of specifications that ultimately result in code and operating procedures, artificial intelligence could radically change and improve the way systems are defined and built. Design analyzers of the type discussed earlier in this chapter could be expanded to examine the preliminary deliverable (such as a context-level data flow diagram) and generate the lower-level structures based on the systems "knowledge" of processes, data, and relations stored in a design dictionary. Similarly, given decomposed data requirements for information systems, AI systems could reconstruct the design.

The concept of intelligent design analyzers could be stretched even further by allowing a flexible *rules database* to govern the analyses of the design analyzer. The rules database could contain the grammars for various design methodologies, as well as a template for the minimum universe of data required to specify (or infer) a software design. This would enable the software engineer to choose the methodology or "language" with which he or she would communicate specifications. A highly sophisticated AI CASE system operating in this mode could generate the code and "show its work" by displaying the interim specifications in the language or methodology chosen. Software engineers could modify the system-inferred design by altering the interim specification and deliverables and resubmitting them to the design analyzer.

Expert design analyzers could also compensate for the deficiencies which might be found in some of the design techniques. If the information captured from the specifications does not meet the minimum universe of required data from which to generate the software (and potentially related operational documentation) the system could query the software engineer to supply the missing parameters.

Expert design systems of this type operate in the *solution domain*. That is, they require the software/systems engineer to identify the problem and the constraints governing the solution. These requirements are then part of the parameter database that feeds the inference engine that produces the resulting system.

For years, the information systems industry has used the term "systems analyst" broadly to describe analysts of existing systems and business problems, who also act as "system designers" for the new applications. Given a sufficient level of expert system technology, systems analysts could become truly analysts, working in the problem domain, and the systems could do the design.

Although nothing is impossible, it is highly unlikely that AI systems will ever be able to operate in the problem domain. If they could, they could run companies or governments. However, the *problem domain*—defining the problem, looking at and describing opportunities, and identifying (or in some cases inventing) data that need to be evaluated will remain a human problem. If an organization's resources could be focused on and dedicated to working in the problem domain, with an intelligent system to capture the definition and generate the system, the productivity implications could be staggering.

How Far Away Are We?

AI CASE systems may not be that far off. Already, CASE companies are building the rudiments of "expert systems." Nastec's Design Analyzer clearly could be the foundation of a system designer. Other firms, such as CGI, Inc. (Paris/New York City), developers of the PACBASE system, are already developing technology which converts solution descriptions to source code. The next logical step is to generate the solution description from the problem description.

Clearly, one of the constraints, as viewed by some, is the limitation of the "von Neumann machine" or the classical central processor–arithmetic unit–memory computer architecture which decomposes the world into binary

1's and 0's. AI experts tell us that new "parallel architectures" and the ability to process symbols as well as numbers are highly important. The Japanese are searching for the "artificial-intelligence machine." While new machines and new hardware will certainly play a role in achieving efficient AI applications, there is an enormous potential to create AI applications on today's mainframes. Even the most sophisticated mainframes, however, are limited in the number of simultaneous applications which they can perform. One of the solutions to the "parallelism" problem may surface in the use of microprocessor networks (Fegenbaum and McCorduck, 1983).

As we demonstrated earlier, one of the advantages of microcomputers for CASE was the ability for multiple users to perform functions simultaneously on multiple, slower processors, without time slicing on a faster but serial processing machine. We cannot overlook the possibilities of networked microprocessors, with multiple data storage paths and concurrent processing capabilities, in solving "inference" problems in which multiple alternatives can be processed simultaneously.

How far away are we? We are perhaps still 10 to 15 years away from multipurpose, business-oriented AI systems which effectively aid management in running a business. However, we may in fact be very close to Kowalski's "new applications" scenario. Software engineering AI systems, systems that build systems, are perhaps less than five years away. How can we prepare ourselves to take advantage of these new systems? By adopting the software engineering approach to building systems, focusing more on better defining the problems and their solutions, focusing less on faster tools to write code, and implementing CASE systems.

CASE systems, which allow the electronic capture of the whole universe of system specifications, represent the most logical "next-step" in the evolution towards AI CASE systems. Current CASE technology can provide, in capturing the software specifications, an on-line database of experience that can serve as the starting point for the next generation of intelligent software engineering systems.

As with any new technology, backtracking is always a problem. CASE systems, in use for the next two- to five-years, can short-circuit the need to backtrack when the expert software engineering systems arrive.

16.6 SUMMARY

Desirable Attributes of a CASE System

From the CASE system architecture described previously, some attributes recommended for a CASE system can be derived:

1. *Flexibility:* The CASE system should support any methodology, allowing the organization to select and implement the life-cycle and design techniques chosen by that organization.

2. *Adaptability:* The CASE system should allow transition to new design techniques and work-breakdown structures and provide a means to create and maintain the life-cycle database. New tools, operating on the standard delivery vehicle or a host, should be accessible through the system.

3. *Integration:* The CASE system should drive the execution of project tasks directly through the project planning process.

4. *Human factors:* The CASE system should provide standard function keys and consistent menu formats throughout all its subsystems. System help information should be easily accessible, and additional help information (such as methodology information and procedures) should be available as an option.

5. *Implementation:* The CASE system should provide subsecond response time, include graphics and word processing, and be able to access the organization's data communications network and host processing environment.

Benefits of Implementing CASE

A CASE system, meeting the requirements set out in Chapter 2, will benefit through

- Improved software quality
- Increased developer efficiency
- Increased management control

This results in

- Lower development costs
- Reduced maintenance workload
- Greater user (customer) satisfaction
- Smaller project backlogs

Efficiency.   Developers' time to create project deliverables can be reduced by up to 30% by implementing text/graphics deliverables preparation systems. The impact of these systems is even more significant in the revision of deliverables (which comprises the bulk of project work). Deliverable revision time can be decreased by up to 80%.* Since final manual preparation is done automatically by a CASE system, only the minimal time for final editing is required. All of the benefits of life cycles and design methodologies are realized because they can be reliably and consistently applied and enforced.

*Nastec Corporation, BASE & DesignAid Customer Surveys, 1984.

Because system design deliverables are stored on-line, with appropriate engineering analysis and design tools, reusable design and code modules can be identified, stored, and recalled when needed, eliminating rewriting and redesigning preexisting primitive processes.

Project managers can save substantial time in creating and modifying project plans and estimates. Since the calculation of estimates and schedules is automated, project managers have more time to devote to aiding developers in the software engineering process.

Quality. With the resulting increase in productivity achieved by implementing a CASE system, software developers can devote more time to exploring design alternatives. The quality assurance process is automated and can be implemented in a real-time fashion, aiding in the early identification and resolution of design problems before they have a cumulative effect on the project. If you wait until a major milestone to review quality, you risk the possibility of compounding design flaws in dependent tasks which get executed prior to the milestone.

Since all project information, including design, is stored on the system and is easily accessible, those adaptation and enhancement projects can be design driven rather than programming driven. By modifying the design, its integrity remains intact, so the software does not deteriorate over time.

By implementing CASE design validation tools, data and process relationships can be evaluated, and requirements can be traced through design. Design changes can be validated to ensure that all related design components are properly updated prior to implementation.

Quality is further assured at the developer level. Standards are developed to help ensure consistency and quality of software. If standards are difficult to access, they are likely to be ignored. Because the standards are implemented on-line in a CASE system, they are easily accessed; therefore, they are a help rather than a hindrance to the developer.

Management control. Virtually all late projects are caused by bad estimates. Either projects are underestimated at the outset, or underestimated changes and enhancements occur. By providing an on-line estimating system, estimates are based on historical information and are therefore more likely to be accurate. Also, with the simulation capabilities of CASE-type systems, changes in staffing and project scope can be accurately evaluated. This provides management with better information with which to make project control decisions.

Projects stay under control with CASE systems because management has real-time visibility of the project progress. Minor project planning changes can be effected during project progress, with those changes being immediately available to the development team.

17

Implementing Software Engineering and CASE

17.1 MECHANICS OF IMPLEMENTATION

Planning the Implementation

The first consideration in implementing any form of software engineering is that it takes both financial and human resources. This requires the commitment of the financial decision makers of the organization. In addition, the implementation of cultural change, as dictated by CASE-type systems, requires constant monitoring and reinforcement at the senior management level.

The implementation and integration of software engineering and CASE within the systems development organization must be approached as a development project. As such, a life-cycle approach to implementation is recommended. Figure 17.1 depicts an eight-phase life cycle for implementing software engineering through computer-aided software engineering.

Defining Constraints and Requirements

The requirements for implementing CASE may vary from organization to organization. Internal application software development shops are usually free to select the design techniques that best meet their needs, while custom-house software developers may be constrained by the life cycles and design techniques of their customer base. Also, certain design techniques are better suited to some types of application development. For example, structured

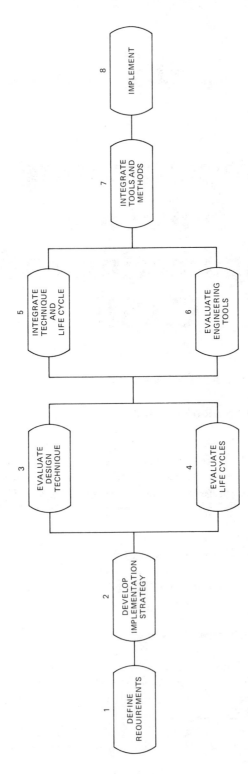

Figure 17.1 Implementing computer-aided software engineering

1 DEFINE REQUIREMENTS

2 DEVELOP IMPLEMENTATION STRATEGY

3 EVALUATE DESIGN TECHNIQUE

4 EVALUATE LIFE CYCLES

5 INTEGRATE TECHNIQUE AND LIFE CYCLE

6 EVALUATE ENGINEERING TOOLS

7 INTEGRATE TOOLS AND METHODS

8 IMPLEMENT

techniques based on data modeling are well suited to business information systems. They do not apply well to real-time command and control systems, where such techniques as state and transition analysis meets the requirements better.

The requirements of the design technique will also indicate whether the development methodology is graphics/text or pure text oriented. This information, combined with the availability, flexibility, and response time of the host environment, will dictate whether a host or workstation (micro)-based solution is appropriate. Typically, CASE systems are workstation based for reasons of response time, graphics ability, and all of the other reasons that people do things like word processing and CAD/CAM on workstations rather than on the host. In addition, since software engineering encompasses the entire gamut of technical and management procedures, things that work well today should be identified and established as constraints for inclusion in any future implementation.

Developing Implementation Strategy

From the requirements definition, a general architecture of a suitable CASE system can be identified, the implementation effort planned and estimated, and resources assigned to the project.

Evaluating Design Techniques/Evaluating Life Cycles

The actual evaluation and selection of the technology and tools begins with these phases. It is immaterial which evaluation is undertaken first, primarily because of the blur in distinction between these two types of commercially available methodologies. Design techniques typically require specific deliverables to be created and specify the sequence and format of the deliverables. While life-cycle methodologies do this also, they do it in the framework of a project-oriented management process and include work steps for quality assurance, project planning, documentation assembly, and project funding. The life cycles provide a hierarchical work-breakdown structure which is typically lacking in pure design technique.

The question to be raised at this point is just what life cycles and techniques are going to be required. Are strategic and tactical planning defined and structured? Do you need a project-oriented system? Do you need a methodology for administering the project selection and decision-making process?

The important (and often overlooked) fact is that a comprehensive, effective software engineering process requires *both* the technique and the project-oriented work-breakdown structure.

Important considerations in the selection of a life cycle are:

1. Does it provide a fine enough work-breakdown structure?

2. Does the WBS have consistency—are deliverables always produced at the lowest level of the hierarchy?
3. Does it provide a dependency network and clearly indicate the predecessor deliverables?
4. Are estimating guidelines and environmental adjustment factors included with the life cycle?
5. Are the project management and control procedures well defined?
6. Does it include tasks for database, communications, and packaged software products evaluation and selection?

The important considerations for the selection of a design technique are:

1. Is it process, data, or state transition based, and is its basis consistent with the types of systems that will be developed?
2. Is it graphics oriented?
3. Is the process well engineered?
4. Are specific deliverables, their format, and syntax well defined?
5. Are there automated tools to support the creation/transformation of design deliverables?

Integrating the Techniques and Life Cycle

Once acceptable techniques and life cycles have been identified, the specific deliverables required by the design technique can be incorporated into the lowest level (work step) of the work-breakdown structure. Generally, there is not a one-to-one mapping, but usually an 80 to 90% mapping can be found. Most life cycles are consistent with design techniques through the third level of the hierarchy, with work steps differing only in graphics/text syntax.

Evaluating and Selecting Engineering Tools

Again, integration of techniques and life cycles and selection of engineering tools can occur concurrently. The place to begin is with the CASE life-cycle management system. The considerations are:

1. Does it support multiple work-breakdown structures?
2. Does it meet the architecture described previously?
3. Does it provide graphics and text support capabilities?
4. Does it provide life-cycle database maintenance facilities?
5. Will it integrate into a network or host environment?
6. Does the vendor provide integration assistance?

Once the life-cycle management system has been identified, detailed tools to support the various life-cycle work steps can be evaluated. Frequently, they operate on the same delivery vehicle as the life-cycle management system or on a host that can be accessed from a workstation-based system. Typically, the vendors of the methodologies and software provide consulting services to assist in the integration.

Integrating Tools and Methods

Once the tools have been acquired, the methodologies can be loaded into machine-readable form for processing by the life-cycle management software. A few of the commercially available methodologies provide machine-readable text of their manuals and procedures, which simplifies the process.

Implementation

As with any new technology, it is advisable to start slowly. A transition to a CASE environment means cultural change, so training and support are crucial. Equally important is the need to identify whether or not the CASE solution constructed works in the proposed environment.

The recommended approach is to plan for the implementation of CASE on a pilot project. In addition to successful completion of the project, it is important to evaluate the effectiveness of the technology and training. Once the pilot exercise has been completed, a more refined plan for transitioning the entire development organization to CASE can be developed.

Conclusion

The answer to the challenges facing the software development industry today are not substantially different from those which faced manufacturing in the past. Software developers need to automate more of their environment. Just as CAD/CAM has spurred tremendous growth in mechanical and electronic engineering—resulting in more performance for less cost—CASE will achieve the benefits of improved quality, productivity, and management control for software development, resulting in high-quality, lower-cost software systems.

Although change always induces some level of stress, a controlled, planned implementation of CASE, rather than ad hoc implementation of piecemeal solutions, will enable software engineering management to meet the software challenge.

17.2 HUMAN ISSUES IN SOFTWARE ENGINEERING IMPLEMENTATION: DECISION MAKING AND CONSENSUS

In all of the discussion of software engineering and computer-aided software engineering, methodologies, design techniques, and workstations, it is easy to lose sight of the fact that for all of the technology surrounding it, the process of building systems is now, and will remain, a human effort. The human effort focuses on communications—between end user and DP, and between system analyst–designer–implementor within DP. The software engineering process must improve and foster this communication.

Norbert Wiener, who coined the term "cybernetics," made an interesting observation on communication methods (Weiner, 1967, p. 257):

> It may seem superficially that even in the absence of a conscious or purposeful interference by nature, the policy of the research scientist should be to play it safe, and always act so that even a malicious and deceitful nature would not prevent his optimum acquisition and transfer of information. This point of view is unjustified. Communication in general, and scientific research in particular, involve a great deal of effort even if it is useful effort, and the fighting of bogies which are not there wastes effort which ought to be economized. We can not go through our communicative or scientific lives shadow-boxing with ghosts. . . .
>
> The devil whom the scientist is fighting is the devil of confusion, not of willful malice.*

The mission of the system developer is to "fight the devil of confusion" in league with the user, to jointly create systems that represent a consensus of need and opinion. It is this consensus, however, which is so often elusive and too frequently is never achieved. Frequently, this is not known until after the system is implemented and fails to provide the solution to some subset of the problem.

There are two major types of consensus that must be achieved in systems development:

1. Consensus on what systems should be built, and when
2. Consensus on what each system should look like

The first type—consensus on what systems should be built, and when—is the problem of achieving consensus in the systems architecture development and strategic and tactical planning processes. The second type of consensus—what each system should look like—is the problem of achieving consensus during

---

*From *The Human Use of Human Beings* by Norbert Wiener. Copyright 1950, 1954 by Norbert Wiener. Copyright © renewed 1977 by Margaret Wiener. Reprinted by permission of Houghton Mifflin Company.

the software engineering transformation process. Both problems revolve around the user being able to communicate with the data processor, and the data processor being able to respond intelligibly to the user.

What Systems Should Be Built, and When

To resolve this issue, some roles must be identified. Who is responsible for what? In fact, systems development is the classical staff organization, paid for by and serving at the pleasure of the user community. Systems development does not decide what business the enterprise is in, nor what information management requires to manage the business effectively. That is the province of the users. Systems development is responsible for ensuring that the needs of the users are articulated and that the methods of capturing the data and providing the information are cost-effective and efficient. Where systems development recognizes inefficiencies or ineffectiveness in an enterprise's transformation process, it should advise management and offer recommendations for solutions. Management ultimately decides what to do. Once the decision has been made, the systems development manager or professional has two choices: abide by the decision or find a new enterprise.

In short, the systems developer is an investigator, who through careful questioning, aids the user in articulating his or her needs in a manner that can be easily understood by the technologists of the organization. The developer must also parrot back the data to the user to verify that they have been faithfully captured. From this point, systems development estimates the funding required to solve the problem. This is the point where most consensus systems break down. Users want the maximum system for the minimum investment at the earliest date, whether or not it is achievable. Reaching balance must be a practice of *negotiation,* not changing estimates to reflect desires, brow-beating development into submission, or other actions often perpetrated by both DP and users.

How to negotiate.   The method used to negotiate which systems will be built and when is to establish these seven rules as corporate policy and then abide by them:

1. The user community and systems development will always be honest and forthright in their communication with each other.
2. The user has the absolute right to state what he or she wants from the system.
3. The user has the absolute right to state how much can be spent on development and implementation.
4. Systems development has the responsibility to seek the lowest-cost method to implement the entire system, determined by quantifiable,

documented techniques, and to inform the user of the true cost, whatever it may be.

5. DP will never say "it can't be done" unless they mean it. That phrase is *not* synonymous with "it takes more time than you want" or "it will cost more than you allocated."

6. If the cost to build exceeds the funding allocated, the users can accept reduced functionality *or* provide more resources.

7. Users will never say "I want it all for less money/in less time."

These seven rules must be applied to strategic, tactical, and project planning consistently, throughout the enterprise.

Establishing priorities. Establishing priorities for development can perhaps be one of the most frustrating endeavors any systems development manager can suffer through. A method to resolve this is to establish a "steering committee" of the most senior-level managers available in the organization who can be convened in a room at one time. Beforehand, have each of them collect (or give to them from your files) all of the projects from all their subordinates. Ask them to rank each project. The ranking should be by net benefit, with adjustments made for absolute requirements to meet legal constraints.

If the financial method of ranking is not feasible, because of lack of data or "intangible benefits"—drop all of the projects with intangible benefits. If the user will not do that, resort to the coin-flip project sorting technique.

The coin-flip project sorting technique. Place a coin (heads up) and the stack of project requests on the desk of the user. Have the user prioritize the number one and number two requests. If they are in priority order, compare number two and number three, and so on. The first time any comparison yields a change in priority, flip the coin over and go through the rest of the stack (leaving the coin alone). If you have not had to flip the coin, the projects are in priority order; if you did, go through the stack again, flipping the coin over when the first priority change is encountered. When you get through the stack without flipping the coin, you are done.

Establishing priorities for the entire enterprise. Have the users arrive at the steering committee meeting with their prioritized stack. Take each number one request from each user and take a vote on each one as to whether it is number one for the enterprise. When the number one is selected, take another request from the stack of requests belonging to the user whose project has been selected, voting on the number two priority. Repeat this process until all projects have been prioritized.

If this method fails, combine all the stacks of requests, putting all number one, number two, number three, and so on, together. Place a coin heads up on the table and use the coin-flip method to sort the priorities. A pair of requests change priority only when the majority of participants votes for the flip. If a deadlock is reached (and it rarely is), invite the lowest-ranking executive to whom the entire group reports and have him or her select the priority.

The effectiveness of the methods.   Although these methods may sound tongue in cheek, they are, in fact, quite serious. Gaining consensus about priorities from a single person is difficult, from a group, nearly impossible, unless the method for selection is simple and binary. Rarely does a person or a group have a difficult time choosing between A and B. Although the method may be time consuming, it is probably less consuming of resource than building the wrong system at the wrong time.

Achieving Consensus on What the System Should Look Like

Once the systems projects have been selected, the next level of consensus is getting the user and the data processing staff to agree on what the system should look like. Occasionally, systems developers interview the users and then go build the system. This is probably not a meritorious approach. Nor is the approach of dumping reams of technical specifications on the user, in some foreign language (from the user's perspective) and asking him or her for a sign-off. That is development by intimidation.

The better approach is to make the user part of the project development team, reviewing deliverables with the user or his or her agent at each step of the project. Many methodologies have "quality review" checkpoints, where documentation is assembled and given to the user for review. Break up the reviews, review it with the user incrementally, and get the "sign-off" at the meeting, only after each facet has been reviewed beforehand.

One of the true benefits of the fourth-generation techniques, such as prototyping, is its ability to paint a picture of the system for the user. Using this technique in that manner is an excellent way to gain consensus (not necessarily to finish the development process).

IBM Corporation is instructing its customers in a technique known as JAD—Joint Application Design.* JAD is essentially a consensus-achievement mechanism as opposed to a life-cycle or development technique. JAD recommends that the user become involved in studying the existing system, as well as the analyst, and that the users, in conjunction with data processing personnel, construct the requirements and first-level design. Formal user-involvement techniques such as JAD help proceduralize and script the user-involvement process and help build user ownership and commitment to the system.

*JAD, Joint Application Design, is a proprietary methodology available from IBM Corporation. Information about JAD is available from your local IBM representative.

Virtually all of the commercial, proprietary systems development life cycles, such as SPECTRUM, SDM/70 and SDM/Structured (from AGS Management Systems, Inc., Philadelphia, Pennsylvania), PRIDE, and others also have built-in procedures for getting systems development and users to work together.

The secret to successful user involvement.   Many developers have found it difficult to get users actively involved in the development process. Often, the reason for this is that the actions that developers want the users to perform are ill defined. Therefore, users are reluctant to commit large amounts of time to a process they do not understand. The "secret," if there is one, is to communicate in a language the user can comprehend, and give the user a task list of well-defined actions that you want the user to perform. If they really want the system and they want it to work, they will perform understood, defined work.

17.3 HUMAN ISSUES IN SOFTWARE ENGINEERING: OVERCOMING TECHNOLOGY SHOCK

Technology Shock Defined

Perhaps one of the biggest barriers to achieving dramatic improvements in systems development productivity is *technology shock.* In any organization, there is a certain amount of inertia, or resistance to change, which must be overcome before any progress can be made. Left to their own devices, a fair number of people will opt to keep doing business the way it has always been done. It seems that this inertia is compounded when applied to systems development. Technology shock is the normal resistance to change, added to by fear of the unknown (new technology and new systems) and multiplied by the staggering costs associated with any aspect of data processing (the fear of getting "canned" for blowing the budget).

Technology shock affects different people in different ways, causing varied responses to the stimulus of a new method or tool. A minority will take to the new system like fish to water. Some people experience an immediate mental paralysis in varying degrees, which prevents them from even learning the rudiments of the new system. Others become subconsciously devious, causing the new system to fail or insisting on following any instruction "to the letter" (which almost invariably produces disastrous results). Some do their best to cope but are less efficient under the new system than they were under the old.

The Impact of Technology Shock

Technology shock can have a graduated impact on the organization. Often, it leads to simple disuse of the system. If the system is a methodology or a mainframe-based tool, the disuse can be unnoticed. If the system is some form of specialized microcomputer, it may become evident by the consistently empty chair in front of the system.

Technology shock is rather expensive. An unused system is capital that may have been thrown out the window. A less effective worker costs the enterprise more each day. With hardware and software, trial periods may alleviate some of the cost if you know it is not working out. Methodologies are another story; a technology shock failure may not be recognized until months after the bill is paid and the consultant is vacationing in Europe.

How to Avoid Technology Shock

The first way to avoid technology shock is to prevent it. The easiest way to prevent it is to avoid the fear of the unknown. Most successful and reputable firms vending tools and methodologies support their products vigorously. Make use of this support, even if it is billable. It is necessary to provide functional training in the tool or methodology, but often, it is the management overview or the global education associated with the tool—why it is better, what it will do for you—that is glossed over. People are more comfortable with a new process if they can see the "big picture." The dollars associated with the education are insignificant compared with the cost of a failure.

Know the Benefits

With any tool or methodology, there are always the canned benefits enumerated in the sales literature and documentation. These benefits are, however, geared toward the decision maker and may not be perceived, or real, benefits to the user of the system. For example, a "project control" system that puts management's finger on the pulse of the project is a great tool for the manager. But what professional, creative programmer wants to be controlled? Many will resist. It is better to find the benefits that fit the user of the system as well. For example, if the same project control system helps develop more realistic estimates, then it helps the project manager to better budget and plan projects and it helps analysts and programmers to avoid unrealistic, high-pressure deadlines. Those are benefits to the user. Failing to recognize these benefits and educate the participants can have disastrous results.

In the mid-1970s the author was co-founder of Maximus Systems Incorporated, where we developed and marketed an application system generator. We told management that it would cut data processing costs in half. Our benchmarks and beta-test installations proved it, but for some time we rarely got past the 90-day test. We later discovered that the programmers viewed it as a way to cut down on or eliminate programmers, or a way to require lesser skills for the programming job. After a period of time, we kept the same management theme, but indicated that the same number of programmers could do more work—help cut the backlog and hence ease the pressure on the data processing staff. We coupled this with an educational program which educated the programmers on the fact that they would be required to spend more time on analysis and design—significantly more professional functions. Sales improved dramatically.

Make It a Big Deal

One method to ensure success is to tell people that it ought to be a success and that it will be a piece of cake for the best and brightest (if you think so). There's a lot to be said for "the emperor's new clothes."

Start Slowly and Ramp Up Quickly

Never install any new technology without a pilot. Make sure that the pilot works—if it doesn't, kick it out. If it does, install it organization-wide as soon as possible. No one wants to be left out. If they are and they feel second class, they will resist when the time comes. Also, the larger the population of users, the more successes there will be. The few inevitable failures, if they happen in the beginning and are part of a statistically insignificant sampling, will taint others' opinions.

Don't Use Second Stringers

Often, in many organizations, the superstars are put on the "hot" projects for the enterprise, the stars are busy, and the average joe gets the assignment to "investigate, evaluate, and pilot" all the new things that you want to try. This is based on the theory that pilots are overhead and the superstar is too valuable to tie up. Let's face it, if you are implementing software engineering or CASE, the potential positive impact on your organization is tremendous. The savings will be high and certainly outweigh the minor cost of devoting your superstar to the project for awhile.

The worst case is that you have a poor performer, so you give this person the "simple" job of evaluating new tools and methodologies. Don't do yourself this favor. It is merely a mechanism to avoid another management problem.

If you are serious, show it. Put your best talent on the project. He or she has been working for the users up to now. You are part of the enterprise and your applications are important, too.

Watch the Progress

Do not trust casual comments on the effectiveness of the system. Take readings and measurements. Watch for signs of disuse.

Involve the Users

The user community will benefit from your new process. In all probability they will participate in it. Educate them, involve them in the decision, give users whose applications will be piloted a role to play in the evaluation. You will always win points with users by asking them for their valued opinions.

____Appendix:____

Software Engineering Life Cycle

Although there are a wide variety of commercially available, proprietary systems development life cycles available, the following represents a model of one that meets the basic work-breakdown structure requirements enumerated in Chapter 13 and is consistent with the concepts in this book. It would be inappropriate to call this a "methodology," since it consists only of the names of the phases, activities, and tasks. The work steps required to complete a particular task would be dependent on the particular development technique employed. The work-breakdown structure is numbered X.YY.ZZ, where XX is the phase number, YY is the activity number, and ZZ is the task number.

A.1 SOFTWARE ENGINEERING LIFE CYCLE

The life-cycle phases are as follows:

1. *Requirements definition:* Identify the problem that must be solved. Analyze the existing system and determine the needs of the user which the system must resolve.
2. *Logical design:* Design the user interface to the system: input forms, screens, and reports. Determine detailed output information requirements, input data requirements, and interfaces to other systems. Document manual and automated processes that must occur, and database design.

3. *Physical design:* Define and design automated processes, specify physical data and user-interface representations, and develop programming specifications.
4. *Programming and unit testing:* Write and test program modules and operating instructions.
5. *System testing:* Run an integrated system test and a user training/user acceptance test.
6. *Installation:* Perform data and procedural conversions and operate the new system.

A.2 ACTIVITIES AND TASKS

Phase 1: Requirements Definition

1.01. Requirements funding
    1.01.01. Review project request
    1.01.02. Establish preliminary justification
    1.01.03. Fund Phase 1
    1.01.04. Prioritize project
    1.01.05. Establish project team
1.02. Define problem or opportunity
    1.02.01. Interview users
    1.02.02. Examine operation/reports
    1.02.03. Document problem from symptoms
    1.02.04. Define project scope
1.03. Analyze existing system
    1.03.01. Assemble documentation on existing system
    1.03.02. Identify data flows
    1.03.03. Identify external interfaces
    1.03.04. Identify problem domain
1.04. Document system requirements
    1.04.01. Document output information requirements
    1.04.02. Document interface constraints
    1.04.03. Document audit trail constraints
    1.04.04. Document turnaround/response time
    1.04.05. Document security constraints
    1.04.06. Document physical environment constraints/requirements
1.05. Validate against systems architecture
    1.05.01. Compare requirements with systems architecture
    1.05.02. Identify possible inconsistencies
    1.05.03. Identify conflicting/concurrent development

1.05.04. Identify recommended changes to systems architecture
1.05.05. Identify recommended changes to strategic implementation plan
1.06. Management review/Phase 2 funding
    1.06.01. Plan next phase
    1.06.02. Reevaluate development costs
    1.06.03. Reevaluate justification
    1.06.04. Obtain user requirements consensus
    1.06.05. Obtain technical consensus

Phase 2: Logical Design

2.01. Identify detailed data requirements
    2.01.01. Identify output requirements
    2.01.02. Decompose output data
    2.01.03. Identify input requirements
    2.01.04. Identify sources of input

2.02. Develop prototype/user system view
    2.02.01. Design interactive screens
    2.02.02. Design reports

2.03. Design database
    2.03.01. Define logical data relations
    2.03.02. Design data structure
    2.03.03. Validate database design
2.04. Structure processes
    2.04.01. Isolate highly related data
    2.04.02. Reconstruct processes to correspond with output requirements
    2.04.03. Identify reusable process structures
2.05. Design interfaces
    2.05.01. Design external data interfaces
    2.05.02. Design human interfaces
    2.05.03. Design intersystem interfaces
2.06. Specify all inputs and outputs
    2.06.01. Define data/interface relations
    2.06.02. Define data/system relations
2.07. Develop preliminary test/conversion procedures
    2.07.01. Identify test requirements
    2.07.02. Create test checklist
    2.07.03. Identify conversion requirements
    2.07.04. Create conversion checklist

2.08. Validate logical design
    2.08.01. Validate data relations
    2.08.02. Validate process relations
    2.08.03. Validate process logic
    2.08.04. Trace requirements to design
2.09. Validate against systems architecture
    2.09.01. Compare logical design with systems architecture
    2.09.02. Identify possible inconsistencies
    2.09.03. Identify conflicting/concurrent development
    2.09.04. Identify recommended changes to systems architecture
    2.09.05. Identify recommended changes to strategic implementation
          plan
2.10. Management review/Phase 3 funding
    2.10.01. Plan next phase
    2.10.02. Reevaluate development costs
    2.10.03. Reevaluate justification
    2.10.04. Obtain user requirements consensus
    2.10.05. Obtain technical consensus

Phase 3: Physical Design

3.01. Design/specify physical database
    3.01.01. Review logical database design
    3.01.02. Determine access method(s) to be used
    3.01.03. Normalize database
    3.01.04. Design database architecture
    3.01.05. Identify reusable database structures
    3.01.06. Develop detailed database layout
    3.01.07. Develop database file/record/schema descriptions
    3.01.08. Develop module calling sequences
    3.01.09. Update data dictionary entries
    3.01.10. Validate physical database design
3.02. Design processing structure
    3.02.01. Compose process structures from data decomposition
    3.02.02. Identify physical subsystems
    3.02.03. Identify physical programs
    3.02.04. Identify reusable programs
    3.02.05. Eliminate process redundancies
    3.02.06. Develop teleprocessing network specifications
3.03. Design processing logic
    3.03.01. Design calling sequences
    3.03.02. Develop calculation specifications
    3.03.03. Design interface logic

3.03.04. Design security logic
3.03.05. Design error recovery logic
3.04. Define procedures
    3.04.01. Review logical system design user interface
    3.04.02. Develop interactive data-entry procedures
    3.04.03. Develop screen specifications
    3.04.04. Design input forms
    3.04.05. Develop physical report specifications
    3.04.06. Develop user operating procedures
    3.04.07. Develop data processing operations run procedures
3.05. Refine test/conversion procedures
    3.05.01. Review test/conversion plans
    3.05.02. Update test/conversion plans
3.06. Validate physical design
    3.06.01. Validate data relations
    3.06.02. Validate process relations
    3.06.03. Validate process logic
    3.06.04. Validate procedures
    3.06.05. Validate teleprocessing network specifications
    3.06.06. Validate system timing and sizing requirements
3.07. Validate against systems architecture
    3.07.01. Compare physical design with systems architecture
    3.07.02. Identify possible inconsistencies
    3.07.03. Identify conflicting/concurrent development
    3.07.04. Identify recommended changes to systems architecture
3.08. Management review/Phase 4 funding
    3.08.01. Plan next phase
    3.08.02. Reevaluate development costs
    3.08.03. Reevaluate justification
    3.08.04. Obtain user requirements consensus
    3.08.05. Obtain technical consensus

Phase 4: Programming and Unit Testing

4.01. Decompose program modules
    4.01.01. Identify program modules
    4.01.02. Identify program module I/Os
    4.01.03. Identify reusable modules
    4.01.04. Eliminate module redundancies
4.02. Develop program modules
    4.02.01. Develop detailed module logic
    4.02.02. Validate module logic
    4.02.03. Code module

4.02.01. Develop module test data
4.02.02. Develop call and called stubs
4.02.03. Unit test program
4.03. Update test/conversion procedures
    4.03.01. Review test/conversion plans
    4.03.02. Update test/conversion plans
4.04. Management review/Phase 5 funding
    4.04.01. Plan next phase
    4.04.02. Reevaluate development costs
    4.04.03. Reevaluate justification
    4.04.04. Obtain user requirements consensus
    4.04.05. Obtain technical consensus

Phase 5: System Testing

5.01. Finalize integrated system test plan
    5.01.01. Review interim test procedures
    5.01.02. Develop integration test procedures
    5.01.03. Develop integration test plan
    5.01.04. Assign integration test responsibilities
    5.01.05. Develop integration test data
    5.01.06. Train data processing personnel
5.02. Finalize user acceptance/training test plan
    5.02.01. Review interim test procedures
    5.02.02. Develop user acceptance criteria
    5.02.03. Develop final user acceptance test procedures
    5.02.04. Develop user acceptance test plan
    5.02.05. Assign user acceptance test responsibilities
    5.02.06. Develop user acceptance test data
    5.02.07. Train users
5.03. Conduct integration test
    5.03.01. Link programs and copy to test libraries
    5.03.02. Establish test files
    5.03.03. Execute integration test
5.04. Conduct user acceptance/training test
    5.04.01. Establish user acceptance test files
    5.04.02. Establish test files
    5.04.03. Execute user acceptance test
5.05. Management review/Phase 6 funding
    5.05.01. Plan next phase
    5.05.02. Reevaluate development costs
    5.05.03. Reevaluate justification
    5.05.04. Obtain user requirements consensus
    5.05.05. Obtain technical consensus

Phase 6: Installation

6.01. Finalize conversion plan
    6.01.01. Review interim conversion procedures
    6.01.02. Develop conversion procedures
    6.01.03. Develop conversion plan
    6.01.04. Assign conversion responsibilities
6.02. Convert files/database
6.03. Install software
6.07. Run systems in parallel
6.08. Turn off old system
6.09. Management review
    6.09.01. Obtain user requirements consensus
    6.09.02. Obtain technical consensus
    6.09.03. Document recommended changes to architecture
    6.09.04. Document recommended enhancements to system

Bibliography

AWAD, ELIAS M., *Business Data Processing,* 4th ed. Englewood Cliffs, N.J.: Prentice-Hall, Inc., 1975.

BIGGS, C., BIRKS, and ATKINS, *Managing the Software Development Process.* Englewood Cliffs, N.J.: Prentice-Hall, Inc., 1980.

BOEHM, BARRY W., *Software, Engineering Economics.* Englewood Cliffs, N.J.: Prentice-Hall, Inc., 1981.

CARLSEN, ROBERT D., and JAMES A. LEWIS, *The Systems Analysis Workbook: A Complete Guide to Project Implementation and Control,* 2nd ed. Englewood Cliffs, N.J.: Prentice-Hall, Inc., 1979.

CASE, ALBERT F., "Automating the Project Management Process: The Computer-Aided Software Engineering Approach," Technical Paper delivered at INFO/SOFTWARE—International Management Exposition and Conference for Software, Chicago, June 13, 1984.

DEMARCO, TOM, *Controlling Software Projects.* New York: Yourdon Press, Inc., 1982.

DRUCKER, PETER, *Managing for Results.* New York: Harper & Row, Publishers, Inc., 1964.

ELLSWORTH, L., and C. BURRILL, "Project Implementation" (Course). New York: IBM System Science Institute, 1979.

FEGENBAUM, EDWARD A., and PAMELA MCCORDUCK, *The Fifth Generation: Artificial Intelligence and Japan's Computer Challenge to the World.* Reading, Mass.: Addison-Wesley Publishing Company, Inc., 1983.

GILLIN, PAUL, "Watch for Prototyping Pitfalls," *Computerworld,* Vol. 18, No. 23, (1984) 49.

JACKSON, MICHAEL, *System Development*. Englewood Cliffs, N.J.: Prentice-Hall, Inc., 1983.

JONES, T. CAPERS, "Laying the Groundwork with Reusable Code," *Computerworld Buyers Guide*, Vol. 18, No. 26A (1984) 12–16.

KOWALSKI, ROBERT, "AI and Software Engineering," *Datamation*, November 1, 1984, 92–102.

LIENTZ, B. P., and E. B. SWANSON, *Software Maintenance Management*. Reading, Mass.: Addison-Wesley Publishing Company, Inc., 1980.

A Management System for the Information Business, Vols. I–IV, GE20-0662-1. White Plains, N.Y.: IBM Corporation, 1983.

MANLEY, JOHN H., "Computer-Aided Software Engineering (CASE): Foundation for Software Factories," IEEE COMPCON '84 FALL CONFERENCE ON THE SMALL COMPUTER (R)EVOLUTION PROCEEDINGS, September 16–20 1984 (Silver Spring, MD: IEEE Computer Society Press, 1984)

MARTIN, JAMES, *Application Development without Programmers*. Englewood Cliffs, N.J.: Prentice-Hall, Inc., 1982.

MARTINS, GARY R., "The Overselling of Expert Systems," *Datamation*, November 1, 1984, 76–80.

MCLEOD, RAYMOND, *Management Information Systems*. Chicago: Science Research Associates, Inc., 1979.

MCNAMIN, STEPHEN M. and JOHN F. PALMERS, *Essential Systems Analysis*. New York: Yourdon Press, Inc., 1984.

Mecca International Suits Corporation-Business Systems Planning Report (SAMPLE), G320-6503-0, White Plains, N.Y.: IBM Corporation, 1980.

METZGER, PHILLIP W., *Managing a Programming Project*. Englewood Cliffs, N.J.: Prentice-Hall, Inc., 1973.

MILLER, G. A., "The Magical Number 7 ± 2: Some Limits on Our Capacity for Processing Information," *Psychological Review*, Vol. 63, March 1956, pp. 81–93.

NAISBETT, JOHN, *Megatrends*. New York: Warner Books, Inc., 1982.

NEIMARK, JILL, "Psych-Out Software," *Datamation*, October 15, 1984, 32–38.

ORR, KEN, *Structured Requirements Definition*. Topeka, Kans.: Kenn Orr & Associates, Inc., 1981.

ORR, KEN, *The One Minute Methodology by E. Z. Systems*. Topeka, Kans.: Ken Orr & Associates, Inc., 1984.

PETERS, LAWRENCE J., *Software Design: Methods and Techniques*. New York: Yourdon Press, Inc., 1981.

PHILLIPS, ROGER, "Can Fifth-Generation Software Replace Fallible Programmers?" *Computerworld* Vol. 18, No. 29, (1984), page In-Depth 27.

PRESSMAN, ROGER S., *Software Engineering: A Practitioner's Approach*. New York: McGraw-Hill Book Company, 1982.

Software Technology for Adaptable, Reliable Systems (STARS) Program Strategy, ADA 128981. Springfield, Va.: U.S. Department of Defense, National Technical Information Service, 1983.

TATE, PAUL, "The Blossoming of European AI," *Datamation*, November 1, 1984, 85–88.

TOELLNER, JOHN D., "Project Management: A Formula for Success," *Computerworld,* November 27, 1978.

TOFFLER, ALVIN, *The Third Wave.* New York: William Morrow & Company, Inc., 1980.

YOURDON, EDWARD and LARRY L. CONSTANTINE, *Structured Design: Fundamentals of a Discipline of Computer Program and System Design.* New York: Yourdon Press, Inc., 1978.

WIENER, NORBERT, *The Human Use of Human Beings: Cybernetics and Society.* New York: Avon Books, 1967.

ZANDERS, KATHERENA LEANNE, "The Next Revolution in Computer Programming," *Fortune Magazine,* October 29, 1984, 81–86.

Index

Abstraction, levels of, 110
Accuracy of estimates, 89–90
Activities, 138–39
Activity and task list, example, 217–22
Adaptability of CASE systems, 201
Adaptation, 80, 133, 179, 201
  cost of, 37
  defined, 64
Ad hoc enhancement, 80
Ad hoc requests, 33
Administration and software
  engineering MIS, 166
Advanced text management system,
  IBM, 193
AGS management systems, 14, 178, 147
AI, (*See* artificial intelligence)
Allocated hours, 75–78
Alternative implementation approaches,
  157–59
Amortized time off, 77, 97
Analysis and design tools, 190–92
Analyzers, problem statement, 181
Analyzers and scanners, 191
Analyzing dependencies, 91–96
Anderson, Arthur, 178
Apollo project, 8
Apollo workstations, 192

Apple Computer Company, 1
Application domain, 58–60, 102
Application planning, 80–81
Architectural dependencies, 64, 91
Architectural validation, 85, 101–2
Architecture:
  components, 39
  development, 39–40
  life cycle, 135
  software engineering MIS, 166–72
Artificial intelligence (AI), 196–200
  life cycle management, 197–98
  life cycle process, 146–47
  software engineering, 196–97
  transformation process, 198–99
Assembly line diagrams, 124
Assembly technique, 120
Assessing technology impact, 82
Assignments, task, 96
ATMS/DCF, 193
Atomism and design, 120
Attributes:
  of CASE system, 200–201
  of fourth generation languages, 154
Automated project control systems, 111
Automation, systems development, 180
Awad, Elias M., 56